FIGHTING WORDS

From War, Rebellion, and Other Combative Capers

CHRISTINE AMMER

NTC Publishing Group

Library of Congress Cataloging-in-Publication Data

Ammer, Christine.
    Fighting words : from war, rebellion, and other combative capers /
Christine Ammer. — 2nd ed.
        p.   cm.
   ISBN 0-8442-0285-1
    1. Military art and science—Terminology.   2. English language—
Terms and phrases.   3. English language—Etymology. I. Title.
U24.A55   1999
355'.0014—dc21   98-33697
                                                   CIP

Cover design by Todd Petersen
Interior design by Point West, Inc.

Published by NTC Publishing Group
A division of NTC/Contemporary Publishing Group, Inc.
4255 West Touhy Avenue, Lincolnwood (Chicago), Illinois 60646-1975 U.S.A.
Printed in the United States of America
International Standard Book Number: 0-8442-0285-1
99 00 01 02 03 04 VL 19 18 17 16 15 14 13 12 11 10 9 8 7 6 5 4 3 2 1

Preface

An astonishing number of words and expressions have entered our language through warfare and other hostilities. Some of them, such as "bazooka," "G.I.," and "jeep," are neologisms, pure inventions. Others are words whose original military meaning has been extended to an altogether different enterprise, such as an advertising "campaign," mountain climber's "bivouac," or football team's pep "rally." Still others have so changed that their original military significance has been quite forgotten—"avant-garde," "deadline," "magazine," "pioneer," "wardrobe."

Since publication of the first edition of this book, various conflicts around the world have given us new terms—"ethnic cleansing," "Gulf War syndrome," "hummer." The nearly 1,000 terms in this revised and augmented second edition are arranged alphabetically. In addition, there is a complete index at the back of the book.

The author is deeply indebted to the many eminent etymologists, linguists, and lexicographers who collectively represent centuries of labor in tracing the origins of the English language. This book is but a modest compilation of the results of their fine scholarship.

Grateful acknowledgment also is made to the many friends and acquaintances who have helped, pointing out terms and sources and verifying current usages. Their assistance has been of immense value. Special thanks are due to World War II aviation ace Robert Curtis, and to that knowledgeable military history buff, Dean Ammer.

about-face, to do an

To reverse a decision. During the American Civil War, "Right about-face!" was a military command to turn 180 degrees at attention. It was—and still is, in the military—performed in a specific way, with the ball of the right foot placed behind the heel of the left foot, which must then pivot 180 degrees to the right (in clockwise direction). The command is often shortened to "About-face!" (In Britain the command for the identical maneuver is "About-turn!") At some time during succeeding decades the military command came to mean simply turning around, and then it acquired the figurative sense of changing a decision or one's opinion or attitude.

according to plan

An ironic euphemism for *not* according to plan. It dates from British communiqués in World War I, where it would be used to excuse a setback, such as a forced retreat. Its use continued into World War II, where it was joined by such phrases as *withdraw to a prepared position* and *strategic advance to the rear*. Thereafter it entered the world of

According to plan

private enterprise and is still used to describe business setbacks, sports defeats, and the like.

Achilles heel

"Ireland, that vulnerable heel of the British Achilles."
—Samuel Taylor Coleridge, 1810

A vulnerable spot or weak area in a person, group, or nation. According to Greek legend, Thetis took her baby son, Achilles, by the foot and dipped him into the River Styx to make him immortal, but the heel by which she held him remained dry. Her son grew up to become the greatest of Greek warriors in the Trojan War. He killed Troy's mighty Hector but was himself slain by Paris, who shot a fatal arrow into his heel. The same story accounts for the name of the *Achilles tendon*, which joins the calf muscles to the heel bone and is frequently injured by athletes.

Another story about Achilles accounts for the botanical name of a genus of plants of the daisy family, *Achillea,* which includes the common yarrow (*Achillea millefolium*). On their way to Troy the

Greeks landed in Mysia and were opposed by Hector's son, Telephus. The god Dionysus caused Telephus to stumble, whereupon Achilles wounded him with his spear. Telephus appealed to the oracle and was told that Achilles would heal his wound. Telephus then promised Achilles he would lead him to Troy in return for his help. Agreeing, Achilles scraped some rust from his spear, and from these filings sprang the yarrow plant, today also called milfoil or sneezewort, which was applied to the wound and healed it. Actually, the healing properties of yarrow have been valued for centuries, infusions (teas) made from it having been used for such diverse maladies as fever, headache, diarrhea, palpitations, and excessive menstrual bleeding. It also works as an insect repellent. Yarrow once was regarded as one of the "witch herbs," and carrying it at weddings supposedly guaranteed seven years of married bliss.

admiral

> "If blood be the price of admiralty, Lord God, we ha' paid in full!"
> —Rudyard Kipling, *The Song of the Dead* (1896)

The commander of a naval fleet. The English word comes from the Arabic *amir*, meaning "commander" or "lord," used with the article *al*, for "of." Thus in Arabic *amir-al-bahr* means "commander of the sea," and *amir-al-ma* means "commander of the waters." British seamen misunderstood the exact sounds and meanings, taking *amir-al* to be a title, and by the end of the twelfth century it became the word admiral. In the U.S. Navy, admiral is the highest rank, but there are several grades, ranging from fleet admiral down through admiral, vice-admiral, and rear admiral. The odd name for the lowest grade comes from the British navy, where the rear admiral commanded the rear, or hindmost, squadron. Among medical students *rear admiral* is jocular slang for the specialist in proctology.

In British terminology the related word *admiralty,* which dates from the fourteenth century, is still applied to numerous objects and affairs connected with the sea—for example, admiralty law and admiralty cloth (melton cloth, used for Navy uniforms). In the United States it has been largely replaced by *maritime* in nonmilitary lingo—for example, maritime law, which governs not only the Navy but also merchant seamen and vessels.

a drag

A tedious experience, a boring undertaking. This term was Army slang during the Civil War and probably alluded to something that impedes progress.

aegis

Protection or patronage. In Greek mythology the *aegia* (or *aigis*) was the protective shield of the god Zeus, covered with goatskin (in Greek, *aix* or *aigos*) and picturing the head of a Gorgon (serpent). In the seventeenth century aegis became an English word meaning "protection" and, by extension, support or sponsorship. Today, therefore, one might speak of a fund-raising drive for a new athletic field that is held under the aegis of the town's Rotary Club.

Agent Orange

A powerful herbicide and defoliant. In the late 1960's U.S. Air Force fliers dumped millions of gallons of this chemical over the thick jungles of war-ravaged South Vietnam. Rained down on more than five million acres, it was intended to strip the land of crops and concealing jungle. Apart from causing widespread devastation, Agent Orange gave rise to a bitter controversy because it contains dioxide, which causes cancer in laboratory animals. After the war thousands of American Vietnam veterans pressed the U.S. government to compensate for injury and illness believed to be caused by Agent Orange. Actually, four herbicides were used in these attacks: Agent Blue, Agent Purple, Agent White, and Agent Orange. They were named for the colored code stripe on each of their containers. Agent Orange, however, was the most toxic and therefore the one most people remember.

airlift

The transport of people or supplies by air during an emergency. The term originated during World War II, when for the first time aircraft were used widely on both the European and Pacific fronts to transport troops and equipment. After the war, when the occupation zones of Germany were so arranged that the city of Berlin was surrounded by Russian-occupied territory, the Soviet Union in June,

1948, imposed an embargo on all land transport to the city. To supply the British and American zones within the city itself, the United States organized an airlift that lasted until May 12, 1949. During these months a total of 195,530 flights transported 1,414,000 tons of food, fuel, and other needed supplies. Since then, there have been numerous airlifts to victims of natural disasters such as floods and avalanches, who are cut off from normal routes of transport, but no prolonged operation on such a large scale.

alarm

> "Love sounds the alarm, and Fear is a flying."
> —John Gay, *Acis and Galatea* (1732)

A warning sound of impending danger; also, the fear caused by such danger. The word comes from the Italian expression *all'armi*, the military command to take up arms. The Italians, too, combined the two words into one, *allarme*, meaning both an alert and the disturbed feelings it may cause. The associations with bellicosity were gone long before the invention of the mechanical alarm, which roused diarist Samuel Pepys from sleep as long ago as the morning of July 16, 1665. (See also FALSE ALARM.)

alert

Wide awake, on guard. This word, which today most often describes a vigilant state of mind, originally came from the Italian *all'erta*, meaning "on the watchtower" and referring to military sentries. During World War II it briefly reacquired its military connotations in the air-raid alert, sounded by sirens warning of the approach of enemy aircraft. After the war, however, its peaceful meanings again took precedence.

all quiet on the Potomac/Western front

> "All quiet along the Potomac tonight,
> No sound save the rush of the river,
> While soft falls the dew on the face of the dead
> The picket's off duty forever."
> —Ethel Lynn Beers, *The Picket Guard* (1861)

All is peaceful for the time being. The phrase "all quiet along the Potomac" dates from the American Civil War, probably originating in dispatches sent by George B. McClellan while commanding the Army of the Potomac from 1861 to 1862. For a period of several months, the river separated the Confederate and Union troops within shooting distance, but virtually no action took place. The dispatches infuriated northerners who wanted to see action, and the expression became an ironic catchphrase. It was quoted in Mrs. Beers's poem, published in *Harper's Weekly* on September 30, 1861, which commented pungently on the official bulletins in another line, "Not an officer lost, only one of the men." The poem was set to music by John Hill Hewitt, and the song "All Quiet Along the Potomac Tonight," published in 1864, became quite popular.

The expression persisted for several decades but was probably obsolete by 1900 or so. However, a similar situation arose on the Western front during World War I, and German military communiqués began to repeat the phrase, *Im Westen nichts Neues* (nothing new in the West), referring to the long-standing stalemate. At the same time, Allied communiqués described it as "all's quiet on the Western front." Now it was not the public who derided the expression, but the soldiers in the trenches, who regarded their situation as anything but serene. The life of the catchphrase was lengthened by Erich Maria Remarque's war novel, *Im Westen Nichts Neues*, translated into English by A. H. Wheen as *All Quiet on the Western Front* and published in the same year as in Germany, 1929.

There is no definitive connection between the nineteenth- and twentieth-century expressions, but lexicographer Eric Partridge believed that the World War I version derived from "all quiet on the Shipka Pass," a phrase current in 1915 and prompted by some bitter cartoons of a Russian soldier being buried in falling snow during the Russian-Turkish War of 1877–78, which saw particularly bloody fighting in this high Balkan mountain pass.

Amazon

> "Old Meg was brave as Margaret Queen
>   And tall as Amazon."
>
> —John Keats, *Meg Merrilies*

A tall, strong, belligerent woman. The name comes from a tribe of women warriors in Asia Minor who were described by the ancient

Greeks. Allegedly they would burn off their right breast so as to draw a bow better. The legendary Greek hero Achilles fought and killed Penthesila, queen of the Amazons, a subject often depicted by Greek sculptors, and the Athenian hero Theseus routed the Amazons for the last time, thereby making Athens impregnable to its enemies. Theseus also had a son by one of the Amazons (either Hippolyta or Antiope—accounts differ), who was named Hippolytus. Among Hercules's twelve labors was stealing the girdle of the Amazon queen, Hippolyta, whom he had to kill in order to do so. According to a colorful account by the Greek historian Herodotus, the Greeks defeated the Amazons in battle, took many of them captive, and sailed away with them. The Amazons then turned on their captors and killed them, but they did not know how to handle boats, so they drifted into Scythian territory. The Scythians at first took them to be men and fought them, but when they discovered their error they tried to get children by them. Scythians and Amazons lived together for a time, but when the Scythians tried to make the arrangement permanent, the Amazons refused to exchange their hunting and riding lifestyle for that of conventional wives, and eventually they parted peacefully.

The great Amazon River of South America was so named by early explorers who believed that some of the native women they saw there resembled the Amazons of Greek antiquity.

ambulance

A specialized vehicle for transporting the ill and injured, usually to a hospital. The name comes from an invention of Napoleon Bonaparte's, *l'hôpital ambulant* (walking hospital), a light litter fitted with bandages and other first-aid equipment that served as a field hospital for wounded soldiers. In time the litters became more elaborate and mechanized, yielding at first to horse-drawn wagons and eventually to motorized ambulances. Today ambulances are standard civilian equipment in all the advanced countries of the world.

amnesty

A pardon. The word comes from the Greek word for "forgetfulness," in English *amnesia,* and supposedly the first to grant amnesty was an ancient Greek general who, instead of punishing defeated enemies as was customary, decided to "forget" the hostilities and grant them a pardon. Today amnesty may be granted by a government, most often for political offenses, or by a court of law, usually for an entire class of offenders (an individual is usually said to be granted a pardon). The organization Amnesty International, which was awarded the Nobel Peace Prize in 1977, works actively to free political prisoners and prevent violations of human rights throughout the world.

Anschluss

Annexation or junction. The word is a legitimate German one and had no special bellicose meaning until Nazi Germany seized neighboring Austria in 1938 and on March 11 of that year proclaimed the country to be part of Germany. There were many protests against this *Anschluss*, but no other nation was prepared to act, and Hitler's argument that he was "liberating" his fellow countrymen in Austria carried the day. Ever since, the word *Anschluss* has carried the burden of that historical event, at least in English.

antebellum

Before the American Civil War. The term comes straight from two Latin words meaning "before the war" and began to be so used in America almost as soon as the Civil War began. Unlike *prewar* and *postwar*, which, since they entered the language about 1905, have been used to mean before/after a variety of wars, in America antebellum firmly attached itself to the Civil War. In the South particularly one finds references to, for example, antebellum architecture (houses built before 1860), agriculture, and a variety of institutions and customs. In Britain, on the other hand, antebellum may refer to the Boer War or to either world war.

appeasement

The act of soothing or pacifying. The word entered the language from the Old French *apaiser* via the Middle English *apaisen* or *apesen* in the fourteenth century and was a perfectly innocuous one—blessed are the peacemakers, says the Bible—until 1938, when, sincerely convinced that "in war there are no winners, there is nothing but suffering and ruin for those who are involved," British Prime

Minister Neville Chamberlain devoted himself to the cause of preventing armed conflict. In March of 1938 Hitler had taken Austria (See ANSCHLUSS) without interference from any foreign power, and the Nazis made no secret of their ambition to take over the largely German-speaking Sudetenland, which was part of Czechoslovakia. Chamberlain saw that a dispute over this area could develop into outright war. Further, was Hitler unreasonable? He said he only wished to help his countrymen in a foreign land. Helping him and avoiding war seemed to Chamberlain a worthy endeavor. Matters came to a head in September, 1938, with the Czechs calling out their troops to quell the Nazi-supported riots of Sudeten Germans. Chamberlain then took the dramatic step of offering to fly to Germany and talk to the German Chancellor. In the end, he made three separate trips to meet with Hitler, whose demands increased each time. The last meeting took place in Munich on September 29, 1938, when Hitler, Mussolini, French Premier Eduard Daladier, and Chamberlain convened and rapidly reached an agreement, the so-called Munich Pact. In exchange for Czech lands that Hitler proclaimed to be German, Hitler agreed never to declare war on Great Britain. It was this agreement that Chamberlain triumphantly waved on his return to England, saying he had "won peace in our time." Within six months Hitler had broken virtually every promise he had made at Munich, and only then did Chamberlain realize that appeasing a dictator would just increase his appetite. He determined to resist further aggression, and in September, 1939, when the Nazis invaded Poland, he issued an ultimatum followed by a declaration of war. Despite Chamberlain's change of heart and policy, he is still identified with appeasement, and some people go further still, contending that if Hitler had been stopped at the outset, World War II might never have taken place.

armada

A fleet of ships, airplanes, or other vehicles. The word came into English in the sixteenth century via Spanish from the Latin *armata*, meaning "equipped with arms," and the most famous such fleet dates from the same period. In 1588 in Lisbon, at the height of the war between Spain and England, the Spaniards amassed a fleet of 130 vessels to invade England. The fleet came to be called the *Invincible Armada*, a name only slightly less ironic than its name in

Spanish, *la felicissima armada* (the most fortunate fleet). The English first sighted the Spanish ships, which carried about 30,000 men, off their southwest shore on July 19, 1588, and during the night the English fleet under Lord Charles Howard slipped out into the English Channel. The clash between the two fleets began the next day and involved a running fight that churned the Channel for more than a week. The tall Spanish galleons tried to maneuver into grappling range so as to swarm onto the English ships and overwhelm their crews. The English fleet, consisting of lower and more maneuverable vessels, was better designed for raids and coastal defense. Neither had adequate supplies, but the English were slightly better off. For six days the Spaniards worked their way up the Channel, while the English moved according to the weather. Then some Spanish ships were lost, but not by gunfire. One suffered an internal explosion, another lost bowsprit and foremast in a collision, and a third drifted toward the French coast. On July 28 the Spaniards anchored off Calais, France, where they were to meet the Duke of Parma and his Army of Flanders to invade England. Parma, however, was not there. That night Lord Howard sent eight fire ships to throw firebrands at the Spaniards, who cut their cables and drifted off in confusion. Finally, weather blew the rest of their fleet into the North Sea, far from their rendezvous with the invasion army. Though few English ships were provisioned well enough to follow them, storms carried on their work, and the reefs of Scotland and Ireland claimed nearly half the remaining galleons. At last the Armada limped home, its numbers reduced by more than half, with an additional 4,000 men lost on the return voyage.

In current usage the word armada has no particular connotations of strength, meaning simply a large group of vehicles moving with a common purpose. (See also FLOTILLA.)

Armageddon

> "We stand at Armageddon and we battle for the Lord."
> — Theodore Roosevelt, speech, June 17, 1912

A decisive battle. According to the Book of Revelation (16:14–16), Armageddon was the site of the final battle that would take place between good and evil on Judgment Day. The word comes from the

Hebrew *har megiddo*, meaning Mountain of Megiddo, which in fact was the site of many real battles. Eventually Armageddon became a figure of speech for any major conflict between good and evil or any great decisive battle. Theodore Roosevelt was seeking the Presidential nomination at the Republican convention of 1912 when he declared that his fight for the nomination against William Howard Taft represented an Armageddon—one that Roosevelt lost. He responded by assuming the leadership of a third party, the Progressive (Bull Moose) Party, thereby dividing the Republican vote and ensuring the victory of Democrat Woodrow Wilson.

armed to the teeth

Fully prepared to do battle, often meaning excessively so. The phrase brings to mind savage tribesmen—or perhaps Marines or commandos—stalking the enemy while holding a knife between their teeth. The phrase is actually very old. It appeared in a fourteenth-century Middle English discourse, *Libeaus Disconus*. In modern English, however, it did not surface again until the mid-nineteenth century, when Richard Ford wrote, in his *Handbook for Travelers in Spain* (1845), "Everybody in Spain travels armed to the teeth." It was then repeated by English industrialist and statesman Richard Cobden in a speech in 1849, in which he deplored the excessive use of the nation's resources for armaments, saying, "Is there any reason why we should be armed to the teeth?" Today the expression is sometimes used figuratively—for example, armed to the teeth against the bitter cold.

assassin

> "Assassination has never changed the course of history."
> —Benjamin Disraeli, speech, May 1, 1865

A murderer, especially one of a prominent person, who acts either from moral conviction or for financial gain (hired assassin). The word comes from members of a fanatic Moslem sect, the Assassins, who in Arabic were called the *hashishin* (hashish users) because their acts of terrorism and murder, directed against the Crusaders, often were carried out under the influence of hashish. Active from about 1090 until 1273 throughout Iraq, Syria, and Persia, they were founded by Hassan ben Sabbah, who wanted to establish a single Islamic empire. They finally were overcome by the Mongols and Mamelukes, but their memory survives in the words assassin and assassinate, which came into English in the sixteenth century. Disraeli's statement in the House of Commons, even if it had not followed the murder of Abraham Lincoln by just two and one-half weeks, is an arguable contention. After all, it was the assassination of the Archduke Ferdinand that set off World War I. Among the world leaders assassinated since then have been Pancho Villa, Leon Trotsky, Mohandas K. Gandhi, President Anastasio Somoza of Nicaragua, Prime Minister Hendrik Verwoerd of South Africa, King Faisal of Saudi Arabia, Indira Gandhi of India, and John F. Kennedy, the fourth U.S. President to die in this way (the others were Lincoln, Garfield, and McKinley).

at full tilt

As fast or as forcefully as possible. This term originally referred to the thrust of a lance or sword in combat but has been used figuratively since approximately 1700. Thus we might say, "Production was running at full tilt in anticipation of the Christmas rush."

at the ready

Prepared for immediate use. This term originally referred to having a firearm prepared to be raised and aimed or to fire. Today it is also used quite loosely, as in "Snow shovels at the ready, we were prepared to deal with the worst of storms."

avant-garde

The individuals or group in any field, but especially in the arts, known for their unorthodox, experimental works and approach. The term was adopted directly from the French term for "front guard" or "advance guard." It originally meant the advance guard of an army, also called the *vanguard*. Both words came into the English language in the late fifteenth century and began to be used in a nonmilitary sense about 1900.

AWOL

Acronym for *absent without official leave*. According to the anonymous author of a particularly fanciful book of etymology, this term originated in the U.S. Army sometime before the Civil War, and during the war Confederate soldiers who were caught absenting themselves from military duties had to walk around camp bearing a sign saying "A.W.O.L." Most reputable lexicographers agree that the acronym first came into use during World War I. During World War II it began to be used in civilian life for anyone absent from a job or other activities without proper explanation or permission, as, for example, a woman extending her maternity leave without authorization from her boss.

Axis

The name given to the alliance of two fascist states, Italy and Germany, in October, 1936, when Italy's dictator, Benito Mussolini, described them as "an axis around which all European states animated by the will to collaboration and peace can also assemble." A year later they were joined by Japan, and today historians sometimes also include Bulgaria, Hungary, and Romania among the Axis countries.

bachelor

An unmarried man. The term comes from the Old French *bacheler*, in turn from the words *bas* and *chevalier*, meaning "below a knight (or horseman)." In medieval times a bachelor was a young man aspiring to knighthood but not old enough to own a horse or display his own banner. Most often he was a squire who served a knight as groom and man-at-arms. Wrote Chaucer in *The Maunciple's Tale*:

> He was the most lusty bachiler
> In al this world and eek the beste archer.

By 1546, when John Heywood published his collection of proverbs, the word had its modern meaning: "Bachelers wives and maides children be well taught"—a sardonic comment on the supposedly wise advice given by bachelors concerning marriage and by unmarried women concerning child raising. In the 1890's a cartoon gave rise to a joke used for decades by comedians in vaudeville and other popular entertainment: "Why do married men live longer than bachelors? They don't; it just seems longer." Demographers, however, tell us that married men do in fact live longer, and divorced and widowed men in particular have a markedly shortened life span.

backroom boys

Anonymous workers who make important contributions in return for little or no credit or publicity. The term comes from a speech made by Lord Beaverbrook in Great Britain during World War II: "To whom must praise be given . . . to the boys in the backroom"—that is, the scientists and technicians who contributed so much to developing scientific warfare and aiding war production. Ever since, the expression has been used for the unsung heroes and heroines whose labors enable scientific and technologic advances.

back to the wall, with one's

Hard-pressed, making a last stand. The expression comes from fighting. Literally backing up against a wall prevents an attack from the rear but also may prevent further retreat. The term has been used since the sixteenth century but became famous near the end of World War I, when General Douglas Haig of Great Britain, according to the London *Times* (April 13, 1918), ordered his troops: "Every position must be held to the last man. . . . With our backs to the wall, and believing in the justice of our cause, each one of us must fight on to the end."

bag and baggage

> "Come, shepherd, let us make an honourable retreat; though not with bag and baggage, yet with scrip and scrippage."
> —William Shakespeare, *As You Like It*

All of one's belongings. It originally (fifteenth century) meant all of an army's property, and to march away with bag and baggage signified not an ignominious retreat but the surrender of nothing of value to the enemy. Touchstone's *scrip and scrippage* (quoted above) was an alliterative counterpart, meaning a purse and the money it contained. In time the connotation of honorable was dropped, and to take bag and baggage simply meant to clear out completely. It appears in this sense in Samuel Richardson's novel *Pamela* of 1741: "'Bag and baggage,' said she, 'I'm glad you're going.'" In 1877 William Ewart Gladstone, leader of Britain's Liberal Party, made a speech urging the victorious Turks to end their occupation and get out of Bulgaria "bag and baggage," giving rise to the name "bag-and-baggage policy" for his anti-imperialist views.

balaclava

A knitted wool cap that pulls over the head and neck, leaving an opening only for the face. Probably few skiers and winter sports enthusiasts know that their warm head covering's official name comes from the town of Balaklava, immortalized by the ill-advised charge of the Light Brigade celebrated in Tennyson's poem. Balaklava today is part of Sevastopol, in the Ukraine. During the Crimean War, on October 25, 1854, there was a disputed error in orders, and as a result the Earl of Cardigan, never a brilliant commander, led an English light-cavalry brigade of 673 men in a hopeless charge on a heavily protected Russian position; 247 of the men were killed or wounded. Although the war eventually ended with Russia's defeat in 1856, the allied soldiers were ill equipped and provisioned. Suffering considerably from the harsh conditions, especially in winter, they adopted various kinds of clothing to keep warm, including the balaclava. For a couple of decades following the war, the name balaclava was also used for a full beard, as worn by those soldiers lucky enough to return from the Crimea.

balkanization

The division of an area into a number of smaller, weaker, contentious units; by extension, the division of a group or organization into smaller warring factions. The word refers to the numerous separate countries and territories on the Balkan Peninsula that resulted from the breakup of the European lands held by the once powerful Ottoman Empire, which was weakened and eventually dissolved in the late nineteenth and early twentieth centuries.

The Balkan Peninsula is bounded by the Adriatic, Aegean, and Black Seas, and the first lands lost by the Turks were those farthest inland on the European continent, Hungary and Transylvania, taken by Austria. Next they lost Podolia and Bessarabia to Russia and then Moldavia, Bosnia, Serbia, Bulgaria, and Romania, along with portions of Greece. Generally speaking, all the European nations wanted to weaken Turkey and therefore encouraged feelings of nationalism and revolt among Turkey's subject peoples. However, each country resented any increase of power by the others. Therefore, although Britain backed the fight for freedom of the various Balkan nationalities within the Ottoman Empire, on several occasions it supported Turkey's territorial claims, mainly because the British regarded Russia, and not Turkey, as their principal enemy. France and Germany took similar positions. Russia's ambitions were blocked when it lost the Crimean War (1856), but it then took advantage of the war between France and Prussia (1871) to renege on an earlier treaty and arm the shores of the Black Sea. Meanwhile Moldavia and Wallachia united and formed Romania, and in 1875 the peasants of Herzegovina, joined by Bosnia, Serbia, and Montenegro, rose up against the Turks, and they were quickly joined by Bulgaria. With the help of Russia, which defeated Turkey, Bulgaria emerged virtually independent and much enlarged.

Once these small territories did attain sovereignty, they did not stop quarreling among themselves. Just before the outbreak of World War I they became embroiled in two brief conflicts, the First and Second Balkan Wars, which, historians believe, set the stage for World War I. After World War I six formerly separate Balkan states—Bosnia, Herzegovina, Serbia, Croatia, Slovenia, and Montenegro—made up a new nation, Yugoslavia, but relations among them, both inside Yugoslavia and with the other Balkan states, remained strained. (In the 1990's they eventually resulted in outright war and the breakup of Yugoslavia.)

It was about this time that the words *balkanize* and *balkanization* were invented. The British historian Arnold Toynbee said the words were first coined by German socialists to describe what the Treaty of Brest-Litovsk had done to the western border of Russia. According to this treaty, which was a separate peace treaty between newly Communist Russia and Germany and Austria-Hungary, signed in March, 1918, Russia recognized the independence of the Ukraine and Georgia, confirmed the independence of Finland, gave up Poland, the Baltic states, and part of Byelorussia to Germany and Austria, and ceded some lands to Turkey. The general armistice of November, 1918, made the treaty null and void. Nevertheless balkanization—the creation of many small states, generally antagonistic and perhaps unviable—continued. After World War II the term was applied to former European colonies in Asia and Africa, which, after attaining independence, broke up into smaller entities based on tribalism and internal rivalries. In this way the former colony of French Equatorial Africa became four separate nations, Ruanda-Urundi became two, the eastern portion of Pakistan became Bangladesh, and so on. The term also is occasionally used for units smaller than nations. For example, a recent newspaper editorial described a formerly cohesive homogeneous neighborhood—Boston's Beacon Hill—as being balkanized through the purchase of property by individuals who treat it as a secondary city residence and spend most of their time elsewhere.

balloon goes up, the

An enterprise or action begins. This term dates from World War I, when the British artillery would send up a balloon to signal gunners along the line to begin firing. Presumably a readily seen balloon was considered more reliable than a courier or some other means of communication. The phrase was adopted by the American military and eventually was broadened in civilian life to mean any beginning, such as the opening of a new store.

bamboo curtain

The barrier of suspicion and mistrust between the People's Republic of China and its allies on the one hand and the non-Communist nations of Asia and the West on the other. It seems to have been coined by *Time* magazine in 1949 ("The Communist bosses of Peiping dropped a bamboo curtain, cutting off Peiping from the world"). A counterpart of the IRON CURTAIN between the Soviets and the non-Communist world, the expression bamboo curtain was never used as widely and may be obsolescent.

banquette

A built-in bench along the wall of a restaurant. The name originally (seventeenth century) was a French word for a gunners' platform erected behind a defensive wall or parapet. The resemblance of the furniture, first so called in the mid-nineteenth century, to the fortification is quite straightforward. In one part of the southern United States, however, the word banquette means a sidewalk, presumably because the early wooden sidewalks of Louisiana and eastern Texas were raised above the muddy soil.

banzai

A war cry or shout. It is actually a Japanese expression that means "May you live 10,000 years" and was uttered on happy occasions until World War II, when it was shouted upon the launching of a suicide attack (See KAMIKAZE). The term was first transliterated in the late nineteenth century, although presumably by then it had been used for many centuries. During and after the war it also came to be used as an adjective—as in *banzai attack*—to mean "suicidal."

baptism of fire

First exposure to the fire of battle; by extension, initial encounter with any ordeal, such as one's first public speech. The term comes from martyrdom—that is, the experience of martyrs who were burned at the stake—but was used in nineteenth-century France to describe a soldier going into battle for the first time. Barry O'Meara's account of Napoleon Bonaparte's exile quotes him as saying, "I love a brave soldier who has undergone the baptism of fire." The term was used similarly in a letter from Napoleon III to the Empress Eugénie, describing their son Louis's participation in the Battle of Saarbruck as *son baptême de feu*. The young Louis later joined his father in exile in England, enlisted in the British army, and died fighting the Zulus in Africa, at the age of twenty-two.

barbarian

An uncivilized person. This term dates from the days of the Roman Empire, when it was used for an outsider, that is, anyone whose language and customs differed. Later its meaning was extended from non-Roman to non-Hellenic and non-Christian, whence its present meaning.

barrage

A sudden and excessive outpouring. It comes from the French *barrage*, meaning "barrier," and was so used from the mid-nineteenth century on. Around the time of World War I, it became more specific—that is, a shortening of the French *tir de barrage*, meaning a curtain or barrier of artillery fire that would destroy everything before it and thereby protect advancing troops. Today the word is used both for a literal outpouring (of fire, artillery, etc.) and figuratively, as in "a barrage of questions from reporters" or "a barrage of insults from a hostile crowd."

barricade

A barrier erected to prevent the passage of troops, automobiles, sea water, etc. Although the practice of building such structures is surely older, the term probably comes from late-sixteenth-century France. In 1588, when Count Henri de Guise returned to Paris in defiance of the hated and incompetent king, Henry III, the King called out the Swiss Guards. Parisians then tore up pavements, threw chains across streets, and piled up barrels (*barriques,* in French) filled with earth and stones, from behind which they shot at the King's soldiers. The King was forced to flee Paris, Henri de Guise took over the throne, and ever since, May 12, 1588, has been called, in French history books, *la Journée des Barricades* (the day of the barricades).

The system of barricades continued to be used in Paris in later times of rebellion. In the mid-nineteenth century, when Napoleon III decided to rebuild the city into a splendid modern capital, the wide boulevards and open squares he had constructed were supposed to prevent the erection of barricades. However, barricades again were used by the revolutionary Commune of Paris, which set itself up against the conservative French government toward the end of the Franco-Prussian War (1871). Today barricades are used to block off a street following a fire, to reroute traffic for a parade, and for similar purposes.

basket case

A person too impaired to function. This term dates from World War I, when it meant a soldier who had lost all four limbs and therefore had to be carried off the field in a litter, or "basket." Later it was transferred to an emotionally or mentally unstable person. It is also occasionally used for something that fails to function.

bastion

> "The wild unrest that lives in woe. . . .
> And topples round the dreary west
> A looming bastion fringed with fire."
> —Alfred Lord Tennyson, *In Memoriam* (1850)

A stronghold or defensive bulwark; by extension, any kind of protection. In the age of chivalry, the bastion, whose name comes from the French, was a five-sided projection in the wall of a fort or castle designed to give the defenders a wider range of fire. From the castle wall itself, the direction in which they could fire was necessarily limited; the bastion gave them almost a full circle of range. From the seventeenth century on, the word also has been used figuratively, as in "Geneva was a bastion of Calvinism."

baton

A stick or wand used by a conductor of music. The word came into English in the sixteenth century, via French, from the Latin *bastum*, for "stick" or "staff," and at that time signified a short, stout club used as a weapon and also carried as a mark of office. Today a baton still is carried by parade marshals, military officers, and other leaders on ceremonial occasions. However, since the nineteenth century the word also has been used for the stick with which conductors direct musicians.

Until the nineteenth century, orchestras rarely had a separate leader. Instead, one of their number—usually a violinist, organist, or harpsichordist—led the group and played his own instrument at the same time. One of the first conductors of note was the French composer Jean-Baptiste Lully, and the baton he used proved to be the death of him. He used a long staff, and while beating time with it he struck himself in the foot and died from the resulting infection.

batten down the hatches

Prepare for action. This term originated in the navy, where it signified preparing for a storm or for battle by fastening down canvas over hatches (openings) in the deck with strips of wood called battens.

batter

> "In households where raised buckwheat cakes were served every morning a cup of batter was left to 'rise' them, instead of fresh yeast."
> —Imogene Walcott, *The Yankee Cookbook* (1939)

A mixture of flour, sugar, eggs, and similar ingredients used to make a cake, bread, pancakes, or some other culinary concoction. The word entered the language in the fourteenth century and comes from the Latin *battere* via the French *battre*, both meaning "to beat" or "to assault." Indeed, it is a beating, whether by hand or electric mixer or food processor, that results in a mixture blended adequately for baking or frying. The word's violent antecedents are retained in *assault and battery,* an unlawful attack on an individual, as well as in the military *battery,* the use of combined artillery against the enemy. New York City's Battery, at the southern end of Manhattan, originally was a fort.

The *battering ram,* so called for the male sheep's proclivity for head butting, was used by the Assyrians as early as the tenth century B.C. and long was considered an essential weapon. It was used to batter down city walls until the invention of gunpowder provided a more efficient method. Originally it consisted simply of a swinging log hand-operated by soldiers, but it soon was elaborated into a long, heavy beam hung by chains from a large frame. About 100 feet long and with an iron-shod head (sometimes made in the form of a ram's head), it was operated by 100 or more soldiers. This form was elaborated further into a wooden tower, roofed and shielded in front with metal plates and moved on wheels. Under the roof was a platform from which archers could pick off the defenders on the city walls.

battle-ax

A colloquial epithet for a woman, often elderly, who is loudly aggressive and unpleasant. It has been so used since at least 1900, often along with the adjective *old,* implying that the woman is unattractive as well. The original battle-ax was a sharp, broad ax used by some of the Gothic tribes. When thrown or wielded, it could penetrate Roman armor and split a shield; the Romans called it *francisca.* In the twentieth century archaeologists dubbed a North European

Knight wields a battle-ax

culture of late Neolithic times the *Battle-ax Culture* because they discovered numerous axes from that period, frequently buried with their deceased owners.

battle cry

> "A good cry is half the battle."
> —George Bernard Shaw, *Man and Superman* (1905)

A slogan used in any campaign or movement. Like the original battle cry, shouted by soldiers going into the fray, the somewhat less bloody battle cry of a Presidential or publicity campaign is intended as much to rally the existing supporters as to gain new ones. Among the most popular songs of the American Civil War was George Frederick Root's *The Battle Cry of Freedom,* also called *Rally 'Round the Flag* (See under RALLY).

battle fatigue

A disabling psychiatric disorder, often involving physical as well as emotional symptoms, that results from the stress of active combat. It also is called *combat fatigue,* but the symptoms do not necessarily include extreme weariness. The term dates from World War II, when it replaced *shell shock,* used for the same syndrome during World War I. The expression sometimes is used figuratively for a person or object exhibiting symptoms or damage resulting from a particularly violent or traumatic experience—for example, a car driven by an inexperienced or reckless teenager may be said to show battle fatigue.

Following the Vietnam War, psychiatrists substituted a new name for it, *post–traumatic stress disorder,* and described it as a wasting condition with such symptoms as depression, sleep disturbances, suicidal tendencies, alcohol and drug abuse, violent outbursts, and a pervasive sense of isolation. According to veterans' groups, it affected about 500,000 Vietnam veterans to some extent, nearly 150,000 of them so severely that without psychotherapy and medication they had little hope for a normal life. Like battle fatigue, the term post–traumatic stress disorder has been extended to survivors of airplane crashes, earthquakes, and similar extreme stresses.

battle of the bulge

A jocular expression for the fight against middle-aged spread. The diet-conscious society of the advanced Western nations has become increasingly absorbed with maintaining a fashionably slender silhouette, a job that becomes more difficult with advancing years. The first Battle of the Bulge began in December, 1944, when the Germans launched their last great drive of the war and Nazi troops "bulged" through the Allied lines deep into Belgium. After a month of heavy fighting, the Germans were forced back, marking the beginning of the European war's end.

Bayonets fixed

bayonet

"A bayonet's contrition
Is nothing to the dead."

—Emily Dickinson, *Glory*

A daggerlike weapon attached to a gun and used in hand-to-hand combat. It is named for the city of Bayonne, in southern France, where it was first made about 1500 (and called *baionette*). The early bayonets were simply short, flat daggers. In the seventeenth century they began to be made with a long, slender handle that was put down the muzzle of a musket, an arrangement exceedingly dangerous to the soldier if he fired while the bayonet was fixed. Later it was attached outside the gun barrel, near the tip. The modern bayonet is fastened to one side of the gun barrel with a spring clip. Infantry soldiers carry it in a scabbard or case worn on either belt or pack and attach it to the gun when the order is given, "Bayonets fixed." Bayonets were especially useful in the days when rifles could not be reloaded rapidly. Although largely replaced by rapid-firing machine guns, they are still used in hand-to-hand fighting under such conditions as those of the jungle warfare of World War II, the Korean War, and the Vietnam War.

A *bayonet socket* is an electrical socket made with slots so that a special lightbulb can be inserted and locked in place, much as the weapon is on a rifle.

bazooka

A comedian's musical instrument and a light, rocket-firing tube used as an antitank weapon. The weapon was named for the instrument, which was popularized by American radio comedian Bob Burns in the 1930's (he actually invented it much earlier, around 1905). According to a letter he wrote to lexicographer Charles Funk, Burns, who grew up in Arkansas, claimed he invented the instrument almost accidentally—first blowing into a piece of gas pipe and then sliding a rolled-up sheet of music in and out of one end, much like the slide of a trombone. It sounded so comical that he decided to embellish it with a second metal pipe, to slide in and out of the first, and soldered a funnel on one end. The name probably came from *bazoo*, a slang word for "mouth" as long ago as 1877 and still used in the 1940's in such expressions as "he blows his bazoo," meaning he talks too much.

The military bazooka used by U.S. troops in World War II is a portable launcher that fires a rocket capable of penetrating several inches of metal armor. According to Burns, it was named for its physical resemblance to his instrument. It consists of a metal tube about four feet long and less than three inches in diameter, and it is carried over the soldier's shoulder.

beachhead

A solid foothold from which one can advance. The term originated in the early years of World War II, when a number of places—Britain, France, the Pacific islands, North Africa—were open to invasion from the sea and the invading force hoped to establish a secure position on shore (the beach) from which to conquer the rest of the country. In 1940 the British still had a foothold on the continent at Dunkirk, on the French coast, but relentless German advances forced them to evacuate, with heavy losses. From that time on a Nazi invasion of Britain by sea, across the English Channel, was an ever-present threat, even though the Royal Navy guarded the approaches to the coast. In the Pacific theater of war, where initially the Japanese had forced American troops off numerous chains of islands, the Americans began to counterattack, and in June, 1942, following the defeat of the Japanese naval forces in the Battle of the Coral Sea, they launched numerous amphibious assaults, landing foot soldiers and tanks from boats and establishing beachhead after beachhead. In August they took Tulagi, as well as Guadalcanal in the Solomon Islands, and began the process of driving the Japanese back to their homeland. Meanwhile, the British and Germans had been fighting bitterly in North Africa. On November 8, 1942, American forces established a beachhead in Algeria, and others were won in Morocco. Among the most dramatic beachheads of the war was that established by the combined Allied forces on D-Day, June 6, 1944, when they launched their long-planned invasion of northern Europe on the Normandy coast. The word is also used figuratively, as in "This exhibit will establish his beachhead in America."

bear the brunt, to

> "No! let me taste the whole of it, fare like my peers
> The heroes of old,
> Bear the brunt, in a minute pay glad life's arrears
> Of pain, darkness and cold."
> —Robert Browning, *Prospice* (1854)

To take the main impact of a blow or assault. The term dates from the early fifteenth century and was first used with reference to armies aligned in the field, where the front ranks took the main force (brunt) of the enemy's assault. Today it is generally used figuratively, meaning to bear the worst of any struggle or misfortune.

beat a retreat, to

> "The expedition was obliged to beat a retreat."
> —Mary Kingsley, *Travels in West Africa* (1897)

To back down. The term comes from the practice of sounding the drums to call troops back to camp or behind the lines. Not only drums were used for this purpose. Indeed, wind instruments were probably used first, since there are several examples in literature of *blowing* or *sounding* a retreat (John Barbour, *The Bruce,* 1375: "Thai had blawen the ratret"; Edward Hall, *Chronicle,* c. 1548: "He caused his trompet to blowe a retreat"). It is difficult to say just when the term began to be used simply for reversing course or backing down from an argument or unpleasant situation, but most likely this happened at some time in the nineteenth century.

beginning of the end, the

The last phase of an ongoing event or process. This phrase is a translation from the French of Talleyrand's assessment of the Battle of Borodino in 1812, when Russian forces under General Mikhail Kutuzov stopped Napoleon's army near Moscow (*"Voilà le commencement de la fin"*). The phrase was repeated in a different context in November, 1942, by Winston Churchill. After the British under Montgomery defeated Rommel's Afrika Korps at El Alamein, the British Prime Minister said, "Now this is not the end. It is not even the beginning of the end. But it is, perhaps, the end of the beginning."

belfry

> "His father's sister had bats in the belfry and was put away."
> —Eden Philpotts, *Peacock House* (1926)

A bell tower, usually one attached to a church. The original belfry was a movable tower used in sieges. The attackers of a walled city or castle were mounted in it and threw missiles and fired arrows at the defenders. The word comes from the Old French *berfrei* or *berfroi,* for "place of safety" (the attackers presumably were safe). With the development of gunpowder the belfry, no longer useful for its original purpose, was moved inside the walls and used as a watchtower and place from which an alarm bell was rung. Eventually even that use was abandoned, but the name continued to be used for a church bell tower.

Belfries were once an important part of the community, sounding the hours in an era when most people did not have pocket watches, as well as calling the faithful to worship services. Today we do not think about belfries much, if at all. Still, having *bats in the belfry* remains a way of saying one is deranged or at least extremely eccentric. The expression probably comes from the seemingly erratic flight of bats, which move about mainly at night and, owing to their specialized sonar system, swerve to avoid solid objects in their path. Bats in the confines of a church tower might well fly about wildly (to avoid hitting the walls), just as peculiar notions fly about in a crazy person's head. The expression originated in the United States shortly after 1900 and is still current.

bell-bottoms

> "Bell bottom trousers, coats of navy blue,
> She loved a sailor, and he loved her too."
> —Moe Jaffee, song, *Bell Bottom Trousers* (1944)

Pants with widely flared legs. Bell-bottoms were introduced by the Royal Navy in 1857 on the assumption that sailors could kick them off easily if they fell in the sea. They were redesigned in the late 1970's with more modest flares, but, worn only by sailors (not officers), they were quite different from trousers worn by the rest of the military. In 1994, they were eliminated because they were considered too costly. The style, however, periodically appears in civilian clothing.

berserk

Wildly crazy. The term comes from one of the great warriors of Scandinavian myth, Berserkr. A fierce and reckless combatant, he always went into battle without armor, covered only with a bearskin. Hence his name—*ber* (bear) + *serkr* (shirt)—which the Saxons turned into *berserk*. Eventually, in the latter half of the nineteenth century, it came to be applied to any frenzied or maniacal behavior, as in "He went berserk with frustration."

besiege, to

To crowd around from all sides. The word comes from medieval France (*siege*, from the Latin word for "seat"), where, as in all of Europe, an army might attack a walled town simply by parking outside the walls and waiting until it surrendered. The word began to be

Krupp's Big Bertha

used in the nonmilitary sense of "pester"—for example, "the students besieged the teacher to find out their final grades"—in the seventeenth century.

A similar word with a similar origin is *beleaguer*, which comes from the Dutch word for a military camp, *leger*. Also once meaning "to attack by surrounding," it is used today in the sense of "harass" or "pester," as in, "the candidate was beleaguered by hostile reporters." (See also SIEGE.)

big Bertha

A large, fat woman; also, a kind of golf club. This U.S. slang term comes from an expression invented by the French during World War I for a German long-range gun used to shell the city of Paris from a range of seventy-five miles. The "Bertha" alludes to Bertha Krupp, matriarch of the German family that became the world's leading producer of guns in the mid-nineteenth century and remained so until the end of World War II. The Germans nicknamed some of their guns *die dicke Bertha* (the fat Bertha), with the same allusion, and the French simply translated it and applied it to the gun that relentlessly shelled their capital for four months in 1918. In the early 1990's the term was also applied to a driver larger than a normal golf club, designed like the wooden driver but made of metal. It has considerable range but rather poor accuracy.

In the United States the slang terms *big gun* and *big shot* have been used since about 1910 for an important, influential individual. One writer claims they were invented by American followers of the Italian patriot Giuseppe Garibaldi, whose forces used a ninety-millimeter cannon against the Austrians, but this origin has not been corroborated.

bigger bang for the buck, a

A better value for one's money. This term dates from 1954, when it specifically meant more efficient use of defense appropriations, relying mainly on nuclear deterrents. The "bang" here alludes to a nuclear explosion. It was U.S. Defense Secretary Charles E. Wilson who said this new policy would provide "a bigger bang for the buck." The phrase subsequently was applied to civilian issues involving a better value. It echoes an older advertising slogan for a carbonated soft drink, "More bounce to the ounce."

big stick, carry a

Influence behavior through the threat of force. Theodore Roosevelt popularized the expression in a speech on September 2, 1901, saying he had always been fond of the West African proverb "Speak softly and carry a big stick." His administration used this tactic in the dispute over Alaska's boundary with Canada (1902–03) as well as in other foreign affairs where the possibility of U.S. military involvement could pose an effective threat. As a government policy it is still historically identified with Roosevelt. However, it obviously applies elsewhere, and there are comparable proverbs in French (*bâton porte paix,* stick brings peace) and other languages.

bikini

A very abbreviated two-piece bathing suit for women; also, the style of brief pants like those of the suit, fitting on or below the hips, worn by men as well as women. The name for the suit was coined by its French designer, Louis Réard, in 1946, a few days after the United States began peacetime nuclear testing by dropping an atom bomb on the chain of Marshall Islands known as Bikini Atoll. Since this event commanded worldwide attention, Réard felt the name would help sales of his design, and it has survived.

bite the bullet, to

To steel oneself against pain or unpleasantness. The term probably comes from the battlefield in times when the wounded had to be treated without anesthesia or painkillers and were asked literally to bite on a soft lead bullet (soft so as not to break the patient's teeth) to brace themselves against the pain. Today the expression is a metaphor for summoning up the courage to deal with a bad situation—for example, "Dad said Tim will simply have to bite the bullet and pay for the broken window."

bivouac

An enforced stopping place without proper shelter against the elements, such as a mountain climber might use when forced to spend the night on a ledge. The word originally comes from the French and Swiss German *biwacht*, meaning an auxiliary patrol, and was used when an entire military encampment had to stand guard at night. By the eighteenth century it meant a military encampment with only improvised shelter and without protection against enemy fire. Later it was extended to include situations one encountered more from choice (such as climbing mountains) than necessity (military service).

Black and Tans

A force of irregulars enlisted by the British government in 1920 to help the Royal Irish Constabulary put down a rebellion in Ireland. They were so called on account of their uniform of khaki (tan) coats and black belts and caps. The Black and Tans became notorious for their use of needless force, and their activities succeeded mainly in strengthening Irish resistance. In 1921 Britain's Prime Minister David Lloyd George entered into negotiations with Eamon de Valera, leader of the strongest rebel group, the Sinn Fein, resulting in the establishment of the Irish Free State (now the Republic of Ireland). The notoriety of the Black and Tans was not forgotten, however, and the name continued to be invoked in the numerous later conflicts between Irish Catholics and Protestants.

black market

Illegal dealing in goods that are rationed, imports that are unauthorized, and the like. The term originated during World War I and was probably a direct translation of the German *Schwarzmarkt*, which referred to illicit selling of rationed items. It was revived in World War II with the same meaning. In peacetime it is used mainly for items that are imported through improper channels to avoid paying customs duties or to escape import quotas.

Black Monday

The Monday when school reopens after a long vacation. So used in Britain since about 1730, the term supposedly originated in France and was first applied to Easter Monday of 1360, when Edward III of England was besieging Paris. That day was so bitter cold that many soldiers and horses died. From that time on the Monday after Easter was called Black Monday, "black" referring to misfortune. More recently, the name Black Monday was given to October 19, 1987, when the New York stock market fell precipitously and the Dow Jones Industrial Average lost more than 500 points in a single day. It was so called mainly by journalists, who likened it to the stock-market collapse of October 29, 1929, a day dubbed Black Friday and often marked as the beginning of the Great Depression.

blackout

A temporary extinguishment of lights, communications, or consciousness. The term may have originated in the theater, where it meant extinguishing stage lights while scenery was being shifted. However, it came into wide use only during World War II, at first in Britain. Beginning in 1939, the British, fearful of German bombing raids, began to take precautions against revealing strategic targets to the enemy. Eventually this practice was extended to showing any lights after dark in London and other population centers, where special blackout shades and curtains were used for the purpose. After the United States entered the war in 1941, similar precautions were taken in American coastal cities, although sometimes only a *brownout*—a partial blackout—was used. By the middle of the war it was obvious that German and Japanese bombers were not going to attack America's coasts, and the practice was largely abandoned. However, it has been revived from time to time during periods when it seemed important to conserve electricity, as in the energy crisis of the mid-1970's.

The word blackout also has been extended to mean a stoppage of communications. The New York newspaper strike of 1962–63, with its citywide shutdown of all New York papers for nearly four months, was termed a *news blackout*. Similarly, a shutdown of radio or television communications, owing to revolution, violent storm, or strike, also may be called a news blackout.

The verb *to black out,* meaning to undergo a temporary loss of consciousness, may have originated with pilots who underwent this experience before pulling out of a power dive. Today it is used as a synonym of fainting, as well as for a period of temporary memory loss.

Black Shirts

Fascists. The term originated in the 1920's in Italy, when Benito Mussolini's followers wore a black shirt as part of their uniform. The name also was used in Germany for the elite Nazi corps, the S.S. (short for *Schutzstaffel,* or defense squadron). In Britain and America the name was sometimes extended to sympathizers of these fascist groups, some of whom went so far as to copy the uniform. (See also BROWN SHIRTS.)

blarney

Deceptive flattery. The term comes from the fifteenth-century Blarney Castle, near the city of Cork, Ireland. Legend had it that in the early seventeenth century the lord of the castle, which had undergone a long siege by the British, agreed to surrender to their commander, Sir George Carew. But day after day the canny Irish lord found ways to put off the actual surrender, coming up with excuse after excuse. Weeks passed and the word got about, to Carew's extreme embarrassment. When Carew cited yet another excuse for the delay, someone—perhaps even Queen Elizabeth herself—termed it more of "the same blarney."

Blarney Castle has a stone in its wall—a triangular piece of limestone placed high up and difficult to reach. From it came the legend that anyone who could reach the stone and kiss it would be rewarded with the ability to cajole and flatter with great eloquence. Hence the saying he or she has *kissed the Blarney stone* for a person who engages in gross flattery. To indulge tourists, the Irish have provided a substitute stone that is easier to reach and that is, they claim, equally effective.

blaze a trail

Find a new path or lead a new enterprise. The term comes from eighteenth-century America, when scouts preceding an armed force moving through a forest would mark the best path by hacking pieces of bark from tree trunks. Although the term still is used literally, for marking a footpath for hikers or travelers, it is more often used figuratively for a pioneering venture, as in "She blazed a trail in computer programming."

blimp

A small, nonrigid, lighter-than-air airship; also, slang for a fat person. The airship, originally developed in England in 1914, was used as an observation balloon in World War I. The origin of the name is disputed. Supposedly there were two different models for the vehicle, one called *A-limp airship* and the other *B-limp airship* (*limp* meaning "nonrigid"). The latter proved to be the better design, and so its name, converted into the one word, *blimp*, was given to all such ships. This theory, however, has been denied by the Goodyear Company, the original manufacturer. Possibly the name was invented by one of the aviators.

In peacetime blimps continued to be used, principally for advertising. The resemblance of a fat person to this balloonlike object gave rise to the slang use; it is sometimes softened to *baby blimp*.

In Britain *blimp* also means a pompous, elderly person noted for his or her unswerving reactionary ideas and self-important stupidity. This usage comes from a cartoon character, *Colonel Blimp,* invented by artist David Low about 1938, depicting a retired army officer displaying all of these unlovable characteristics.

blitz

A swift, sudden onslaught. In German *Blitz* means "lightning," and early in World War II the Nazis coined the word *Blitzkrieg*, or "lightning war," for the species of warfare they carried on in their conquests of Czechoslovakia and Poland—a sudden concentrated attack by land and air resulting in a quick overwhelming victory. The British shortened it to blitz and, probably because of its resemblance to "blast," used it to mean an aerial bombing attack; in fact, they soon called Hitler's air raids over their country *the blitz*. The American columnist Walter Winchell turned it into a joke, coining *blisskrieg* for a quick romance, a common practice among servicemen in wartime. After the war the word blitz, used as a verb as well as a noun, was broadened to mean any intensive campaign resulting in rapid victory, in business, sports, or other areas. In American football blitz also means the defense taking the offensive and directly charging the passer.

blockade

A barrier that prevents passage on a road or railway owing to snow, an accident, or some other circumstance. This term was transferred from the military blockade, which prevents the entry of supplies or ammunition by means of ships or other forces. Blockades were used in the Napoleonic Wars and the War of 1812. In the latter the British shut off commerce from Chesapeake Bay and Delaware Bay in 1812, and later to the mouth of the Mississippi, as well as the ports and harbors of New York, Charleston, Port Royal, Savannah, and eventually, in 1814, New England. During the American Civil War the North began a blockade of the Confederate coast in 1862. This move gave rise to the term *blockade runner*, for a vessel or person evading or trying to evade a blockade.

blockbuster

A tremendous success; also, an overwhelmingly forceful individual or object. The term originated in Britain during World War II as R.A.F (Royal Air Force) slang for a heavy bomb of great penetrating power, enough to break up whole blocks of buildings and pavements. In the 1950's it became a colloquial term for a book, theatrical performance, or other product that was lavishly produced and heavily advertised in the expectation that it would be an immense popular success.

The term *blockbusting* also was used to describe an unscrupulous practice of realtors and speculators who would make huge profits from housing they bought very cheaply as a result of using scare tactics—warning that the property was about to lose most of its value due to a change in the ethnic or racial makeup of the neighborhood. Since this charge was fictitious, they could then resell at a much higher price.

bloodbath

Wholesale extermination, a ruthless slaughter. This term originated during World War I, when German soldiers termed a battle with many casualties *ein Blutbad*. Allied soldiers translated and adopted the term, which is roughly a synonym for "massacre." During the Vietnam War, supporters of American involvement held that if the United States pulled out, the North Vietnamese would kill thousands of American allies in a terrible bloodbath. Although this feared eventuality never occurred in Vietnam, it did happen in Cambodia, where the victorious Khmer Rouge killed an estimated million inhabitants.

bloody Mary

A cocktail consisting of tomato juice, vodka, and seasonings. The name refers to Queen Mary I (Mary Tudor) of England and Ireland, who during her reign (1553–58) became infamous for her persecution of Protestants. At least 300 of them were burned at the stake, including the eminent Archbishop Thomas Cranmer. In London the name is also a nickname for a red-brick church, St. Paul's, so called for its resemblance to St. Mary's in Cambridge.

bluchers

Half boots made of heavy leather. They were named for Field Marshal Gebhart Leberecht von Blücher (1742–1819), a Prussian general who was instrumental in defeating Napoleon at Waterloo. Later the name *bluchers* was used also for a style of man's leather shoe in which vamp and tongue are made of one piece and the top overlaps the vamp and is tied over the instep. (See also CARDIGAN; EISENHOWER JACKET; RAGLAN; WELLINGTONS.)

blue ribbon

Of outstanding excellence; also, the highest honor attainable, first prize. The name comes from a wide blue ribbon that is the badge of honor of the Garter, the most coveted British order of knighthood. It originally was founded by King Edward III about 1350 and was reestablished in the nineteenth century. Edward's reign was marked by foreign wars and dissension with the church, and consequently he was heavily dependent on the support of loyal noblemen, whom he rewarded with this exclusive honor. The choice of a blue garter, according to popular legend, arose from an incident at a court ball. One of the ladies present accidentally lost her blue garter, which was picked up by the King. Noting the circumspect looks of those who saw him, he bound the garter around his own leg and said, *Honi soit qui mal y pense* ("Shame on him who thinks evil"), which became the motto of the Order of the Garter. It was limited to members of the royal family and twenty-five other knights, but in the twentieth century it began to be awarded to a few commoners, among them Sir Winston Churchill (in 1953). (See also CORDON BLEU.)

boat people

Refugees who escape a country by boat. This term dates from the end of the Vietnam War (about 1975), when it was applied to the thousands who left South Vietnam by sea after it fell to the North Vietnamese. They, and other refugees of this kind, usually leave with few of their possessions, inadequate supplies, and no definite destination, since many countries refuse them entry. Often they fall prey to unscrupulous shipowners and, in Asian waters, even to pirates.

body count

The number of troops killed in a specific action or period of time. This term dates from the Vietnam War. It is occasionally used for the casualties of civilian disasters, such as floods or earthquakes.

bombshell, to drop a

To deliver sudden and extremely surprising news. The term began to be so used shortly after World War I and undoubtedly referred to the instantaneous devastation caused by a falling bomb. A similar meaning, although referring to a rather different devastation, is conveyed by *blonde bombshell*, a slang term dating from about 1940 for an extremely attractive, sexy woman with blonde hair.

The noun *bomb*, apart from its military meaning of a highly explosive missile, is used in the American and British theaters in two wholly opposite senses. In Britain "It went like a bomb" is said of a great success—at first, in the 1950's, of a play or show that was a big hit and later of a party, love affair, vacation, or any other event. In contrast, in the United States a play is said "to be a bomb" (or "to bomb") when it is a complete failure. Further, in America *to be bombed* also has been, since the mid-1930's, a slang term for being intoxicated or high on drugs. (See also TIME BOMB.)

booby trap

A hidden hazard set out to disconcert someone. A classic example known to schoolchildren for generations is putting a pail of water on top of a door so that it falls on whoever opens it. The name for this basically harmless amusement comes from a deadly device—a bomb or other explosive concealed and arranged to go off when it is tampered with. The unlucky victim is the booby, a word thought to come from the Spanish *bobo*, for stupid, and adopted into English about 1600. Although both such a device and its name were used earlier, the term booby trap gained currency during World War II, when it also became a verb, *to booby-trap*, meaning to rig such a device. (See also TIME BOMB.)

boomerang

An action or statement that backfires—that is, turns against its maker. The name comes from a weapon of the Australian aborigines, which consists of a curved wooden throwing club. One edge is convex, so that when it is thrown properly the weapon returns to the thrower.

boondocks, the

The backcountry, the provinces, the "sticks." The word comes from the Tagalog *bundok*, meaning "hill" or "mountain." From it the U.S. Marines stationed in the Philippines during World War II coined "boondocks" for the rough hill country, with its thick brush, jungle, and marshes. It soon became generally used for any remote rural area; often abbreviated as *boonies*.

boot camp

A training camp for U.S. Navy and Marine recruits. The new recruits themselves are called *boots*, a term that dates from World War I. It may have originated, according to William and Mary Morris, from an old-time Navy custom of scrubbing the decks barefooted, a matter of pride in very cold weather. However, a group of new recruits from the Midwest considered the practice ridiculous and bought themselves rubber boots to wear in cold weather. Consequently, they were called, with some contempt, "rubber-boot sailors," a term shortened first to "rubber boots" and then simply to "boots." From this also comes *boot training*, meaning the Navy's and Marine Corps' basic training for recruits. (See also DIE WITH ONE'S BOOTS ON.)

booty

Any prize or gain. The word comes from the Middle Low German *bute*, meaning a distribution or sharing out, and in English it first meant sharing the plunder of war or piracy. Today it still means such loot, but not necessarily taken after a military action. A related but now obsolete expression is *to play booty*, which meant to act as a decoy for one's confederates, or to collude in a shady or criminal transaction. It was used from the sixteenth to the late nineteenth centuries.

Another related term is *freebooter*, from the Dutch *vrijbuiter*, meaning a person in search of booty—in other words, a pirate or buccaneer. It gave rise to FILIBUSTER.

boulevard

A broad avenue, often with one or more strips of plantings (grass, trees, flower beds) on both sides and/or down the center. The name originally meant the same as *bulwark* and came from the same source, the Middle Low German *bolwerk*, the top of the wide rampart—often twenty or more feet wide—that served as the defensive wall of medieval towns. As more sophisticated weaponry rendered such structures obsolete (they could simply be blown up), they sometimes were razed to ground level and used as a wide street on the town's perimeter. The city of Vienna has such a broad boulevard, called the Ring, circling the old town on the site of its original city walls.

bowie knife

A single-edged heavy knife, used by hunters, campers, and other outdoor enthusiasts. It is named for Colonel James Bowie (1799–1836), an American pioneer, adventurer, and soldier who died in Texas at the siege of the Alamo. The knife was designed either by Bowie himself or by his brother, Rezin Pleasant Bowie, but it was the Colonel who popularized it. Supposedly Bowie used such a knife in a general melee following a duel in 1827 and killed at least one person with it. It was so admired that thereafter he decided to have copies marketed under his name.

brainwashing

Subjecting an individual to a barrage of ideas or messages in order to convince him or her to embrace them. The term, which is a direct translation of the Mandarin Chinese words meaning "to wash" and "brain," first appeared in English in the late 1940's. At that time the technique was used by the Chinese Communists to win over their own countrymen to their political beliefs. Brainwashing also was practiced during the Korean War by the North Koreans, who used it to persuade American prisoners to denounce their own side. The results, shown on television, horrified the American public. In a controlled environment such as a prison, brainwashing can be a very potent psychological weapon, often involving physical as well as mental torture, and in fact it did result in some defections to the enemy camp.

Since the Korean conflict, the word has been applied to the overzealous methods used by extremist religious sects to gain converts, who, in this process, are persuaded to give up friends, family, and possessions, and to devote their lives entirely to proselytizing and fund-raising on behalf of their new religion. It also has been used loosely for less intensive forms of indoctrination—in consumer advertising (seeking converts to a brand), political campaigning, and the like.

brass hat/top brass

The highest-ranking officials or executives in an organization. Most etymologists believe that the term *brass hat* originated in the late nineteenth century in the British army, where the senior officers had gold oak leaves on the brim of their caps. John Ciardi, however, believed it refers to the cocked hat worn by Napoleon and his officers, which was folded and carried under the arm indoors. In French they were called *chapeaux à bras* (hats in arms), and the British, said Ciardi, anglicized *bras* to *brass*.

By World War I brass hat referred to all high-ranking officers, and by World War II, in both Britain and America, such synonyms as *the brass, the big brass,* and *the top brass* all were in common use. After the war these terms began to be applied to the top executives in business and other hierarchical organizations, a usage that has persisted.

briefing

Giving detailed instructions about the nature of a specific assignment. The term dates from the 1860's, perhaps originating in the legal brief, and came into common use during World War II to signify giving the details of an attack plan or other mission to the officers and troops assigned to carry it out. From this also came *briefing session,* for the meeting at which such instructions were given.

Also originating in World War II is *debriefing,* for interrogating a person returning from a mission about its results and other details of the operation. Both briefing and debriefing now are used to describe the same process for civilian assignments, such as a diplomatic mission, space travel, a business trip, an investigation, or the like.

brinkmanship

Flirting with extreme danger; seeing how far one can go to the edge of an already hazardous situation. The term originated during the

COLD WAR between the United States and the Soviet Union. In 1956 the American statesman Adlai E. Stevenson referred to Secretary of State John Foster Dulles's hard-line, uncompromising diplomatic policy, which seemed to him to invite direct confrontation, as brinkmanship—that is, as leading the country to the brink of war. Stevenson was not sure if he had invented the word himself or had heard it somewhere, but it continued to be used for taking a risky stand rather than making any concessions.

broadside, a

> "Broadside and broadside our cannon balls did fly.
> And small shot like hailstones on the deck did lie.
> The masts and rigging were all shot away."
> —*Nelson's Death and Victory,* street ballad, early 1800's

A strong verbal attack. This term comes from naval warfare, where it signifies the simultaneous discharge of all the artillery on one side of a ship of war. The naval term was already used in Shakespeare's day.

Brown Shirts

Members of Hitler's Nazi Party, so called for the color of their shirts. By extension, all Nazis. (See also BLACK SHIRTS.)

brushfire

Limited in scope or confined to a small area. This meaning comes from the term *brushfire war,* a localized conflict in which only conventional weapons (as opposed to nuclear ones) are used. Such conflicts are believed to be inevitable, but the deterrent of full-scale nuclear war prevents them from developing into major conflicts.

buccaneer

A pirate. The name originated in the West Indies in the seventeenth century, when sea rovers and pirates haunted the Caribbean. It originally was a French word, *boucanier,* in turn from the West Indian *buccan*—a wooden grill used by the islanders to smoke the meat of wild ox and boar. The French took up this culinary practice and, since many of them took to piracy as well, the term came to be used for both endeavors.

bug out, to

To leave suddenly or rapidly. This term probably originated in World War II and came into wide use during the Korean War. By the mid-1950's it was also civilian slang.

bully for you

Good for you. This expression became a popular catchphrase during the American Civil War.

bulwark

> "A mighty fortress is our God,
>   A bulwark never failing."
> > —Martin Luther, hymn, *Ein' feste Burg*

A strong defense or support. Originally a strong defensive rampart made of earth or other materials, the bulwark has been so called since about 1400. By the late 1500's the word was in more general and figurative use, as in the translation of Luther's famous hymn.

bum/to bum

A lazy, worthless person; a tramp. Also, to loaf or wander or beg. These words came into use shortly before the American Civil War, during which they became widespread. During the war a soldier who left his ranks and plundered was called a *bummer,* and during William Tecumseh Sherman's famous drive from Atlanta to Savannah, his March to the Sea (1864), *Sherman's bummers* was the name given to stragglers who robbed civilians. Some may have been part of Sherman's army, but many others were deserters and some even civilians.

bumped, to be

To be refused a seat on an airplane because the flight was over-booked and there is no room for all of the passengers who have reservations. John Ciardi believed the term originated during World War II, when civilian passengers were forced to make way for military officers or others with higher priority. In Britain, however, *getting bumped* was a Royal Navy term for being torpedoed, as well as meaning a demotion for noncommissioned officers.

burn one's bridges, to

To commit oneself irrevocably to a course of action, cutting off any possibility of retreat or reversal. The term, along with its British version, *to burn one's boats*, comes from ancient military history, when invaders crossing a river or other body of water literally burned the bridge or boats they had used to cross so that they were forced either to vanquish the enemy or die. Of course, a similar tactic may be used by a retreating force, which burns its bridges to foil the pursuing enemy.

The same meaning is conveyed by *to cross the Rubicon*. The Rubicon is a river between ancient Italy and Cisalpine Gaul that Julius Caesar crossed in 49 B.C., thereby invading Italy and starting a war against Pompey and the Roman Senate. Once he had invaded Italy, there was no turning back. According to Suetonius's account, Caesar had halted his forces at Ravenna while he waited to hear whether the Senate would accept the tribunes' veto on the issue of disbanding his army. When news reached him that the Senate indeed intended to disband his forces, Caesar went to join his advance guard on the banks of the Rubicon and told his staff, "We may still draw back but once across that little bridge we will have to fight it out." He then led his army across and begged them to stand faithfully by him.

bury the hatchet, to

"Buried was the bloody hatchet."
—Henry Wadsworth Longfellow, *The Song of Hiawatha* (1855)

To make peace and end hostilities. The term comes from the Native American custom of proclaiming peace by literally burying a tomahawk in the ground. It was first described by Samuel Sewall in 1680 in the New England Historical Register and was referred to again by Robert Beverley in 1705, in an account of Virginia history,

Bury the hatchet!

so the custom appears to have existed among a number of eastern tribes.

A similar British term, *hang up the hatchet*, dates from the early fourteenth century but appears to have had a quite different meaning. Rather, it refers to the hatchet as a tool and simply means to put one's tools away for a time and take a rest.

bushwhacking

Making one's way through forest or underbrush where there is no trail. Originally referring to backwoodsmen's whacking bushes to get them out of the way, in the early 1800's this term began to be used for guerrilla warfare. It gained much wider currency during the American Civil War, when it was applied to the activities of Confederate guerrillas or plunderers, and also to deserters or draft dodgers who hid in the bushes.

bust, to

To demote. Originally, in the late nineteenth century, it was a colloquial military term for downgrading a noncommissioned officer (See BUMPED, TO BE). Gradually, it was extended to mean any reduction in rank or status.

buy it, to

To die. This term, originating during World War I, is thought to be a shortening of the Royal Air Force (R.A.F.) term *to buy a packet*, meaning to be killed. An American variant, dating from about 1950, is *to buy the farm*. According to J. E. Lighter, when a U.S. Air Force training flight crashes on a farm, the farmer sues the government for damages sufficient to pay his mortgage and buy the farm outright. Since pilots in such crashes usually died, they "bought the farm" with their lives.

by George

"By George! she's got it!"
—Alan Jay Lerner, *My Fair Lady* (1956)

An expletive or mild oath used less often today than far ruder exclamations. "By St. George!" was the battle cry of English soldiers and referred to the patron saint of England, who is generally believed to have been a Roman officer martyred early in the fourth century. The "St." was gradually dropped, as the term entered civilian language. It may be obsolescent.

by the numbers

In a prescribed routine way. This term comes from World War II, when recruits were taught certain basic operations, such as putting on a gas mask, by the numbers—that is, at the count of one, the carrier was unfastened, at two the mask was removed, and so on.

by the seat of one's pants

By using intuition or by improvising, as opposed to a learned method or experience. This term was invented by World War II aviators to describe flying when instruments did not work properly or weather limited visibility. It soon came into broader use after the war, as in "Recipe? I just made this cake by the seat of my pants."

cabal

A small, elite, secret group that hatches plots; a junta. For some time this word was thought to be an acronym for the cabinet of King Charles II, whose principal advisers from 1667 to 1673 were named *C*lifford, *A*shley, *B*uckingham, *A*rlington, and *L*auderdale. In fact, however, the members of this cabinet often disagreed and were involved in separate intrigues. Further, the word was already in use much earlier and meant the king's inner group of advisers. Nevertheless, the coincidence of the cabinet members' initials helped bring the word into common use. Its actual origin is now thought to be from the Hebrew qabbālāh, meaning a doctrine received or handed down directly from Moses. In the eleventh and twelfth centuries it referred to an occult theosophy developed by certain rabbis and based on a mystical interpretation of the Scriptures supposedly received from Moses and handed down.

caddie

A person hired to carry a golfer's clubs and chase down lost balls. Although the motorized golf cart has made caddies an endangered species, the name persists in *caddie cart*. The origin of golf is not precisely known, but the game has been closely associated with Scotland since the mid-fifteenth century, and the word "caddie" in Scotland has long meant "errand boy." It came from the French word *cadet*, for younger son, which some say was introduced by the French-born Mary, Queen of Scots. In noble families the younger son did not inherit either family title or fortune and consequently often joined the army. The word "cadet" retained this military meaning in Scotland, but it then acquired the further connotation of someone who hung around waiting to be called on to carry messages or do other errands, and this kind of cadet was then abbreviated to caddie. In England the word cadet similarly came to mean a menial helper, in particular one who did odd jobs for students at Oxford University. Because such a person usually lived in the town rather than at the college, the contempt of "gown versus town" attached itself to him. This kind of cadet was shortened to *cad*, from whom the useful tasks were somehow detached, leaving only the pejorative meaning of nongentleman or rogue. In America both *cad* and *caddie* were adopted, but *cadet* also retained part of its original sense, that is, a military trainee.

Cadmean victory

"They joined battle, and the Phocaeans won, yet it was but a Cadmean victory."

—Herodotus, c. 450 B.C.

A victory that costs the winner as much as it does the loser. There are two possible origins for the term, both from Greek myth. According to one legend, Polynices and Eteocles, the sons of Oedipus and descendants of Cadmus, fought over the possession of Thebes and killed each other. The other story concerns Cadmus himself, who killed a sacred dragon and gave its teeth to Jason to sow, hoping that armed men would spring from the teeth and kill him. But Jason, acting on the advice of Medea, threw a stone among them, and they killed each other instead. (See also PYRRHIC VICTORY.)

cadre

A framework. The word comes from the Latin *quadro*, for "square," via French and Italian, and originally referred to the permanent establishment of a regiment—that is, the framework into which the troops fitted. Today it is also used figuratively for a small group of trained individuals who are capable of forming and training a larger organization, such as a union, political party, or military unit.

Caesar

"Thou'rt an emperor, Caesar, Keisar, and Pheezar."
—William Shakespeare, *The Merry Wives of Windsor*

A dictator or tyrant. A classic American gangster film starring Edward G. Robinson as a character modeled after the notorious Al Capone (1899–1947), who in the 1920's came to control practically all of Chicago's underworld by killing off most of his rivals, was entitled *Little Caesar* (1930).

Caesar is an ancient Roman name. It was the family name of Caius Julius Caesar (102–44 B.C.), statesman and general, a military hero who became Rome's dictator for life. The name Caesar was assumed by his male successors and by the heir apparent to the imperial throne, the most famous of whom was Caesar Augustus (63 B.C.–A.D. 14). Both the German and Russian words for emperor, *Kaiser* and *Tsar*, are derived from Caesar.

The medical term for surgical delivery of a baby, *cesarean section*, supposedly is derived from the fact that Julius Caesar's mother died just before he was born and he was taken from her surgically opened womb. (Some etymologists disagree, believing that the medical term comes from the related Latin verb *caedere*, to cut.) A wide-ranging warrior, Julius Caesar gave his name to the Spanish city of Caesaris, which became Jerez and in turn gave its name to its most famous export, a wine whose name was anglicized as *sherry*.

caisson

A watertight chamber used in construction. In the early days of gunpowder, a caisson was a chest used to store this explosive safely; the word is French and came into English in the seventeenth century. In time the word began to be used for a two-wheeled wagon used to carry artillery ammunition on the battlefield. It is this meaning that is preserved in the U.S. Army song:

> Over hill, over dale, we will hit the dusty trail,
> And those caissons go rolling along.

calculated risk

An action taken despite the known possibility of failure, because doing nothing or something else may be still more dangerous. The term comes from World War II, when the chances for losing bombers were taken into consideration before a bombing mission was sent out, the possible loss of personnel and equipment being weighed against the benefits of damaging the enemy. After the war the term was adopted in such areas as politics and business, where taking an uncertain step is often considered necessary to ultimate success.

camouflage

Deliberate disguise or pretense. The underlying principle of camouflage, used in warfare to conceal military objectives from the enemy, is that of the protective coloring found in nature. A classic example is the chameleon, a lizard whose skin color changes so that it blends in with its surroundings; another is the Arctic weasel, whose brown summer fur changes to white in winter (and is called ermine), so that it blends in with the snow.

Although it certainly originated much earlier, the practice of camouflage became quite elaborate during World War I, which is when the word, derived from the French *camoufler* (to disguise), came into English. The French used elaborate techniques to conceal industrial installations, even creating fake landscapes by wiring foliage to large screens. They also dazzle-painted ships, making it hard to discern their course. In World War II practically all of the belligerent nations used camouflage, especially in the Pacific and Southeast Asia. Uniforms, tents, and other fabrics as well as the paint on tanks, jeeps, airplanes, and other vehicles sported a mottled green-and-brown design, intended to blend in with vegetation, while ships were painted gray so as to blend in with the sea.

Today camouflage is often used figuratively (and as a verb) to mean any stratagem used for concealment. Thus the cut of a maternity dress may be designed to camouflage a woman's pregnancy, or loud boisterous behavior may be said to camouflage a teenager's underlying shyness. (See also SMOKE SCREEN.)

campaign

An all-out effort to accomplish a particular goal. A political campaign is undertaken to secure the election of a candidate to office; an

Camp followers

advertising campaign is mounted to persuade people to buy a product or support an issue. The word campaign comes, via the French *campagne*, from the Latin *campus*, for "field," specifically a field of battle. Indeed, a military campaign still signifies a series of operations mounted to achieve a particular wartime objective.

The same roots also produced the word *camp*, which originally meant a field where an army or troops were temporarily deployed and sheltered in tents. Later it was extended to mean any temporary lodging set up for people in the countryside for an outing, vacation, or similar purpose. (See also CAMP FOLLOWER.)

camp follower

"I hope she has more prudence than to follow the camp."
—George Farquar, *The Recruiting Officer* (1706)

A hanger-on, one who clings to a group without being part of it. The practice of so attaching oneself probably originated with the families of recruits, and also prostitutes, who, making a rational business decision, settled near an army encampment. It then was extended to other civilians who were connected to and benefited from but were not part of military installations—vendors of products, for example. "Suffer me to follow the camp," wrote Lucan in his account of the Roman civil wars in A.D. 60. The term camp follower as such, however, is much newer. It has been traced to a letter written by the Duke of Wellington in 1810 and probably originated about that time.

In America the camp follower of popular musical ensembles, sports teams, or other celebrities has, since the 1960's, been called a *groupie*—also a follower, but not a member, of the group.

Cannae

Any major defeat that marks the turning point for a successful leader. It refers to the Battle of Cannae, where the Carthaginian general Hannibal defeated the Romans on August 3, 216 B.C. Under the Roman system, each of two consuls took turns commanding the army on alternate days. On August 3 it was Terentius Varro's turn, and he made the disastrous decision, against the advice of the other consul, Lucius Emilius, to attack Hannibal's forces. Nearly 50,000 of the Roman troops and their allies were killed. Emilius was wounded, although Varro himself managed to escape. A similar turning point occurred in 1812, when Napoleon Bonaparte occupied Moscow, which, it turned out, had been deserted except for a small number of Russian civilians and in the next few days was largely burned down. Left without provisions or winter quarters for his troops, Napoleon was forced to retreat westward over hundreds of miles of Russian soil, with terrible losses.

cannibalize, to

To salvage parts from vehicles or machinery, or employees or assets from a business, in order to repair or build up another. The term, adapted from the savage practice of eating one's own species in order to survive, or for magical purposes or some other compelling reason, began to be used in this newer, figurative sense in the armed forces during World War II. During the war mechanics often took necessary parts from badly damaged planes and tanks and jeeps to put other vehicles into good working order. Soon the term was applied also to taking personnel from some military units to build up others. The word retained the same meanings in peacetime. Indeed, in the United States there is a sizable automobile "used parts" industry that capitalizes on just such repair work.

cannonball

Anything that moves very fast, notably an express train and, in tennis, a very fast serve. In tennis Bill Tilden is supposed to have been the first to use the expression, about 1920, to describe a decisive overhead smash. The term *cannonball express* (train) dates from about 1888. And swimmers call a jump into water from a curled-up position, with the arms grasping the upheld knees, a *cannonball dive*. All these meanings are derived from the military cannonball, a round iron or steel missile fired from a cannon, which came into use in the late sixteenth century, replacing the stone missiles of earlier times.

cannon fodder

Personnel who are expendable. The term, dating from the late nineteenth century, originated as a translation from the German *Kanonenfutter*, meaning military personnel considered likely to be killed or wounded in combat. Later it was occasionally transferred to anyone regarded as expendable, such as an inexperienced salesperson, or employees most likely to be laid off if a company had to downsize.

canteen

"I left my heart at the stagedoor canteen,
I left it there with a girl named Eileen."
—Irving Berlin, *This Is the Army* (1942)

A portable flask; also a cafeteria, snack bar, or other informal place where refreshments are sold. The name comes from the Italian *cantina*, first meaning a cellar where soldiers drank. Eventually it came to mean any bar or tavern (in both Italian and Spanish), but in eighteenth-century Britain it also came to mean a portable bar, that is, a container for carrying drinks. At first such canteens were used mainly by soldiers but later also by travelers, hikers, and others on the move.

cardigan

A collarless sweater that buttons down the front. The style was named for a British cavalry officer, James Thomas Brudnell, Seventh Earl of Cardigan (1797–1868), who popularized it. It was he who led the ill-fated charge of the light brigade at Balaklava (See BALA-CLAVA) in 1854. It is odd that his name should have attached itself to any garment, for he was widely considered an obnoxious and incompetent officer. Worn by British troops under their tunics to protect themselves against the bitter cold of the Crimean battle-fields, the cardigan was praised by Queen Victoria but condemned by military experts. An extraordinary number of garments got their names in this war. (See also RAGLAN.)

care package

A gift of food and/or small necessities sent to a needy person, student, or camper. The original CARE (Cooperative for American Remittances to Europe) was founded in 1944 by twenty-two organizations to work together in helping victims of World War II. On May 11, 1946, the first CARE food packages were delivered in Le Havre, France, and soon packages were being delivered in eleven other European countries. In 1948 CARE airlifted food to Berliners through the Russian blockade (See also AIRLIFT). By the early 1950's, as Europe recovered, CARE turned its attention to needy persons in other parts of the world and continued to assist victims of war, drought, famine, and civil strife, as it still does. By then the organization was so well known that the name "care package" began to be used for packages of food and other treats sent by relatives to summer campers, boarding school and college students, or simply to anyone as a gift.

carpetbagger

An outsider who seeks to exploit an area for personal gain, especially of a political nature. The name dates from the period just after the American Civil War, when northern political adventurers traveled to the South seeking to build up the Radical Republican Party by getting the newly enfranchised southern African-Americans to support it. Southerners referred to any northerner who came there as a carpetbagger because they thought of all northerners as opportunists who had hastily thrown their meager possessions into a carpetbag—a bag made from pieces of carpet that was a standard style of luggage at this time—and rushed down to plunder the defenseless people of the defeated side. Actually some of the carpetbaggers were sincere and believed that the redemption of the South and the blacks could come only through democracy. Others were fortune hunters, and still others were bent on aiding the Republican Party in order to gain public office for themselves. And some were legitimate businessmen who sought investment opportunities for themselves or their companies in the South. Whatever their aims, many of the carpetbaggers worked their way into positions where they could direct the black vote for the benefit of the Republicans. They found partners in the *scalawags*, southerners who for one reason or another were willing to work for the Republicans.

Carpetbags have long since been replaced by other kinds of luggage, but carpetbagger still retains its pejorative meaning, that is, an outsider who seeks to benefit from the misfortune of the indigenous population. In recent years it also has been applied to politicians who seek office in a state other than their own.

car pool

An arrangement whereby each of a group of automobile owners in turn drives all of the others to or from a particular place, such as work or school, on a regular basis. The term originated during World War II, when shortages and rationing made it practical to conserve gas, oil, and tires in this way.

carte blanche

Unlimited power; complete freedom. The term is a French one and literally means "blank paper," in the same sense as a blank check—that is, one bearing only the signature so that the recipient can fill in any amount of money. It originally (seventeenth century) was used for an unconditional military surrender, in which the victorious side dictated all the terms. It then became part of the language

Giving carte blanche

of diplomacy (which in Europe actually was the French language until World War I) and thereafter was used for civilian concerns, as in "While the company president was away, his second-in-command had carte blanche for hiring and firing."

cartel

A combination of businesses formed to regulate prices, or of political interest groups to promote a particular cause or legislation. The word comes from the Italian *cartello* and in the sixteenth century meant a written challenge to a duel. In the seventeenth century it came to mean an agreement between opponents, specifically one between warring nations concerning the exchange of prisoners of war. Only in the twentieth century did it acquire its meaning of an association of producers of the same or similar goods who seek to obtain monopoly advantages for their members. In the United States antitrust laws have outlawed cartels except where they involve a patented product or where they are concerned solely with the export trade of their members. Since World War II many European governments have invoked similar restraints. Before World War II, however, cartels were not only common but perfectly legal in most of Western Europe.

Today the term cartel refers chiefly to international associations seeking to control a world market by setting prices, restricting production, and/or allocating sales territories or a fixed market share among their members. One of the best known cartels is the Organization of Petroleum Exporting Countries (OPEC), which made its power felt in 1973 by cutting off oil sales to some nations entirely and quadrupling prices to its remaining customers.

cartridge

A container for a liquid, powder, gas, film, or tape. The name comes from the Italian *carta*, the principal kind of paper available in the fifteenth century. Closer to modern cardboard than paper, it was used as a wrapper for costly commodities, such as spices and drugs, and soon it also was used as a container for gunpowder, which was made by rolling up a *carta* into a *cartoccio*. Thus the powder charges could be measured in advance of firing and each be rolled inside a cartoccio, which the soldier opened at one end and inserted into his weapon. In France the container was called a *cartouche*. By 1650 it was customary to include a bullet or shot with each dose of powder, and indeed the modern ballistic cartridge does just that. In the twentieth century a similar device proved convenient for holding the ink of a ballpoint pen or computer printer, camera film, recording tape, and other materials where the convenience of inserting an entire cartridge replaced earlier, more cumbersome methods (filling a fountain pen, loading a camera, etc.).

Cassandra

A person who prophesies doom or disaster. The name alludes to a daughter of the Trojan King Priam, who warned her father not to allow the huge wooden horse built by the Greeks as an offering to the gods inside the city walls. He ignored her warning, and the Trojans dragged the horse inside. There, under cover of night, the Greek soldiers concealed in the horse got out and opened the city gates to their troops, who then sacked and burned Troy.

catapult, to

To hurl something or to move suddenly, as, for example, a rocket catapults a satellite into space. The name comes from the ancient Greek *catapeltes*, meaning "to hurl down" (not up), via the Latin *catapulta*. Numerous ancient peoples had war machines for hurling missiles, at first stones and later arrows. In the sixteenth century the word catapult was used for a variety of missile engines so employed. By the nineteenth century catapult also meant a much smaller device of this kind, a slingshot, which can be lethal in the hands of a skilled user. In the twentieth century the noun became a verb that is used figuratively as well as literally; thus one might say "The Nobel Prize catapulted this obscure economist to worldwide fame."

cataract

> "We shall throw a cataract over his eyes."
> —Plautus, *Miles Gloriosus* (c. 200 B.C.)

An eye condition in which the lens becomes opaque, giving it a filmy appearance. The word comes from the Greek *katarractes*, which not only means "waterfall," as does the English word cataract, but also what in medieval castles was called a *portcullis*, a gate that could be quickly lowered, by means of weights, to close off the entrance to the castle. Originally simply a door, it came to be made like a heavy iron grill. Often it had spikes at the bottom, to catch and injure an invader who managed to enter before it was completely lowered. Because the development of an opaque film in the eye resembles closing off an entrance, this condition began, in the sixteenth century, to be called a cataract.

Catch-22

A no-win dilemma in which one is trapped by a paradox. The term comes from the title of a war novel by Joseph Heller, published in 1961. It refers to an Air Force rule whereby a pilot is considered insane if he continues to fly combat missions without asking to be relieved, but if he does make such a request he is considered sane enough to continue flying. The novel was made into a highly successful motion picture, which further popularized the term. Today it is used to describe such common dilemmas as that faced by a person who is refused employment owing to a lack of experience in that kind of work, which, however, cannot be acquired without getting such a job.

cavalcade

A procession. The word comes from the Italian *cavalcata* (in turn from the Latin *caballus*, for "horse"), which at first meant a raid by men on horseback. In time (seventeenth century) it came to mean a parade of horsemen, especially for a festive occasion of some kind, and soon it was extended to horse-drawn carriages as well. About 1910 a new version was born, the *motorcade*, a procession of cars. Today cavalcade is used more loosely, both literally for any kind of procession and figuratively, as in the early television extravaganza called *Cavalcade of Stars*.

cavalier

A gentleman; also, haughty, disdainful. Like CAVALCADE, this word stems from the Latin *caballus*, for "horse," but in this case came into English via Old French. Originally it meant an armed horseman, that is, a knight. Since knights far outranked foot soldiers, it came to be a synonym for a nobleman and later simply a gentleman. In the seventeenth century, during the English civil war (1642–47), the royalists, who supported King Charles I, were called Cavaliers, whereas those who sided with Parliament were called Roundheads (because they wore their hair cut short). Similarly, a particularly brilliant group of poets at the court of Charles I came to be known, because of their royal affiliation, as the Cavalier poets. The term was actually used quite loosely; the poets were not formally organized in any way, but they all wrote elegant verses on courtly themes and subjects (love, beauty, loyalty). The principal Cavalier poets were Robert Herrick (1591–1674), Thomas Carew (1595–1639?), Sir John Suckling (1609–42), and Richard Lovelace (1618–58). During this same period the term cavalier began to be used as an adjective describing the behavior of some gentlemen—that is, curt, supercilious, haughty, and condescending.

chain reaction

A series of occurrences in which each is caused by the preceding one and in turn causes the next. Although the term originated in chemistry in the mid-1920's, it was confined to specific scientific applications until the end of World War II. The detonation of the first atomic bomb, which in effect ended the war, was followed by a proliferation of information concerning nuclear fission, in which the chain reaction plays a central role. Soon afterward the term began to be transferred to any series of events in which *A* sets off *B*, *B* sets off *C*, etc.—for example, a chain reaction of lawsuits arising from a single case of medical malpractice.

chauvinism

A blind, unswerving, and exaggerated faith in the superiority of one's country, sex, group, or cause. The word comes from Nicolas Chauvin, a soldier under Napoleon Bonaparte who, although he was frequently wounded in battle and finally retired on a modest pension, continued to proclaim his devotion to Napoleon even in defeat. In the mid-nineteenth century several French playwrights caricatured him in their plays, among them Eugène Scribe in *Le Soldat laboureur* and Cogniard in *La Cocarde tricolore* (1831), and his name soon became synonymous with blustering patriotism.

Chauvin may have had an American counterpart in Stephen Decatur, naval officer and stubborn patriot. In April, 1816, a few months after the War of 1812 had ended in a stalemate, Decatur proposed a toast: "Our country! In her intercourse with foreign nations may she always be in the right; but our country, right or wrong."

In the course of the nineteenth century chauvinism became linked with national rivalry, imperialism, and militarism. (See also JINGOISM.) Today the term has been extended to other areas of blind bias, as in *male chauvinism*, an unreasoning belief in the natural superiority of the male sex. Feminist opponents of this attitude, which they so named in the late 1960's, also coined the term *male chauvinist pig*, or *MCP*, for any adherent to it.

chicken shit

Petty regulations, make-work chores, and the like. This term was coined by G.I.'s during World War II. John Ciardi suggested that it alludes to the unending work of shoveling up droppings on a chicken farm. In the next decade, by the time of the Korean War, the term was also used adjectivally as a synonym for "petty."

chink in one's armor, a

A vulnerable point or weakness. The medieval knight was sheathed from head to foot in armor made of mail, that is, interlinked rings or scales of metal that were jointed at various points. At times one or more cracks would develop between the links or joints, leaving him less protected against an enemy spear or arrow. From this comes the present term, which has been used figuratively for a vulnerability or weakness that provides an opening for attack.

chop-chop

Food or any allusion to it; also, quickly, immediately. The latter adverb is also used in verb form, *to chop-chop* meaning to hurry. Both usages are pidgin English brought home from Asia by sailors and soldiers. The noun dates from the time of the Korean War, and the adverb from the late 1800's.

chopper

Nickname for helicopter. The term appears to have originated as military slang during the Korean War, replacing earlier nicknames like *whirlybird* and *copter*. It came into wide use during the Vietnam War, in which helicopters played a major role, flying troops and supplies in and out of otherwise virtually inaccessible places. Etymologists are divided on the source of the name, one saying it came from the belief that helicopter blades could chop off a person's head and another that it arose from the chop-chop noise made by the rotors; the latter seems more likely.

chow

Food. This term was originally brought to America in the mid-1800's by sailors from East Asia or possibly by Chinese workers on the West Coast. By the late 1800's it was used in the military for mess, or mealtime, as well as being used verbally, *to chow* meaning to eat. It also gave rise to numerous variations, such as *chow line*, for any line in which people wait for food, and *chow hound*, for an extremely enthusiastic eater. By the time of World War II these military terms were widely used by civilians.

classified

Secret; permitted to be seen only by authorized individuals. Although the word "classified"—something being put into classes or categories—is much older, this particular meaning originated during World War II, when secrecy concerning military plans took on more importance than ever before, largely because this was the first war in which rapid dissemination of information by radio and other electronic means played a role. "Loose lips sink ships," American defense-plant workers were warned in posters and radio commercials. After the war the term was adopted first in government agencies and then in business and other areas where it was important to keep production and design plans a closely guarded secret from competitors.

clear the decks, to

To prepare for action. The term comes from naval warfare, when a crew prepared for battle by removing or fastening down all loose objects on deck that might otherwise get in the way of the guns or be knocked down and injure a sailor. The procedure was important mainly in the days of sailing ships, since the modern battleship requires far fewer preparations of this nature. The transfer of the term to other areas, where it means to take care of minor details so as to cope with a major undertaking, dates from at least the eighteenth century. Robert Burns, in his poem *The Jolly Beggars*, wrote:

> Their tricks an' craft hae put me daft,
> They've ta'en me in, an' a' that,
> But clear your decks, an' "here's the Sex!"
> I like the jads [women] for a' that.

click, klick

Abbreviations for kilometer. These terms came into use during the Vietnam War and soon came to be used in nonmilitary contexts.

climb the walls, to

Also, *to be up the wall*. To feel so restless or frustrated that one is driven to action. One of the earliest uses of this expression appears in the Old Testament Book of Joel, in which the writer prophesies that a great army will come upon the Israelites, and "They shall run like mighty men; they shall climb the wall like men of war . . ." (Joel 2:7). Indeed, until the invention of gunpowder made them obsolete, cities and towns were surrounded by defensive walls, which had to be climbed or otherwise breached by their attackers. While the military climbers of city walls scarcely did so from sheer restlessness or frustration, their attack no doubt seemed fierce and frenzied, giving some support to the idea that one could be driven up the wall in this fashion.

clobber, to

To batter, pound, or destroy. This verb, of unknown origin, began to be widely used by airmen during World War II, both in the present sense and to mean shooting down enemy aircraft or killing or wounding someone. It quickly entered civilian terminology in both the literal sense of physically beating someone up or defeating someone, and figuratively, as in brutally criticizing someone. All these usages remain current.

close quarters

A confined space; crowded. The term comes from naval warfare. In the eighteenth century wooden barriers were placed at various points on a ship. When it was boarded by the enemy, the crew would retreat behind the barriers, which were fitted with loopholes through which they could fire. In this situation they were fighting in close quarters, that is, in immediate contact with the enemy. In time the term came to be used figuratively for any crowded or confined situation.

close ranks, to

To present a united front. In the old-time European army the soldiers were aligned side by side, in neat rows, or ranks, on the battlefield.

When the enemy attacked, officers would order the troops to close ranks, that is, to move the rows close together, so that the enemy faced a seemingly impregnable mass of men. This standard order of battle proved useless in the face of guerrilla warfare, such as the British encountered in North America when they fought against Native Americans. With the development of modern weapons, it was eventually abandoned altogether. However, the term remained in the language in its figurative sense of individuals banding together and presenting a single view to the public, even though they might have differences among themselves in private. One writer in 1739 described the barons and clergy closing ranks and standing "firm like a stone wall."

coat of arms

"A threadbare coat is armour-proof against highwaymen."
—Thomas Fuller, *Gnomologia* (1732)

A heraldic device that bears special symbols denoting the bearer's family history. The original coat of arms was a linen or silk overcoat worn by medieval knights to protect their armor against the elements; it was probably first used by Crusaders to protect their valuable armor against the sun and dirt they encountered on their travels to the Holy Land. These coats were not plain but were embroidered with various markings showing how each knight was entitled to bear arms by virtue of his family crest. When costly metal armor was rendered obsolete, the coat of arms lost its "coat" and became a purely decorative and ceremonial object. However, it is still of great interest to genealogists who trace the details of family history, often with a view to uncovering a background of nobility. Today some individuals even take pains to design a family coat of arms for themselves as a kind of status symbol.

cohort

"The Assyrian came down like the wolf on the fold
And his cohorts were gleaming in purple and gold."
—Lord Byron, *The Destruction of Sennacherib* (1815)

A companion or associate; also, a group or company united in some enterprise. Originally a cohort was one of the ten divisions of a Roman legion, consisting of 300 to 600 soldiers. The term then

Cold feet

became attached to the army camp where such a division was quartered, and in the Middle Ages it was transferred to a farm enclosure, that is, a barnyard. The meaning of individuals banded together persisted, however, and today one may speak of, for example, a gang leader and his cohorts (accomplices in crime) or, more benignly, a law student and her cohorts (colleagues) in the study group.

cold enough to freeze the balls off a brass monkey

Extremely cold, frigid. This term is widely believed to come from naval warfare, when large sailing ships could carry numerous cannon, but the cannonballs occupied too much space. Therefore they were stacked in pyramids on brass trays called *monkeys*. During very cold weather the metal would shrink and balls would fall off the monkey. The theory may be fanciful, but "monkey" also was at one time a name for a gun or cannon (seventeenth century), so there may be an element of truth in it.

cold feet, to get/have

To be timid; to back away from some undertaking. One highly imaginative etymologist claims this term came from the fact that frozen feet were a common infantry hazard until about 1900, and that a soldier so afflicted will not rush into battle but will advance slowly, if at all. This view is allegedly borne out by pictures of retreating troops whose feet are wrapped in rags, as in Napoleon's retreat from Moscow. Another writer points out the chilling effects of fear, which he believes gave rise to this metaphor for losing one's nerve. The precise source of the term is, in fact, not known, but it has been used since about 1890.

cold war

Tension between nations that view one another with extreme distrust and hostility. The term was invented by Herbert Bayard Swope just before World War II, as an alternative to a *shooting war*, which some Americans were talking of entering with Germany. In 1946 Swope first used the phrase publicly in a speech he wrote for Bernard Baruch to describe the state of affairs between the United States and the Soviet Union, which by then had emerged as the world's two superpowers. Baruch, however, considered the phrase too severe and did not use it until the following year, when he finally decided it was appropriate. Although America and Russia were the principal "belligerents," the cold war of that period centered on the conflict between all of the Communist and non-Communist nations, and it finally erupted into actual fighting in the Korean War (1950–53). Since then the term has continued to be used for nations hostile to one another but not actually at war. It also has been extended to antagonists on a smaller scale—rival business firms, for example—when their relations become extremely unfriendly.

colonel

> "Where the corn is full of kernels
> And the 'colonels' full of corn."
> —William James Lampton (1859–1951), *Kentucky*

In the American South, an honorific, that is, a title of respect; elsewhere, a military rank. The English word is derived from the Italian *colonello*, in turn from *colonella*, for column, because this was the name given to the officer who led a column of soldiers. The military meaning persists in the colonel of the U.S. Army, Air Force, and

Marine Corps—a commissioned officer who ranks above a lieutenant colonel but below a brigadier general and is equal in rank to
a captain in the U.S. Navy.

The southern honorific colonel has existed since the mid-
eighteenth century, often being created by a state governor who
confers the title on some prominent citizen or crony. Apparently
this practice was so prevalent in Kentucky that since the mid-1930's
"colonel" has been a common colloquialism for a native or resident
of that state.

The image of the southern colonel—a courtly, old-fashioned
gentleman—became a famous trademark in the 1950's when
Colonel Harlan Sanders, who had been made an honorary colonel
by Kentucky Governor Ruby Laffoon in 1936, took to the road to
promote his newly incorporated fast-food enterprise, Kentucky Fried
Chicken. Soon the image of the white-haired Colonel, with his goa-
tee, white suit, black string tie, black elastic-sided gaiters, and cane,
was seen all over the United States on billboards, storefronts, television commercials and talk shows, motion pictures, and millions of
containers holding the product of his invention. In 1964 he sold
the business to a large corporation but was given a lifetime job as the
company's goodwill ambassador, and he continued to travel thousands of miles a year for promotion, almost until his death at the age
of ninety (in 1980).

combat zone

In large cities, a sex district—that is, a kind of legal no-man's-land
where pornographic film operators, topless dancers, prostitutes, and
pimps ply their trade with little or no interference from the authorities. The term apparently comes from the analogy to a military
combat zone—the area where fighting actually takes place—in that
such districts are wide open and, further, that they often appeal to
soldiers and sailors far from home who seek solace in "adult" entertainment. The authorities presumably tolerate such districts because
they are confined to a specific small area.

The military combat zone is defined as the area extending from
the front line back as far as the communications area. In World War
II in the European sector, however, it was extremely difficult to
determine the precise location of a combat zone, because it was
often hard to distinguish between front lines and support personnel

(communications, supply lines, etc.). The front line of contact with the enemy was generally held by a string of rifle companies, and behind them lay, in turn, what were called the battalion sector, division sector, corps area, and communications zone.

commandeer, to

To seize arbitrarily and illegally. The term came into English from South Africa during the late nineteenth century, when the Afrikaans word *commandeer*, meaning to compel military service or to appropriate for military purposes, became familiar to English soldiers. By the time of the Boer War (1900) it had been transferred to nonmilitary uses—as in "The motion-picture director commandeered the town's main thoroughfare to shoot a scene."

The Boers also gave us the word *commando,* in English meaning a member of an assault unit specially trained for hit-and-run tactics in enemy territory. In Afrikaans the word originally meant an armed troop of Boer cavalry (the entire troop, not an individual serving in it). During the Boer War it referred to an army unit made up of the militia of an electoral district. In World War II the British adopted the name for elite troops made up of volunteers for particularly hazardous duty, and the name applied to both the unit and the individuals in it.

comrade

> "A comrade is a familiar male friend."
> —William Dampier, *Voyages* (1697)

Fellow member, colleague, friend, crony. The word comes from the Spanish *camarada*, which originally meant a room in which soldiers were billeted together and later was applied to the soldiers who shared such a room. It was in the latter sense that the word came into English in the late sixteenth century and then was extended to the more general meaning it has today. The old military sense is retained in the term *comrade in arms*, which since the nineteenth century has meant fellow soldier, but which also is used loosely for a fellow worker or anyone engaged in the same struggle.

In the twentieth century comrade also acquired the connotation of membership in the Communist Party, because *tovarich*, the Russian word for comrade, became, from the time of the revolution, a term of address in the former Soviet Union.

concentration camp

A place for detaining large numbers of individuals who are considered undesirable for one reason or another and therefore are "concentrated" in a single place where they can be closely controlled. The concentration camp was invented about 1900 during the Boer War. The British commander Lord Horatio Kitchener was encountering massive guerrilla resistance, so he moved his troops systematically through enemy territory and rounded up not only Boer soldiers but their wives and children as well. All of the captives were thrown into hastily improvised camps where, under terrible living conditions, many of them died.

Even more notorious were the concentration camps in which, beginning in the 1930's, the Nazis confined political opponents, Jews, and other "undesirables," resulting in the death of millions—by execution and from disease and starvation—by the end of World War II. During that war the United States confined hundreds of Japanese-Americans, considered enemy aliens, under somewhat more humane but still prison conditions, in so-called *internment camps*. In 1988 Congress somewhat belatedly passed a law making some monetary restitution to former inmates of these camps. Some of the camps in which displaced persons have been confined—notably those for Cambodian refugees in Thailand—are in effect concentration camps in all but name.

conk out, to

To slow down or stop; to go to sleep or to lose consciousness. This colloquial term was originated by aviators during World War I, probably in imitation of the coughing noise an engine makes before stopping completely. The word *conk* alone is much older. It first was a slang word for head (early nineteenth century) and later, in Britain, for nose, and then for penis or vagina (perhaps owing to its similarity to cock for the former and cunt for the latter).

conscientious objector

A person who refuses to perform a required duty on moral, ethical, or religious grounds. The earliest use of the term dates from about 1900 and referred to an individual who refused to be vaccinated, contrary to legal requirements. Since World War I, however, the term has been used almost exclusively for a person who refuses to render military service. During World War II, Americans often abbreviated it to *C.O.* (and Britons to *conchie* or *conshy*).

containment

Stopping an advance by limiting the object or person to a circumscribed area. At one time (about 1900) it simply meant stopping enemy troops from advancing. After World War II, during the cold war, it began to mean specifically stopping the spread of Soviet communism. This meaning persists in an expanded version among those who believe that the United States has an obligation to assist, militarily and in any other way, any nation that it believes might otherwise turn to communism; in the 1980's Nicaragua was a prime target for such activities.

In the mid-1970's economists began to speak of *cost containment* with reference to the galloping inflation that affected certain sectors of the economy. For example, the cost of health care in the United States rose at about twice the rate of inflation between the mid-1970's and mid-1980's, making cost containment in this area a major priority.

contras

Opponents of an established government. The word is short for the Spanish *contrarevolucionario*, or counterrevolutionary, and was (and is) used specifically for a guerrilla group active in Nicaragua that opposed the Sandinista government, which took over by force in 1979. The Nicaraguan contras were ultraconservative and were long aided by the United States; the Sandinistas were considered Marxist and were aided by the Soviet Union. In 1987 the contras helped touch off a political scandal in the United States when it was discovered that American intelligence agencies had been supplying arms and other aid to the contras in contravention of a congressional decision to limit U.S. interference.

convoy

A protective escort. The word entered the English language as long ago as the fourteenth century, coming from the Latin *conviare*, "to travel with," via the Old French *conveier* or *convoier*, "to accompany." However, it acquired the specific connotation of protection only during the sixteenth century. During World War I, beginning with the sinking of the passenger liner *Lusitania* in 1915, German submarine attacks on Allied shipping became an ever-increasing hazard, so that Allied troops and supply ships were obliged to travel in convoys protected by destroyers. The same practice continued during World War II. Both as a noun and as a verb, convoy retains the military sense of protection against the enemy, but it also is used in civilian affairs, as in "A motorcycle is convoying the visiting dignitary."

Copperhead

A traitor or enemy sympathizer. The copperhead is a poisonous snake of the eastern and southern United States that gives no warning before it strikes. During the Civil War, many in the North, especially among the Democrats, opposed the war. Their fellow northerners considered them traitors to the Union cause and called them Copperheads. In the late 1930's President Franklin D. Roosevelt revived the term, using it for those who opposed his New Deal legislation and again during World War II for Americans who supported Axis propaganda.

cordon bleu

Gourmet—that is, describing distinguished food and those who indulge in it. The term, French for "blue ribbon," originally was the emblem of the highest order of French knighthood, the Order of the Holy Ghost (St. Esprit), comparable to the BLUE RIBBON of Britain's Order of the Garter. The French knights would hold dinner meetings that became famous for their fine food, and the name cordon bleu therefore became attached to *haute cuisine* (elegant cookery), eventually becoming a synonym for it.

corps

A group of individuals who act together or have a common purpose. The word comes from the Latin *corpus*, which meant not only "body" but also "a body of soldiers." It entered the English language in the thirteenth century with its military meaning, which has persisted to the present. The official name of the U.S. Marines is United States Marine Corps. In the U.S. Army a corps is a specific unit, a ground combat force made up of two or more divisions. However, the word also began to be used for such civilian groups as press corps, ballet corps, and diplomatic corps, each describing a body of individuals associated in a common enterprise.

Also from the military came *esprit de corps*, a French term, literally meaning "corps spirit," adopted into English in the eighteenth century and meaning a sense of unified purpose, team spirit, or fellowship.

countdown

Last-minute preparations for an important occasion or project. The term comes from nuclear-weapons testing, where counting backward to the final moment of launching a rocket or setting off an explosion became common procedure. However, one writer holds that the procedure originated in the German director Fritz Lang's science fiction film, *The Lady in the Moon* (*Die Frau im Mond*, 1929), which featured a rocket launching. It then was adopted in early German rocket testing and brought to the United States by German scientists who came to work there in the 1930's.

The process—in its simplest form, 10, 9, 8 . . . 1, blast off!— even entered the realm of children's games, where it replaced the much older "1, 2, 3, go!" Soon the term was extended figuratively to any final preparations for an important event—for example, the countdown for a vote on a new law or for unveiling a new automobile model.

coup

A very successful and somewhat unexpected move; a sudden victory. The word is French for "stroke" or "blow" and meant, among the North American Plains Indians, a special honor earned by a warrior's act of unusual bravery or recklessness—for example, striking an armed enemy with the bare hand or openly stealing an enemy's horse or weapon. Each such act earned a coup, and the warriors with the greatest number of coups had special status in their tribe. In the present use of coup, the connotation of recklessness has been replaced by unexpectedness, as in "Harry's admission to the prestigious Century Club was a great coup." (See also COUP DE GRACE; COUP D'ÉTAT.)

coup de grace

A finishing stroke. The term is French for a death blow ("blow of mercy," literally) given to end a wounded person's suffering. It most likely originated in dueling or other sword fighting and was adopted into English by 1700. Later it was transferred to mean the finishing touch on any project or undertaking.

coup d'état

The seizure of power by force. The term is French for "stroke of the state." One of its most famous uses was for Louis Napoleon's seizure of the French throne on December 2, 1851. However, it was already known two centuries earlier, when a French historian used it to describe Cardinal Richelieu's accession to power.

cover story

An elaborate lie. This expression originated in the intelligence community during World War II (and perhaps even earlier), when it was used to describe the wholly fabricated, seemingly legitimate background given to a spy. The term was perpetuated in war and espionage novels beginning in the 1950's. It now is used for any elaborate pretense used to disguise a true purpose, such as a cover story given to the press concerning a politican's financial backers.

The use of "cover" to mean a pretense or deliberate concealment is much older, dating from at least 1599, when Shakespeare wrote, "Death is the fairest cover for her shame" (*Much Ado About Nothing*).

crack the code, to

To solve a very difficult problem or mystery. This term comes from World War II, where it signified deciphering coded intelligence. After the war it was transferred to similar problems, especially to cracking the genetic code.

cravat

Necktie. The name for this standard item of male attire comes from Croatian mercenaries who guarded the Turkish front of the Hapsburg Empire during the centuries when it was threatened by the Ottoman Empire. Their distinctive neckwear, a lace-trimmed scarf knotted about the neck, with long flowing ends, appealed particularly to the style-conscious French, who adopted it first for their troops and later for high-society dress. The French name for Croat is *cravate*, which in English became cravat (and in German, *Kravatte*).

credibility gap

Distrust of a public statement or position. The term was first used in the 1960's during the Vietnam War, when numerous Americans began to have serious doubts about the truth of official statements and policies expressed by the government and President Lyndon B. Johnson concerning the conduct of the war. For example, military victories would be proclaimed, but no real progress toward the war's

Crusaders

ending appeared to follow. Since then, the term has been applied to individuals, corporations, government agencies, and the government as a whole whenever the public experiences a lack of confidence in the veracity of their statements or perceives large discrepancies between word and deed.

crusade

A vigorous campaign for or against some issue or cause. It originated in the Crusades, the series of wars undertaken by European Christians between the eleventh and fourteenth centuries to recover the Holy Land from Islam. The word itself comes from the Spanish *cruzada*—from *cruz*, for "cross"—because the Crusaders' breastplates or shields nearly always bore the sign of the Christian cross. Since the late eighteenth century the word has been transferred to other undertakings. In 1786 Thomas Jefferson spoke of a crusade against ignorance, and today one might speak of a crusade against cigarette smoking or a crusade for civil rights.

date of infamy

An instance of base treachery. The term comes from President Franklin D. Roosevelt's speech to Congress following the Japanese attack on Pearl Harbor: "Yesterday, December 7, 1941—a date which will live in infamy—the United States of America was suddenly and deliberately attacked by naval and air forces of the Empire of Japan." The term is often misquoted as *day of infamy*.

D-Day

Any day marking a particularly important event or occasion. The term began to be used during World War I as a code designation for the Allied offensive at Saint-Mihiel. The most famous use of it, however, was in World War II, when it designated the start of the Allied invasion of the Normandy coast. It originally was planned to be June 5, 1944, but was postponed until June 6 owing to bad weather. The "D" has no special significance, simply standing for "day," much as the "H" in *H-hour* stands for "hour." However, one writer points out that all amphibious operations have a "departed date," for which D-day may serve as an abbreviation.

deadbeat

A loafer or sponger. This term dates from the Civil War, when it, along with *beat*, was applied to soldiers who shirked their duty. This meaning persisted after the war, as well as a broader one, for any worthless person. The term also was extended to a person who would not or could not pay his or her debts, a sense that is still current.

deadline

A time or date when something must be completed. Originally, during the American Civil War, a deadline was a line of demarcation around the inner stockade of a prison camp. At the notorious Confederate camp at Andersonville, a line was actually marked out some distance from the outer wire fence. Any prisoner crossing this line was shot on sight. After the war the term continued to be used in the South in games of marbles, where it meant a line drawn near the ring. If on the first shot a player's marble fell short of the line, he was "dead," that is, had to drop out of the game.

According to Irving Lewis Allen, in 1880 a quasi-official deadline was designated by New York City's Police Inspector Thomas Byrnes, who decreed that any professional swindler known to the police would be arrested if seen south of Fulton Street (in lower Manhattan). A few years later the city's 14th Street was informally known as the deadline, whose crossing meant breaching class lines (the area south of that street was considered a slum).

By 1920 the term was in common use for a time limit, such as a newspaper's deadline, and the penalty for passing beyond it was considerably less lethal than the original usage.

Dear John

A letter terminating a romantic relationship. The term was first used during World War II for a letter from the wife or sweetheart of a serviceman stationed overseas or far away, telling him that she was no longer willing to wait for his return (or that she had found a replacement for him). Although only single American men were drafted at first, by the spring of 1943 some 30 percent of all U.S. troops were married men. In India some soldiers formed a Brush-Off Club, with admission only by a Dear John letter. In Texas there was a Jilted G.I. Club, with the same entrance requirement, and its theme song was the popular song *Somebody Else Is Taking My Place* (1937). Some servicemen called the letter a "green banana," but this term foundered, and Dear John entered the language more or less permanently.

death march

A forced march or other cruel and unusual punishment. In 1942, after taking Bataan, the Japanese imposed on their prisoners a terrible forced march in which thousands of Americans and Filipinos died. It gave rise to the term, which is still most closely associated with that occasion but has since been used for similar events in other parts of the world.

decimate, to

To destroy or annihilate; to kill many people. The word comes from the Latin *decimo*, for "tenth," or *decimare*, "to kill every tenth man." The Romans in fact did punish a mutiny by executing every tenth man involved in it; sometimes they also lined up a defeated army and chose by lot one of every ten soldiers, who was killed. This meaning of the word persisted in English until the nineteenth century, when it came to mean simply the destruction of a large number of persons. Thus today one speaks, for example, of an epidemic of cholera that decimated the population.

defenestration

Jumping or being thrown out of a window. The term entered the language in the early seventeenth century with reference to an event that occurred just before the outbreak of the Thirty Years' War. Two leading Roman Catholic members of the royal council, as well as the council's secretary, were thrown out of the window of Hradcany Castle in Prague on May 21, 1618, by Protestant nobles who believed that the country's liberties were being threatened by Emperor Matthias. By some extraordinary stroke of luck they landed in the moat of the castle and sustained only minor injuries.

This, in fact, was the *second* defenestration of Prague. The first had taken place almost exactly two centuries earlier. During the outburst of protest that followed the burning at the stake of the religious reformer John Huss, several town councilors appointed by the king were thrown from the windows of the Prague town hall on July 30, 1419, and were killed. This event set off the Hussite Wars, a series of conflicts that lasted until 1478. The second defenestration, in 1618, set off the Thirty Years' War, which began as a religious struggle between Catholic and Protestant nations but eventually became a political struggle between the Hapsburg Empire and its opponents.

In 1948 there may or may not have been a *third* defenestration in Prague. Jan Masaryk, son of the country's leading statesman, first president, and principal founder, had served as foreign minister of the Czech government in exile during World War II. He continued in this post after the government returned to Prague in 1945 and remained in office after the Communists took over the government in February, 1948. A few days later, however, it was announced that he had committed suicide by throwing himself out of a window. It has never been determined if he actually did so or was murdered.

Defenestration is not an exclusively Czech phenomenon, although the Czech capital seems to have had more than its share of notable instances. Following the Wall Street crash of October, 1929, quite a number of brokers and investors who found themselves financially ruined committed suicide by jumping from high office buildings in New York City. In the 1970's the chief executive of the United Fruit Company threw himself from a New York skyscraper when his involvement in illegal financial doings was exposed. The stock debacle of October, 1987 (see under BLACK MONDAY) appears to have been taken in better stride; no specific defenestrations seem to have followed it.

defoliation

The destruction or loss of leaves. The term comes from the Vietnam War, when incendiary and chemical weapons such as NAPALM and AGENT ORANGE were used by the U.S. Air Force to expose jungle supply lines. During the 1964 Presidential campaign Senator Barry Goldwater suggested using atomic weapons for the same purpose, a statement that cost him considerable support.

Desert Fox

Nickname for German Field Marshal Erwin Rommel (1891–1944), a brilliant soldier who rose through the ranks beginning in World War I and particularly distinguished himself in World War II as commander of the Afrika Korps. His campaigns in the Sahara earned him the nickname. Toward the end of the war he turned against Hitler and supposedly took poison after it was discovered that he had taken part in a plot to assassinate Hitler, but he was buried with military honors.

desert rats

Nickname of Britain's Seventh Armoured Division, which fought in North Africa during World War II. Its divisional sign was the desert rat (jerboa), whose tactics of scurrying and biting it adopted with great success. The desert rats fought in Libya and then took part in the Normandy invasion, fighting their way to Berlin.

détente

The easing of hostility and tension, especially between nations. The word is French for "slackening" and first referred to the trigger of a gun or other firing arm, which was held back ("detained") in order to be fired. It then came to be used figuratively in both French and English for a relaxation of tension (which is, in a sense, what happens when one pulls the trigger). The international language of diplomacy was for many centuries French, and so the term was borrowed to describe the easing of tension between countries by means of negotiation, forging of new agreements, and similar diplomatic measures. It has been so used in English since about 1910 and came into particular prominence as a goal of various summit meetings held by the heads of state of important world powers, especially the United States and the Soviet Union, beginning in the early 1960's. By this time détente meant a long-range policy of improving relations between nations at opposite ends of the political spectrum so as to avoid a confrontation that could conceivably end in nuclear war and mutual annihilation. By the 1970's détente was an important element of American foreign policy, leading to prolonged negotiations with the Soviet Union over limiting nuclear weapons and testing, as well as interference in the affairs of smaller countries, such as Afghanistan.

deterrence

The act of preventing or discouraging an action through fear of the consequences. The verb *to deter*, meaning to discourage or prevent, came into English in the late sixteenth century. Although its root is the Latin *deterrere*, meaning "to frighten away," it long had a fairly benign meaning, as in, for example, "Applying creosote deters wood from rotting." Only since World War II has deterrence acquired a sinister connotation, as nations hastened to arm themselves with nuclear weapons, thereby acquiring the potential for mutual annihilation. Today deterrence and deterrent nearly always imply *nuclear deterrents,* that is, possessing nuclear armaments in order to prevent violent confrontation lest, in retaliation, these weapons will actually be employed.

diehard

An individual who never gives up, no matter how hopeless the cause or position appears to be. The word supposedly comes from the words of a British colonel, Sir John Inglis, who took command of the Fourth Battalion of the 57th Regiment of Foot against Napoleon's forces in 1811 at the Battle of Albuera, in Spain. Although badly wounded himself, the Colonel told his men, "Never surrender. Die hard, my men, die hard." Some three-fourths of the battalion were killed or wounded in the battle. Thereafter the regiment was nicknamed the Die-Hards, and in time the term was transferred to anyone who persists in taking a hopeless stand against overwhelming odds.

In 1911 a group of peers in Britain's House of Lords refused to agree to any diminishment of their veto power over the House of Commons, and they became known as the Diehards. Thereafter diehard also sometimes meant a political ultraconservative, who refuses to change with the times.

die is cast, the

A final decision has been made. The term comes from Suetonius's account of Julius Caesar's invasion of Italy in 49 B.C. When Caesar

Dying with his boots on

crossed the River Rubicon into Italy, thereby advancing against Pompey and the Roman Senate, he supposedly said, *"Jacta alea est"* ("The dice have been thrown"), meaning that now there was no turning back.

die with one's boots on, to

To die while still actively employed. Presumably the expression comes from soldiers who died on active duty. A related term is to *die in harness,* that is, like the plough horse that works to the end. Shakespeare used "harness" in the sense of armor in *Macbeth*; "Blow, wind! Come, wrack! At least we'll die with harness on our back," cried Macbeth as he rode into battle against Macduff.

digging in

Standing firm in one's position or views. The term comes from the trench warfare of World War I, where the soldiers of both sides dug trenches and held them, with neither side advancing or retreating measurably, for months on end.

dirty tricks

Secret operations and deceitful tactics. Although originating in the late 1600's, this term became well known when applied to the covert intelligence operations carried out during the cold war by the Central Intelligence Agency, which actually was nicknamed "department of dirty tricks." In the 1970's it was applied to unethical political campaign practices, such as the notorious Watergate break-in that ultimately led to President Richard Nixon's resignation from office.

dive-bombing

Attacking from above. The military technique of dive-bombing dates from the 1930's, when it was discovered that fighter bombers could wreak enormous damage if they released their load while they were in a steep dive down toward the enemy. It was used with devastating effect in the Spanish Civil War and later in World War II. Since then the term has been transferred to attacks by mosquitoes, insect sprayers, and the like.

divide and rule

Win by getting one's opponents to fight among themselves. Although surely discovered to be a successful technique by the most ancient of adversaries, and already a maxim in Roman times (*divide et impera*, in Latin), it was quoted particularly often during the seventeenth century. Sir Francis Bacon advised King James I in 1615: "*Separa et impera.*" A few years later Sir Edward Coke said that *Divide et impera* was the motto of Philip of Macedon and of Louis XI of France in dealing with his nobles, as well as the traditional motto of Austria. It is also put as *divide and conquer*.

The saying's truth has been borne out in more recent times by the experience of various third-party political movements. When a group of dissidents breaks away from Major Party *B* to form a new party, *C*, it is almost invariably Party *A*, which has remained intact, that wins the next election.

Dixie

The American South. The term was popularized through Daniel Decatur Emmett's song *Dixie's Land* (1859) and gained currency throughout the Civil War.

dogfight

A battle of two or more airplanes. This term dates from the end of World War I but was not widely used until World War II.

dog tag

Nickname for an identification bracelet or tag. The term was widely used for the identification tags issued to the U.S. Armed Forces in World War II but had already come into use by the end of World War I, when someone likened these disks to the tags that dog owners attach to canine collars. The term *dog tag on file* was a euphemism for "dead and buried." Dog tag soon was applied to any similar identification device attached to one's person or to personal possessions such as luggage.

dollar-a-year man

A person who serves the government for patriotic reasons. This term originated during World War I, when volunteers of this kind were paid that sum in order to make their contracts legally binding.

dollar diplomacy

The use of U.S. military and economic power to further the interests of American business abroad or to persuade other nations to follow American political leadership. In the early 1900's, U.S. Marines helped American business open new markets in Latin America, establishing protectorates over Cuba, Haiti, Nicaragua, and Santo Domingo. The policy was so described in a *Harper's Weekly* article in 1910 and later defended by President William Howard Taft, who spoke of "substituting dollars for bullets." Since then it has become a term of criticism of the United States's strong-arm economic tactics in various parts of the world.

domino theory

The idea that if one event takes place it will give rise to a whole series of similar events. The term was used by President Dwight D. Eisenhower in 1954 to explain his decision to aid the South Vietnamese government of Ngo Dinh Diem. If the Communists were allowed to prevail in South Vietnam, it was claimed, the rest of Southeast Asia would also fall to communism, like a row of dominoes (in the game). The term continued to be so used throughout the Vietnam War, when in effect it was the excuse for American intervention there. Since then the term, sometimes expressed as *domino effect* or *domino reaction*, has been applied not only to intervention in such instances as Bosnia's civil war but also more loosely to any kind of CHAIN REACTION.

don't give up the ship

Don't lose heart; keep on fighting. This phrase dates from the War of 1812. In June, 1813, Captain James Lawrence, in command of the U.S.S. *Chesapeake*, engaged the British frigate *Shannon* outside Boston Harbor. The *Chesapeake* was soon severely damaged, and as Lawrence lay dying from his wounds, he told his men, "Fight till she sinks, boys . . . don't give up the ship." The Americans did have to surrender, but their captain's words have lived on. Commodore Oliver Perry had them stitched onto a flag he flew during the decisive Battle of Lake Erie a few months later, and this flag is still on display at the U.S. Naval Academy in Annapolis. On the same occasion Perry himself gave rise to another famous saying, "We have met the enemy and they are ours."

double-barreled

Serving a double purpose, or having two aspects or parts. The term alludes to the double-barreled firearm. Early firearms were loaded from the muzzle by first pouring powder into place and then ramming a bullet on top of the powder. Consequently, a gun could fire only a single shot and then had to be reloaded. One way of overcoming this considerable handicap was to create more than one barrel, and indeed some gunsmiths went so far as to make six- or seven-barreled pistols. More common, however, was the double barrel, which survives not only in today's double-barreled shotgun but in the metaphoric use of the adjective, as in "Let's give the baby a double-barreled name, for both of the grandmothers," or "They intended to launch a double-barreled attack on government spending," or, if we really want to give someone a message (or a hard time), "We'll let him have it *with both barrels*."

double-edged

Cutting both ways, that is, having opposite effects simultaneously. The word comes from an ancient weapon, a sword with two cutting edges, usually wielded with both hands. The adjective has been used figuratively since at least the eighteenth century. Boswell's *Life of Johnson* describes a "strong-pointed double-edged wit." Similarly, one speaks of a double-edged argument, which supports both the pro and the con of an issue, or a double-edged compliment, which can be taken as either insult or compliment. A double-edged sword was sometimes called a *Delphic sword*, with reference to the ambiguities of the Delphic oracle of ancient times, whose pronouncements could often be taken in two ways. Thus the poet John Dryden wrote, in *The Hind and the Panther* (1686):

> "Your Delphic sword," the panther then replied,
> "Is double-edged and cuts on either side."

In this, Dryden's most famous religious satire, the hind is a symbol of the Roman Catholic Church, to which the poet had converted, and the panther represents the Church of England.

double time

A musical direction to play twice as fast. It comes from the military order to march twice as fast as normally.

doughboy

> "She was so accustomed to fast riding with our cavalry . . . she
> does not know how to treat a doughboy."
> —Mrs. George A. Custer, letter (March, 1867)

A nickname for U.S. infantrymen since about 1867. There are several theories as to its origin, the most common being that their uniform's large brass buttons resembled a pastry called doughboy. Another, to which H. L. Mencken subscribed, is that pipe clay was used to whiten their uniforms, and when it rained they therefore became soggy and doughlike. According to William and Mary Morris, the pastry dough-boy became known to British troops during the Napoleonic Wars. In the Battle of Tulanera, Spain, in 1809, the Duke of Wellington was forced to retreat to Almaraz, where there was a severe food shortage. Therefore the British rifle brigade took grain from the surrounding fields to make bread and christened the site Doughboy Hill.

D.P.'s

Abbreviation for *displaced persons*, meaning any individuals who are uprooted from their homeland owing to revolution, war, famine, or some other violent disruption. The term originated toward the end of World War II, when literally millions of persons were driven from their countries and ended up with no place to live. In Europe survivors of concentration camps, as well as citizens of Eastern Europe who did not wish to live under Communist regimes, ended up in West Germany and Austria, where thousands had to live in internment camps for many months until a new homeland could be found for them.

draft dodger

A person who evades military service. The term originated in Britain during World War II, when it first meant a person who tried to avoid being sent overseas to fight. In the United States, however, it meant someone avoiding conscription. The word *draft* came into English from the Old English *dragan*, meaning "to draw" or "pull," and is still used in this sense, as in "draft animal." It came to mean military conscription only in the early eighteenth century in Great Britain, and then in America during the Civil War (the Union Draft Law was passed in 1863). Those conscripted during World War I were called *draftees,* but official fiat changed this to the euphemism *selectees* during World War II.

In American politics "draft" usually refers to a Presidential draft. In 1880 Congressman James A. Garfield of Ohio graciously consented to break a three-man deadlock among President Ulysses S. Grant, James Blaine of Maine, and John Cooper of Ohio, and on the thirty-sixth ballot Garfield was in fact drafted. Franklin Delano Roosevelt felt he had to be drafted in 1940 to avoid accusations of megalomania in running for an unprecedented third term in office. A more authentic draft was that of Adlai E. Stevenson in 1952. Stevenson truly did not seek the nomination but was drafted by Democratic delegates who did not like the leading candidate, Senator Estes Kefauver.

dragoon, to

> "If you want a receipt for that popular mystery
> Known to the world as a heavy dragoon . . ."
> —W. S. Gilbert, *Patience* (1881)

To coerce or persecute. The term comes from the seventeenth-century French name for a carbine, *dragon,* which was so called because, like the legendary beast, it spouted fire. (Some authorities, however, believe it was so named for the shape of its hammer.) The carbine was used at first by mounted infantrymen and then by cavalrymen, who themselves came to be called *dragoons*, a name that later was attached to some British cavalry regiments. The verb form originally (late seventeenth century) meant to set dragoons—that is, a heavily armed troop—on someone and about the same time was extended to mean "to coerce." By now the word has lost all of its military significance, so today one might say, "The class president was dragooned into organizing the reunion."

draw a bead on, to

To take careful aim. The term, originating in the United States about 1830, comes from aiming a revolver or rifle, the bead in question being a small knob in the foresight. By 1930 the term was being used figuratively for taking aim at any kind of opponent, as in "The school's champion debater drew a bead on her chief opponent."

drawbridge

A bridge that can be raised so that tall vessels can pass through. The first drawbridges were built over the moat of a castle and were raised to prevent attackers from reaching the castle walls. Their civilian use dates from the nineteenth century.

draw the long bow, to

> "He's a long-bow man, a liar."
>   —John Ray, *English Proverbs* (1678)

To exaggerate greatly; to lie. The term comes from the days of military archers and rests on the fact that with a long bow one can shoot farther than with a shorter crossbow. It was used figuratively from the seventeenth century on, by Lord Byron, O. Henry, and numerous other writers, but is heard less often today.

dreadnought

A heavily armed battleship, so called because it fears (dreads) nothing (nought); also, a thick, heavy coat or cloak that gives good protection against extreme cold. The best-known example of the former was the British ship H.M.S. *Dreadnought*, a 17,900-ton battleship completed in 1906, which was the first of a famous class of warships. The same name had been used three centuries earlier for a ship in the navy of Queen Elizabeth I, presumably with a similar implication of invincibility. The twentieth-century *Dreadnought*, built at a time when Britain wanted to maintain its traditional rule of the seas, was the largest battleship in the world, armed with ten twelve-inch guns and attaining a speed of twenty-one knots. This ship changed naval history, at least for a while, and enabled Britain to win important naval victories during World War I. Modern weaponry has outmoded such vessels, but the term dreadnought today is occasionally used for a formidable woman (ships traditionally being "female").

drill

> "So I'll meet him later on
>   At the place where 'e is gone—
>   Where it's always double drills and no canteen."
>   —Rudyard Kipling, *Gunga Din* (1890)

Any kind of exercise or practice, such as a fire drill, in which people practice safe evacuation of a building. The word appears to come from a form of military training used in the sixteenth century, in which troops were taught to turn about in a circle, resembling the movement made by the boring instrument then—and still—called a drill. Eventually the term was extended to all kinds of exercise, including those used in education for testing or teaching a particular skill, such as a vocabulary drill. The original military meaning persists in *drill sergeant*, the noncommissioned army officer charged with training recruits in basic exercises.

drum up, to

To gather together or summon; to find. Today one might speak of drumming up trade by means of vigorous advertising campaigns, or drumming up customers or choir members or other needed individuals, or drumming up new interest in a cause. Beating drums is rarely, if ever, part of such an enterprise. Further, drums do not enter into *beating the drum* for something in the modern colloquial sense of promoting a product ("Beating the drum for Clean-All Soap") or in being *drummed out*, that is, being fired from a job. In the armies of the seventeenth to nineteenth centuries, however, drumming was an essential means of communicating orders. Soldiers were gathered together by drumming (were drummed up), were told to retreat by drums (See also BEAT A RETREAT), and were drummed out (dismissed) to drumbeats.

dry run

A rehearsal or practice exercise. This term comes from World War II, when it was used for a practice bombing flight in which no bombs were actually dropped. After the war it was transferred to numerous civilian undertakings, as in "Bill decided to make a dry run to the hospital so he'd know the way when his wife went into labor."

dub, to

To give a name to. The word comes from the eleventh century, when it meant to invest a person with a special dignity or title, specifically that of knighthood, which involved a military obligation. It in turn comes from a Germanic root meaning "to strike," and the ceremony of conferring knighthood involved, at its conclusion, a light stroke of the sword on the recipient's shoulder. This origin persists in the golf term *to dub*, which means to hit a ball poorly or misplay a shot. Acoustic *dubbing*, on the other hand, as in supplying a foreign film with an English-language soundtrack, has nothing to do with striking or knighthood; it comes from abbreviating *doubling*.

dud

A colloquial term for "failure." It originally was a contemptuous word for a person (in Britain about 1825) and by the end of the nineteenth century meant "counterfeit." It then acquired a specific meaning during World War I, when it was used for a shell that failed to explode. After the war it was extended to mean any kind of failure, including a person or an enterprise, as well as an object.

Dunkirk

An emergency requiring drastic measures; a hasty and complete withdrawal. Dunkirk is a seaport in northern France that once was a notorious haunt for pirates. The modern meaning, however, comes from World War II. From May 26 to June 4, 1940, a major Allied expeditionary force of 300,000 was forced to withdraw by sea in order to avoid complete annihilation. The evacuation was directed by Vice Admiral Bertram Home Ramsay, a career naval officer, who used destroyers, pleasure yachts, and any other available craft, manned in part by civilian volunteers, to rescue as many British troops as possible. Although the operation saved many lives, it still was regarded as a disastrous defeat, which is the meaning Dunkirk has retained.

Dutch courage

Bravery induced by strong (alcoholic) drink. During the seventeenth-century wars between England and the Netherlands, it was the practice of some Dutch admirals to allow their crews to drink a substantial amount of gin before a battle. The English then derided the enemy by saying their valor was in exact proportion to the amount of alcohol they consumed. Nevertheless, the term has persisted, and some individuals swear by having a stiff drink before facing an ordeal.

earshot

The range in which a human ear can perceive sound. The word has been part of the English language since about 1600, a time when measurements frequently were based on such imprecise means as counting footsteps (foot), shooting an arrow as far as possible (bowshot), and the like. "Within earshot" therefore meant within the distance that a gunshot could be heard. (See also FAR CRY.)

eat crow, to

To admit one is wrong and humbly make amends. This expression is said to come from the fact that crow meat is notoriously unpalatable and from a story told about the War of 1812. Toward the end of the war, during a temporary truce, a New Englander went hunting and mistakenly crossed over to the British lines. There he shot a crow. The shot was heard by a British officer, who came upon the American and decided to punish him. However, he was unarmed, so he complimented the man on his fine shooting and asked to see his gun. When the ingenuous American handed it over, the officer pointed the gun at him and, since he was guilty of trespassing, told him to take a bite out of the crow. The soldier had to obey, but when the officer returned the weapon with a warning, the American took his revenge, pointed the gun at him, and forced him to eat the rest of the bird.

echelon

A group with a certain authority or rank. The word comes from the French *echélon*, which meant originally (and still does) the rung of a ladder. In the standing army of the eighteenth and early nineteenth centuries, an echelon was a military formation in parallel lines but with no two rows in the same alignment, so that the overall appearance was that of a series of steps, or staircase. By the mid-twentieth century the word was being used figuratively, as it most often is today, when one speaks of the top echelon (highest rank) of a company's executives or the lower echelons (least important positions) of city government.

egg on, to

To urge on; to encourage. This term has nothing whatever to do with eggs. Rather, it comes from the Old Norse word *eggja*, "to put an edge on," which in turn is thought to be related to the Latin *acies*, for "edge of a sword," and *acer*, "sharp." Presumably the modern sense comes from an older, none too gentle urging-on of workers or prisoners with the edge of a sword or some other persuasively sharp instrument. Indeed, the expression to egg on was phrased, until the mid-sixteenth century, as *to edge*, but this locution is now obsolete.

Eisenhower jacket

A short, fitted, belted jacket. It is named for General Dwight D. Eisenhower, who often wore it during World War II. Since then the style has continued to appear in civilian clothes.

Elba

A place of exile. The name comes from the Italian island in the Mediterranean Sea to which Napoleon Bonaparte was exiled following his unconditional surrender on April 12, 1814. The allies gave him the small island as a sovereign principality, but before a year had passed Napoleon gathered a handful of followers and landed near Cannes, France, from which he began a triumphant march northward to Paris. This effort at a comeback soon failed. He was defeated at Waterloo and again abdicated, surrendering himself to the British. He hoped for asylum in England but instead was sent as a prisoner of war to the very isolated island of St. Helena, where he remained until his death in 1821. Oddly enough, although Napoleon spent a much longer and more genuine exile at St. Helena, it is Elba that became synonymous with exile.

emigré

A person who leaves his or her own country, especially one who does so owing to war, revolution, or political upheaval. The word, which is French, was first used during the French Revolution for royalists, mainly members of the high nobility and clergy, who fled and took up residence in a foreign land. Because many of them tried to persuade foreign powers to support the French crown and some of them even plotted to form a counterrevolutionary army, severe laws were passed against them, including perpetual banishment from France and confiscation of their property. From about 1802 on, however, Napoleon permitted some emigrés to return to France, and after 1814 all were granted amnesty. They gradually became a strong conservative force in France, working to restore the monarchy, and they helped to bring about the July Revolution of 1830.

Following the Russian Revolution of 1917, many White Russians (who opposed the Red Russians, or Communists) became emigrés, a word probably used because so many of them settled in France (although numerous others went elsewhere). They included not only aristocrats but some who opposed communism on ideological grounds and others who simply wanted to pursue their own interests without government interference.

enemy alien

A citizen of a nation that is at war with the one in which he or she is currently residing. The term dates from World War II. When the United States entered the war following the Japanese attack on Pearl

Harbor, it had numerous Japanese residents, especially along the West Coast. Owing to concern that some of them might be spies for the Japanese government, as well as general hostility against Japan, thousands of them were forced to leave their homes and be interned in special camps for the duration of the war. (There was similar hostility against Germans during World War I, but no such formal measures were taken against them.) In carrying out this measure, there was a shameful lack of discrimination. Numerous persons who had lived in America for decades, as well as many who were Nisei—persons of Japanese descent but born and educated in the United States—were interned along with more recently arrived immigrants. (See also under CONCENTRATION CAMP.)

ersatz

Serving as a substitute, usually an artificial or inferior one. The word comes from German, where it means "replacement" or "compensation." Although it began to be used in English in the late nineteenth century, it was not very common until World War I, when first British and then American troops picked it up. Eric Partridge held that *ersatz girl*, for a temporary sweetheart or a prostitute, was British prisoner-of-war slang as early as 1916.

During World War II the word was widely used again, for various substitutes for scarce and strictly rationed goods, such as ersatz coffee (made from grain) and ersatz silk stockings (leg makeup). It is still used as a synonym for substitutions of this kind.

escalate, to

To increase the level or intensity of something by successive stages. Although this word, which came from the moving staircase called an *escalator*, had been used since the early twentieth century to describe increases in prices, wages, and similar nonmilitary matters, it acquired a new meaning during the cold war and the Vietnam War. In the 1950's escalation began to mean an increase in military activity, either to prepare for or to fight an actual war. It also could refer to a changeover from conventional weapons to nuclear warheads. Then, during the mid-1960's, various American officials, dismayed by the heavy casualties and seeming lack of military progress in Vietnam, were anxious to avoid public discouragement and began to use a number of euphemisms to describe the conflict. Thus, they said the war had "escalated" rather than worsened, they called bombing "air support," and they termed killing the Viet Cong (Communist guerrillas) who were hiding in small villages "pacification." (See also *Pentagonese*, under PENTAGON.) Today we have again transferred the word to other arenas, so that one speaks of, for example, drug use that escalates from marijuana to heroin or a book royalty that escalates according to the number of copies sold.

An earlier related word, *escalade*, coming directly from French into English about 1600, denoted scaling a city or castle wall by means of ladders, a basic tactic of early warfare. However, it is not a current synonym for escalation.

ethnic cleansing

The murder or removal of an ethnic group from an area. This euphemism became popular in the 1980's as a synonym for GENO-CIDE, particularly in relation to the conflict between the Armenians and Azerbaijanis, each of whom was trying to drive out the other. In the 1990's it was used with respect to the battles between Hutu and Tutsi in Rwanda and between Serb and Muslim in the former Yugoslavia. In the latter, as the war in Bosnia entered its last weeks in 1995, an estimated 16,000 Bosnians were listed as missing, most of them presumed to be dead and buried in secret mass graves, victims of ethnic cleansing.

expendables

Persons or things that can be done without. In both world wars this term was jargon for servicemen who were about to die. In fact the American journalist William L. White wrote a book, *They Were Expendable* (1942), about the story of the Philippine campaign as told by four officers of a U.S. Navy motor torpedo squad. The word dates from about 1800, but for the first 100 years of its life it was used mainly to describe property or supplies that could be spared. Before that, however, in the 1700's, *to be expended* was naval jargon for being killed. According to Grose's *Dictionary* (1796), this usage referred to the gunner's accounts, in which an item that was consumed was charged as *expended*, a term later extended to a sailor's life as well.

eyeball to eyeball

A direct confrontation; in close contact with the enemy. This phrase, from African-American English, gained currency from its use during the Korean War. When General MacArthur's headquarters sent a dispatch to the 24th Regiment, which was all black, to ask if they had contact with the enemy, they responded, "We is eyeball to eyeball." The message was widely quoted, and a decade later the term was used with reference to the Cuban missile crisis (it was charged that Russian missiles were being sent to Cuba), when the cold war threatened to become a hot one.

eyewash

An outward prettying up; a sham. This term probably originated during World War I, when it was used to describe cleaning up the barracks and grounds for inspection. Over the years it has been used as slang for other kinds of cover-up intended to make something look better than it actually was, as in "Appointing two students to the faculty council is just eyewash; they have no voice in any decisions."

fall-back position

An alternative to be resorted to in case of failure. The noun *fallback* originated in America in the mid-eighteenth century (from the verb *to fall back*, meaning "to retreat") and referred to a previously prepared military position that was to be taken should a strategic retreat be necessary. In the mid-twentieth century it became government jargon for an excuse prepared ahead of time in the event that a particular plan or project failed. It was also used in American politics in the late 1960's to describe various strategies for securing the nomination of a widely acceptable candidate by selecting a second person if the party's first choice should fail.

fall in line with, to

> "I came to fall in, and not to fall out."
> —John Heywood, *Proverbs* (1546)

To agree with someone or something. The term originally meant a soldier's taking his place in the ranks; occasionally it was abbreviated to *fall in*, which is still used as a military command.

fallout, falling-out

By-product or side effect; quarrel or disagreement. The nonhyphen-ated fallout dates from about 1945 and originally meant the atmos-pheric particles resulting from fire or explosion, specifically the *radioactive fallout* from a nuclear blast. Since then the word has been transferred to the undesirable side effects of almost anything, such as the emotional problems that are the fallout of a custody fight or the psychological distress that is the fallout of being mugged.

The hyphenated falling-out, meaning a quarrel or disagreement between those who were originally close, most likely comes from the military term *to fall out,* meaning to disperse from the ranks or to be dismissed from formation (See also FALL IN LINE WITH). Leaving a formerly close companion or friend—in spirit or in opinion—became analogous to leaving one's place in the ranks. This type of falling-out has been part of the language since the sixteenth cen-tury. The English theologian and hymnist Isaac Watts (1674–1748) wrote, in *Divine Songs for Children*:

> Birds in their little nest agree
> And 'tis a shameful sight
> When children of one family
> Fall out, and chide, and fight.

false alarm

An alarm raised when there is no fire or other emergency. It may be sounded by mistake or, as it was originally, in a deliberate effort to deceive. The noun *alarm* originally meant a call to arms (See ALARM), and sounding a false alarm became a standard military tactic to con-fuse and harass the enemy, forcing them to remain ready for battle even when no attack was planned.

false colors, to sail under

> "I had so much wisdom as to sail under false colours."
> —Robert Louis Stevenson, *St. Ives* (1897)

To pretend to have a different view or character so as to deceive; deliberately misrepresent. The term comes from a tactic used by pirates, maritime robbers who roamed the seas and attacked the vessels of all nations. Especially rampant during times of unrest, pirates preyed on commerce from the times of the ancient Phoenicians and Greeks until about 1825, when a concerted effort by the United States and Great Britain finally destroyed their last North African, European, and West Indian strongholds. To deceive the ships they preyed on, pirates would often run a "friendly" flag— that is, they displayed false colors to fool their victims and lure them close enough so they could be overwhelmed. The term false colors had begun to be used figuratively by 1700 or even earlier. The so-called pirate flag, the Jolly Roger, showing a white skull and crossbones on a black field, was a fairly recent device in the long history of piracy, dating only from the late eighteenth century.

Well after their elimination from European and Caribbean waters, pirates continued to operate in Asia, especially in the China seas and the Straits of Malacca, where even today they pose a hazard to Thai and Vietnamese fishing boats.

far cry, a

> "One of the Campbells replied, 'It is a far cry to Lochow,' a proverbial expression of the tribe, meaning that their ancient hereditary domains lay beyond the reach of an invading army."
> —Sir Walter Scott, *The Legend of Montrose* (1819)

A long way; very different. This measure of distance presumably pre-dates even EARSHOT, the human voice having been around much longer than firearms, and like it probably originated in measuring one's distance from an enemy. It began to be used figuratively—as in "To be nominated is a far cry from being elected"—as early as 1800 and, according to Eric Partridge, was a cliché by the mid-nineteenth century.

fascist

Totalitarian and dictatorial; extremely conservative or politically reactionary. The modern term dates from an Italian political movement originating about 1915 and led by Benito Mussolini from the early 1920's until the end of World War II. It took its name from the Latin *fasces*, a bundle of rods from which an ax projected, which in ancient Rome served as a symbol of authority. It was carried by special guards, called *lictors*, marching before a consul, dictator, or emperor. It also symbolized unity, and indeed the modern Italian fascists strongly proclaimed that there is strength in union. By the 1920's the term fascist was being applied to similar totalitarian movements in other countries, especially Hitler's Germany and Franco's Spain, and acquired the connotations of ruthless crushing of opposition, aggressive nationalism, racism, and similar reprehensible policies. After World War II the term also began to be used more loosely for various ultraconservative ideologies and their adherents.

fatigues

A casual style of dress, describing certain boots, shirts, and pants. It is in direct imitation of military fatigue clothes, so called since the 1830's but presumably worn even longer in the armed forces for so-called *fatigue duty*, nonmilitary tasks of maintenance such as kitchen duty, digging drainage ditches and latrines, etc. The style of clothing became popular in the 1950's, especially among young people, who at first bought leftovers from World War II in military surplus stores; later it became fashionable enough so that civilian clothing manufacturers produced it. Among the favorite items are *combat boots*, which had been introduced by the U.S. Army in 1943, field jackets, shirts, and shorts.

feather in one's cap, a

"Their favour in an author's cap a feather."
—Lord Byron, *Don Juan*, Canto I (1818)

A special honor or accomplishment. The term comes from the ancient custom of numerous peoples—Native American tribes, Hungarians, Turks, Himalayan peoples—of placing a feather in a soldier's cap for every enemy killed. According to an early account, in sixteenth-century Hungary a soldier could wear a feather only if he had killed a Turk, and the number of feathers in the cap showed the precise number killed. The custom was so well known that putting a feather in one's cap was already being used figuratively,

A feather for every dead enemy

as it still is, by the early seventeenth century, and it was virtually a cliché by the time Laurence Sterne wrote "The feather put into his cap of having been abroad. . . ." (*Tristram Shandy*, 1761–67).

fed up

Disgusted, bored, having had enough. This expression, probably a euphemism for a more vulgar F-word, is believed to have originated among Australian troops during the Boer War and became widely known during World War I.

fellow traveler

A person who sympathizes with a political party or movement but is not an active member of it. This expression was especially popular in the United States from the 1930's to the 1950's, when it described Communist or leftist sympathizers who strongly approved of the changes wrought by the Communist Revolution in the Soviet Union. Since the Communists also were called Reds, another name for such sympathizers was *parlor pinks* (or *pinkos* or *pinks*). The term fellow traveler—*poputchik* in Russian—was allegedly coined by Leon Trotsky for several Russian writers who seemed to be interested in the Revolution and its goals but were not dedicated to working actively for it.

fief

The domain of an individual, group, organization, or political unit. In the feudal era of the Middle Ages, a king or lord gave a knight a grant of land, called a fief, and serfs (laborers) in exchange for his military services. Later the term was broadened to signify any particular domain, as in "Keep your hands off Dad's computer; that's his fief."

field day

An occasion of great enjoyment and excitement. The term dates from the mid-eighteenth century and originally denoted a special day set aside for troop maneuvers and exercises, a meaning that is still current in the military. However, early in the nineteenth century it began to be used for such wholly civilian occasions as the annual school picnic and, even more figuratively, for any experience of jubilant pleasure, as in "David had a field day with his new tape recorder."

fifth column

A group of traitors; treachery. This term, unlike many, can be traced to a specific person and date. In 1936, during the Spanish Civil War, General Emilio Mola, second in command to Franco, led four columns to attack the city of Madrid. In a radio broadcast on October 16, 1936, he told listeners that he had a fifth column—*una quinta columna*—of supporters inside the city who would join his troops when he attacked. This claim was in fact true, and as a result many innocent citizens were rounded up and shot. The term caught on, perpetuated in English by novelist Ernest Hemingway, who in 1937 used it for the title of his only play, a melodrama. During World War II it was extended to secret Nazi supporters who engaged in espionage, sabotage, and similar subversive activities. Later it was loosely applied to Communist sympathizers in the United States, and today it continues to signify traitors.

filibuster

Organized obstructionist tactics used by a minority to prevent passage of a law by the majority who favor it. It is used specifically for the use of such tactics in the United States Senate, which are based on the Senate's long-standing tradition of free debate, provided for by Rule 22. (The House of Representatives rules limit debate, as does the British House of Commons.) The traditional filibuster consisted of extremely long speeches; for example, in 1957 Senator Strom Thurmond of South Carolina held the floor for twenty-four hours and eighteen minutes talking against a proposed civil rights bill. Beginning in the 1970's, however, this form of filibuster began to give way to more subtle means, such as the use of multiple amendments to a proposed bill, consecutive roll calls, and other parliamentary devices to prevent a vote. For example, one senator might refuse to vote on the usually routine motion of approving the journal of the previous day's proceedings because he had not read the journal. Under the rules, the entire Senate must vote to excuse one member from voting. A roll-call vote is ordered for this purpose, and then another senator (supporting the first) might refuse to vote on the ground that no senator should vote so as to compel another's vote. Next a roll call must be ordered on this refusal, and eventually a complete bottleneck can result. Indeed, on one occasion the United States Senate had to table the Lord's Prayer, which a senator had offered as an amendment to a bill.

The word filibuster comes from the older English word *freebooter*, for "pirate" or "buccaneer" (in Dutch *vrijbuiter*), which the Spaniards turned into *filibustero*, which in turn became filibuster. The original filibusters were English and French pirates who operated out of the West Indies during the sixteenth century to prey on Spanish shipping. In the nineteenth century the word was applied to adventurers who, under private auspices, organized themselves into bands in order to invade certain Spanish-American lands and effect revolutions there. Some of these filibustering expeditions came from the United States and were directed against Cuba, Mexico, and other Latin nations, such as William Walker's expedition against Sonora (1853–54); others were directed by rebellious citizens of the countries themselves who were trying to overthrow their government, like that of Narciso Lopez against Cuba. By the mid-nineteenth century filibuster had also begun to be used in its modern sense of a means of obstructing legislation.

final solution

Mass murder. The term originated in Nazi Germany, being a translation of the German *endgültige Lösung* and referring to the so-called Jewish population. It was used by Franz Stuckart, who drafted the Nuremberg Laws of 1935, whereby German Jews were stripped of their citizenship and most of their civil rights. Although it still refers to that specific Nazi program, it occasionally has been used since then whenever a policy of GENOCIDE has been suspected or discerned.

firestorm

An explosion of criticism or protest; an uproar. Although this term originally referred to a severe fire in which the rising column of air above the fire draws in heavy winds, in the mid-1900's it was applied to the intense fire created by nuclear explosion. Since then it has been transferred to figurative storms, as in "If he doesn't withdraw the nomination, the committee will turn the hearings into a firestorm."

fireworks

A loud display of anger. This term originally was slang for "gunfire," "bombardment," or "shelling." One writer believes it was applied to night bombardment, when the flash of artillery fire could be readily seen, but it appears also to have been used more generally. By the late 1800's it also was used figuratively, as in "There'll be fireworks when Mom finds out you took her car."

first light

At dawn. According to Ivor H. Evans, the phrase came from World War II, when it meant the earliest time of day that the infantry could advance. Similarly, *last light* meant the latest hour at which operations could still be carried out.

first rate

> "His natural parts were not of the first rate."
> —Henry Fielding, *Tom Jones* (1749)

Excellent, of the best quality. The Royal Navy's warships were at one time rated on a scale of one to six according to their size and the weight of weapons they carried. This system was later transferred to general use, as in Fielding's novel.

flagship

The foremost member of an organization or system. The term originated in the Royal Navy, where the flagship is the vessel carrying an admiral or other top-ranking officer and displaying the officer's flag. It later was adopted by commercial shipping lines, which called their principal vessel their flagship, and then by airlines, which used the name for their largest or most important plane. Almost any large business organization today may refer to some leading division, store, or other element as its flagship. Thus the Four Seasons Hotel in Vancouver is known as the Four Seasons Corporation's flagship.

flak

Colloquial term for severe criticism or noisy opposition; also, slang for a press agent, also spelled *flack*. The word originated in World War II as an acronym for the German word for anti-aircraft fire, **Fliegerabwehrkanone**, clearly a mouthful for any non-German. Some etymologists hold that the word actually dates from World War I but at that time was used only among fliers, and was revived and popularized from about 1940 on, when air warfare played a much more important role.

After the war flak became a slang term for "press agent," a person who, like the puffs of smoke generated by exploding shells, puffs up (inflates or exaggerates) clients to obtain good publicity.

Flanders poppies

> "In Flanders fields the poppies blow
> Between the crosses, row on row."
>   —John McCare, *In Flanders Fields* (1915)

Artificial red flowers sold on Veterans Day (in Britain called Remembrance Day) to commemorate the troops who lost their lives for their country. The association comes from a poem published in the British magazine *Punch* on December 8, 1915, written by a member of the Canadian Army Medical Corps who was dead by 1918. The poppy, botanically called *Papaver rhoeas*, commonly grows wild in European grain fields such as those that covered Flanders before it became the scene of continuous fighting in World War I. Ever since, this flower, which is also called corn poppy or field poppy, has been associated with wartime casualties, the image of this minor poet having caught the imagination more lastingly than many works of more exalted literary quality.

flap

Slang for a situation of great excitement; a panic. The term comes from the late nineteenth century, when it was used, according to Eric Partridge, for any sudden movement on board or in a fleet of warships, especially the commotion following the issuance of an emergency order. By World War I it was service jargon in the army as well and, according to H. L. Mencken, was used by British aviators to denote an air raid. Most probably all these usages come from the image of agitated birds madly flapping their wings. Eventually the word was transferred to civilian emergencies, including a political flap, which might well be more a commotion than a true crisis. Today we are apt to say, "Don't get in a flap" when we mean "Don't panic" or "Calm down."

From politics comes the adjective *unflappable*, for someone who remains calm and imperturbable in the face of a crisis. It was widely used to describe Britain's Chancellor of the Exchequer, Harold Macmillan, during the Suez crisis of 1956, when Egypt under Colonel Nasser took over the Suez Canal twelve years earlier than the date set by international agreement, triggering invasions of Egypt by Israel, Great Britain, and France. Macmillan's reputation

Flash in the pan

for unflappability extended into his tenure as prime minister (1957–63) during a variety of domestic crises.

flash in the pan

A short-lived success, or a failure following a showy start. The term comes from the seventeenth-century flintlock musket. Often an attempt to fire it would end with a flash in the lockpan, a depression that held the priming powder, which would fail to explode the main charge. This left the gun *hanging fire*, that is, slow to fire a charge, an expression that became a general synonym for delaying or being indecisive. Long after flintlocks had been replaced by superior weapons, the term flash in the pan remained in the language, and it is still used for a person or project that shows early promise but fails to fulfill it.

Florence Nightingale

A nurse; also, anyone who nurses the sick. The real Florence Nightingale (1820–1910), a reformer of hospital and nursing methods, became world-famous during the Crimean War, when, learning of the high death rate among British soldiers, she organized a hospital unit of thirty-eight nurses. Her work there helped reduce the death rate of the wounded from about 40 percent to 2 percent. Today her name is sometimes used loosely for any nurse or a nonprofessional devoted to caring for the sick.

flotilla

A small group of individuals or vehicles moving together; a flock. The word comes from the Spanish *flotilla*, a diminutive of *flota*, or fleet, and meant a small fleet. It retains a military meaning today, that is, a group of small naval vessels, specifically a unit consisting of two or more squadrons. However it also has been transferred to human beings, as in "The winning team was followed by a flotilla of reporters and photographers."

flying blind

Groping one's way. The term originated during World War II when poor visibility would force pilots to rely solely on instruments. Although such instruments have been improved greatly since then, the figurative meaning of not being able to see very well, and therefore having to proceed mainly by guesswork, persists.

flying colors, with

> "We came off with flying colours."
> —George Farquar, *The Beaux's Stratagem* (1706)

Victorious; extremely successful. The term comes from the practice of a victorious fleet sailing into port with flags flying from all the mastheads. By 1700 or so it was being used figuratively, signifying any kind of triumph. (See also FALSE COLORS).

fly right

Behave properly. This term comes from World War II aviators' slang and was given greater currency through the title of Nat King Cole's popular song, *Straighten Up and Fly Right* (1944).

footlocker

A small trunk. The name comes from army usage in World War II, when every soldier was issued a small olive-drab trunk to store his clothes and personal belongings. It usually was placed at the foot of his bed, whence the name. After the war the name survived for similar trunks used by campers and college students.

foot soldier

A person relied on to do minor but necessary tasks in some endeavor. The earliest armed force consisted of fighting men on foot, called *infantry* since the late 1500's and foot soldiers since the early 1600's. Not only did they constitute the bulk of early armies in terms of sheer numbers, but they were relied on to do much of the "dirty work" of fighting. From this comes our figurative use of foot soldier, as in "Students are serving as the campaign's foot soldiers, ringing doorbells for signatures and distributing leaflets."

forecastle

The forward part of a ship. Its name comes from the fact that in medieval warships the front was raised and fortified like a castle, so that it loomed above the enemy's deck, upon which troops could then aim. (The rear, or aft part of the ship, now called quarterdeck or afterdeck, was at that time called *aftercastle*.) Later it became customary to put the crew's quarters in the forecastle and house the officers in the afterdeck. The word forecastle is often spelled *fo'c's'le* and usually is pronounced "foke-sil."

forlorn hope

An enterprise with little chance of success. This expression comes from the Dutch term *verloren hoop*, which meant "lost troop" (not hope) and signified a picked group of soldiers, usually volunteers, who were selected to start an attack. The English mistook *hoop* for *hope* and converted the meaning to "a desperate undertaking," with faint hope of success. It was already so used in the seventeenth century, and in fact Eric Partridge claimed it was a term used by gamblers from the late seventeenth century through the nineteenth century for their last stake.

foxhole

"The foxes have holes, and the birds of the air have nests."
—Gospel of Matthew 8:20

A small slit trench dug to shelter one or more soldiers in combat. The name, alluding to its resemblance to the animal's hole, originated in the trench warfare of World War I. However, the use of foxholes in this conflict was rare. Instead, both sides dug thousands of miles of opposing trenches, which held thousands of troops. Although rapid-firing small arms and artillery had ruled out the infantry charges of earlier wars, the general staffs of both sides still clung to the idea of an uninterrupted line of defense. The lack of a decisive weapon to break through the enemy's trenches created a stalemate and war of attrition.

The foxhole played a much more important role in World War II and subsequent conflicts. However, practical considerations limit its use to terrain where a shallow but man-sized hole can be dug quickly with a primitive shovel.

frank

"Frankness invites frankness."
—Ralph Waldo Emerson, *Essay on Prudence* (1841)

Candid, straightforward, free. This common adjective, part of the English language since the thirteenth century, came from Old French and Latin words meaning a member of the Franks, a Germanic people who settled along the Rhine River valley in the third century. They were so called because they used spears (*Franken*) as opposed to the short swords (*Sachsen*) of the Saxons. Through a series of conquests their domain grew, until by the eighth century it included most of France, the Low Countries, Germany west of the Elbe, Austria, Switzerland, and northern and central Italy. Their most powerful ruler was Charlemagne. Because of their dominance, the Franks were considered the only "free" men or nobles; indeed, in Old French *franc* meant "of noble birth." Hence the adjective frank acquired the connotation of being free to act or to speak, without fear of the consequences. This implication persists in modern speech, where "to be frank" or "frankly" frequently accompanies the disclosure of an unpleasant truth or unpopular opinion.

fraternize, to

To associate in a friendly fashion. The word for this seemingly harmless activity, from the Latin *frater*, for "brother," acquired suspect connotations during World War I, or perhaps even earlier, when it was used to describe friendly contact with enemy troops or with the inhabitants of an occupied country. By World War II it often had the specific significance of soldiers associating closely with women of enemy nationality or of an occupied country. Following the war, many of the Frenchwomen who had fraternized with German soldiers during the Nazi occupation of their country were publicly exposed and punished by their fellow citizens.

free lance

An individual who works on a fee-paid assignment basis for numerous employers rather than on a regular salary basis for one employer. This kind of employment is particularly common for writers, artists, photographers, filmmakers, interior decorators, and musicians. The term comes from the medieval knight who was not, like most knights, committed to a feudal lord and therefore hired himself and his lance out to anyone willing to pay for his military services. Eric Partridge points out that in earlier times such a soldier was called a *free companion*, and it was Sir Walter Scott, in his medieval romance *Ivanhoe* (1820), who renamed him. Actually freelance soldiers, today more often called *mercenaries*, still operate, frequently playing an important role in civil wars and other internal strife.

free world

The countries of the world that are not under Communist domination. The term, which often is capitalized (Free World), is thought to have originated during World War I to signify those nations not under German domination and continued to be used between the world wars and during World War II for countries not under Axis control. It was after that, especially during the cold war, that the expression came into prominent use among Western democracies. It has always implied bias on the part of its users and is heard less often today.

friendly fire

An attack on one's own troops, allies, or friends, presumably by accident. The term originated in an investigation of the death in 1970 of an American soldier in Vietnam, which revealed that he was a "nonhostile casualty of friendly artillery fire"—that is, he was killed by shrapnel when an American shell hit a tree over his foxhole, owing to the fact that the cannon had been erroneously aimed too low. Presumably this was neither the first nor the last time that such an accident of battle occurred. At least one historian presumes that in the fray of earlier battles "friendly" sword cuts could have the same result. (For another early example, see under MARTINET.)

During World War II, where this situation was called *amicicide* (from Latin roots for "friend" and "killing"), the most common such mistake was the landing of artillery rounds among friendly troops. However, U.S. aircraft attacks on U.S. troops apparently occurred often enough for the G.I.'s in Europe to call the Ninth Air Force "the American Luftwaffe." The most spectacular episode of this sort, according to Lee Kennett's *G.I.: The American Soldier in World War II*, occurred in July, 1944, during a massive air strike against the Germans in the St.-Lô area. Bombing errors there led to more than 800 U.S. casualties, with 131 dead, including General McNair. Ground amicicide was even more widespread in the Pacific theater, especially when Americans used perimeter defense against Japanese infiltrations, and inexperienced or just plain nervous G.I.'s fired at anything they heard or saw in any direction, including the interior of their own perimeter. According to that old adage of uncertain origin, "With friends like that, who needs enemies?"

frogmen

Swimmers equipped for underwater diving, with special suits, fins, face masks, and air tanks. The term originated during World War II for seamen trained and equipped to perform underwater sabotage by attaching explosives to enemy ships. After the war it was used first for workers employed in underwater salvage operations, and later came into general use for anyone who did deep-sea diving, for sport, pleasure, scientific investigation, or similar purposes.

front line

The forefront or position of greatest prominence in any undertaking. The term comes from the front line of military operations, where actual combat takes place. The military term as such was first used during the nineteenth century, although the word *front*, in the sense of foremost military line, is much older, dating from the fourteenth century. The term was soon transferred to civilian spheres. Today one might speak, for example, of an activist who is in the front line of the civil rights struggle or a reporter who is in the front line of local politics.

Führer

Adolf Hitler. This word, which is simply German for "leader," was taken as a title by Hitler after the death of Hindenburg in 1934 and has ever since been identified with the Nazi dictator of Germany and his programs for world conquest and the extermination of Jews, Communists, and whoever else he perceived as an opponent.

furlough

A leave of absence or a temporary layoff. This word came from the Dutch *verlof*, for "permission," and was originally (seventeenth century) used only in the sense of an official military leave, a meaning still current. However, beginning about the mid-eighteenth century, it began to be applied to any leave of absence, from regular employment, imprisonment, etc.

gadget

A mechanical device of some kind; an ingenious contrivance. There are several theories as to this word's origin, which is not known, but it was probably first used in the 1850's by seamen of the Royal Navy. One writer suggests it is a corruption of *gorget*, an ornament worn by French officers during the seventeenth and eighteenth centuries (and in Britain by officers of the Royal Marine). The term in its present meaning was used by U.S. seamen from the early 1900's on.

galley slave

> "I am a galley slave to pen and ink."
> —Honoré de Balzac, letter (1832)

A person who performs menial or tedious tasks. Ancient Greek and Roman warships were galleys with one or more banks of oars. The rowers often were slaves or condemned criminals. The present usage is a half-joking transfer from this practice.

Gang of Four

Four radical members of China's Communist Party, who in 1965 launched the Great Proletarian Cultural Revolution, a massive attempt to instruct a new generation in basic revolutionary principles. One of them was Jiang Qing, wife of party Chairman Mao Zedong. Their policy involved large-scale purges and a program of forcibly relocating millions of urban teenagers into the countryside, as well as requiring scientists, educators, and other intellectuals to abandon their professions and take up manual labor. The movement continued for about three years, but fighting between the radical Communists led by the Gang of Four and more moderate factions continued throughout this period. It worsened with the death of both Mao and Premier Zhou Enlai in 1976. The radicals then were defeated, and the new ruling group modified their policies in education, culture, and industry, as well as seeking better relationships with non-Communist nations.

garret

A small room at the top of a building; an attic room. The word comes from the French *guérite* (and earlier Old French *garite*), for "watchtower," and originally (fourteenth century) meant a turret or watchtower. From the fifteenth century on, however, it was transferred to the space from which one watched, that is, an attic room. It also acquired the connotation of being small and miserable, an abode for someone who could afford no better. In the romantic nineteenth century the garret became associated with impecunious artists, poets, and students, who "starved in a garret" while producing their great masterpieces. This image is forcefully presented in Puccini's famous opera *La Bohème* (*Bohemian Life*), based on H. Murger's novel, portraying the life of artists and students in a Parisian garret.

gat

American underworld slang for a gun. It comes from the Gatling gun, a manually operated machine gun developed by Richard J. Gatling (1818–1903), which was perfected during the Civil War. It fired 350 shots a minute and had a range of more than one mile, a remarkable achievement for this period. Although the Union Army

Gatling gun

was not quick to adopt the gun, news of it had a demoralizing effect on the Confederates. Eventually it was widely adopted and used until about 1900. Well after it had become obsolete, about 1920, the writer of a mystery story had the killer call his revolver a *gatling*, and a story published later that year abbreviated it to *gat*. The word caught on, in both detective stories and gangster films, where criminals invariably called a pistol or revolver a "gat" and influenced real-life mobsters to use this name as well, along with *rod* and *heater*.

gatehouse

A house or other structure at the entrance of a fenced area where a guard controls the entryway. This feature and its name come from the medieval castle, where gatehouses—a series of towers, bridges, and barriers—protected each entrance to the fortification or town. Today it appears, in much simpler form, outside modern housing developments or apartment complexes whose security-conscious residents prefer to limit access in this way. The word is also used for a structure at the gate of a reservoir or dam that is equipped to regulate the flow of water.

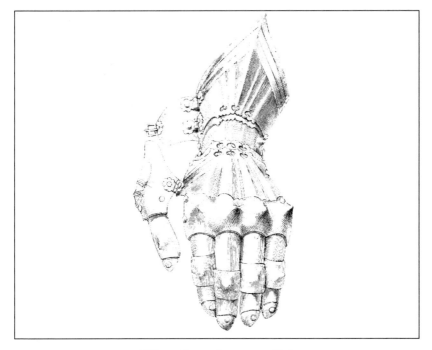

Fifteenth-century gauntlet

gauntlet, to run the/throw down the

To risk danger or severe criticism; to issue a challenge. The first expression originated during the Thirty Years' War, when the Germans adopted a military punishment from the Swedes. It consisted of stripping a man to the waist and making him run between two rows of soldiers, who struck him with sticks or knotted cords or rope ends. The passage he ran was called *gatloppe* in Swedish and became *gantloppe* or *gantlope* in German. The method was adopted in the American colonies as a civilian punishment, and also was used by Native Americans on captives during King Philip's War, or so the Puritan writer Increase Mather reported. It was variously spelled *gantlet* or *gauntlet*, and although modern lexicographers still do not entirely agree on this point, gauntlet seems to be the preferred spelling, at least in the United States. "They have run the gauntlet of the years," wrote Oliver Wendell Holmes in *The Autocrat of the Breakfast-Table* (1858).

Throwing down the gauntlet, on the other hand, is an even older term, dating from the days of knights in armor. The gauntlet was a glove of mail, which protected the knight's hand. Throwing down the gauntlet was a challenge to combat, and the term was so used in the sixteenth century in Edward Hall's *Chronicles.* "I cast them my Gauntlet, take it up who dares," wrote Thomas Nashe in *Pasquil's Apologie* (1590).

Both expressions are still used figuratively today.

generalissimo

A supreme commander, usually of several forces. In the military, the title was first used by Cardinal Richelieu, who took command of the French armies in Italy in 1629. Since then it has been used by Marshal Foch, who commanded the combined Allied forces in France in 1918; Josef Stalin, who was made general of all the Soviet forces in 1943; Francisco Franco, who declared himself chief of the Spanish army in 1939; and Marshal Chiang Kai-shek, leader of the Kuomintang, in power in China from 1927 to 1949.

genocide

The extermination of a racial, ethnic, or national group. The word was coined in 1944 by Professor Raphael Lemkin of Duke University and used in drafting the official indictment of World War II war criminals in 1945. In 1948 the United Nations General Assembly declared genocide a crime in international law.

Although Lemkin's original intent was the characterization of the Nazi plan to exterminate Europe's Jews, the practice of genocide long preceded the coining of the word—the Old Testament of the Bible is full of examples. Moreover, since the 1940's the word has also been used more loosely than originally intended—to describe, for example, a relatively bloodless ruling such as eliminating the requirement for Gaelic studies from Scottish schools, which opponents attack as genocide directed against the native Scots heritage. But it also retains its original meaning for bloody conflicts seemingly aimed at exterminating a people in Bosnia, Rwanda, and elsewhere in the world. (See also ETHNIC CLEANSING.)

Geronimo

An exclamation that means, "Here goes!" It originated during World War II among American paratroopers, who shouted "Geronimo!" when they jumped. It is believed to come from a motion picture seen by members of the first unit of paratroops, about Geronimo, the fierce and colorful Apache chieftain (c. 1829–1909), and his exploits. After seeing it, they began to shout out his name in derisive reference to the mock heroics of practice jumping.

Gestapo

Describing brutal suppression tactics. The Gestapo was an acronym for *Geheime **Sta**atspolizei*, the secret state police formed in Nazi Germany by Hermann Göring and later led by Heinrich Himmler. By 1933 their tactics of terrorism and torture had made them hated and feared throughout Germany. The Gestapo had vast powers, spying on the military as well as on civilians. Virtually anyone suspected of "disloyalty" to the Nazi regime or of social aberration (being Jewish, a Gypsy, homosexual, mentally defective, etc.) could be summarily arrested, executed, or sent to a concentration camp. In 1946 the Nuremberg War Crimes Tribunal declared the Gestapo a criminal organization. Since then, the name Gestapo has been used for any brutal secret police operations or tactics.

G.I.

An American enlisted man or woman. The term began to be used about 1941 by soldiers, replacing the DOUGHBOY of earlier times. It may have originated in a cartoon of 1941 by Corporal Dave Breger, entitled "G.I. Joe." There is some dispute as to what the initials stand for. Some say "Government Issue," which applied first to the soldiers' uniforms and then to the troops themselves. Others say it was for "Garrison Issue," meaning originally items used in garrison (barracks) rather than in the field. H. L. Mencken even suggested that it originally (before World War I) stood for "galvanized iron," as in G.I. (ash) can. Although the precise origin is debated, G.I. was used for government-issued objects prior to World War II. One writer holds that the Regular Army used it as a derogatory name for early draftees, since they wore what the Army provided rather than buying their own, more stylish, and better-fitting uniforms.

The expression *too G.I.* meant, by 1942, too-rigid adherence to regulations. When the Army magazine *Yank* was first published, on June 14, 1942, the staff said that the magazine was "not G.I." except in the sense that "we are G.I." That same issue contained Dave Breger's cartoon.

Although government issue might be considered a self-deprecating putdown, most writers agree that enlisted soldiers did not consider G.I. an insulting term, at least not when it was used among themselves. After the war its use was perpetuated in the G.I. Bill of Rights, a law signed on June 22, 1944, which provided numerous benefits for World War II veterans. In 1951, during the Korean War, the Defense Department barred all Army public relations officers from using G.I. instead of soldier, on the ground that it was undignified, but the name has survived.

Gibraltar

A pillar of defense. The figurative use of the word derives from the Rock of Gibraltar, a long, steep mountain that was, in ancient legend, one of the Pillars of Hercules. It lies at the southern tip of Spain, overlooking a narrow strait between the European and African continents, which guards the only entrance to the Mediterranean from the Atlantic. Its ancient name was Calpe, and the other "Pillar," on the African coast, was called Abyla.

The name Gibraltar comes from the Arab *Gebel-al-Tarik*, meaning "hill of Tarik," a brilliant Saracen leader who defeated the King of Spain in the year 711 and built a castle on this strategic spot. The Moors held this fortification until 1462, when the Spaniards took it back from them. In 1704 the British took it over, and despite a number of unsuccessful sieges by the Spaniards and the French, they have held it to this day. Formally it is a British crown colony.

Gibraltar served as a naval station in World War I, and in World War II its fortifications were strengthened and most of the civilian population was evacuated. Despite frequent bombing, no important damage was done to it. Since then, Spain has tried to regain possession, but the population of Gibraltar has resisted all such attempts and it remains in British hands.

gismo

A mechanical device or part for which one does not know or remember the correct name. The term was used during World War II by G.I.'s as a synonym for *doohickey, thingamajig, whatchamacallit,* etc. One etymologist believes it was derived from the Arabic *shu ismo,* which means the same thing and was picked up by G.I.'s during the North African campaign. At any rate, it survived the war; it is sometimes spelled *gizmo.*

A similar word is *gidget,* which also became current during World War II. William Morris reports hearing from a sailor who defined it as "a gidget for a gadget"—in other words, some part of a mechanical device. Like gismo, it survived, but it is somewhat less common.

go ballistic, to

To lose control. This term originally applied to a missile whose course was unguided, that is, did not follow its assigned trajectory. By the 1980's the term had been transferred to an expression of human rage, that is, losing control of one's temper.

gobbledygook

Pretentious nonsense as it appears in bureaucratic jargon, that is, inflated and obscure. This word was allegedly coined during World War II by former Texas Congressman Maury Maverick, who served as chairman of the Smaller War Plants Corporation. Fed up with the bureaucratic jargon he encountered, he characterized it as gobbledygook, which he later explained (in the *New York Times Magazine* of May 21, 1944) as a combination of the old turkey gobbler gobbledy-gobbling about with ludicrous pomposity and ending in a sort of gook. However, William Morris cites several sources that trace the word to different and older origins. One was a World War I mess sergeant who described as gobbledygook the answers he got from the Quartermaster Corps when he complained about receiving a shipment of beans instead of potatoes. Another writer traced the word to his childhood in northwestern Pennsylvania. Whatever the ultimate origin, the word became well known from about 1945 on and has remained in the language ever since.

God's country

An especially beautiful rural area; also, one's own country. During the Civil War, Union soldiers used this term to describe the North, which seemed a wonderful place compared to the heat, humidity, and other miserable conditions of southern battlefields. During World War II, G.I.'s overseas used it as a synonym for the United States. Today it is used less specifically.

goldbricker

A person who shirks duties or responsibilities. The noun gold-brick was used in the mid-nineteenth century United States for a fraud or swindle, derived from the practice of enterprising con men who sold a brick of "gold"—actually lead or stone that was painted gold—to unsuspecting customers. During World War I soldiers began to use the word for any of their number who loafed instead of working and consequently were as worthless as such a brick. It also was used as a verb—to goldbrick, meaning to shirk—and this usage has remained entrenched in colloquial American speech.

go off half-cocked, to

To act prematurely or without adequate preparation. This term, also put as *to go off at half-cock*, alludes to the old flintlock rifle, which was the first weapon to use a spring-loaded device called a *cock*. Pulling the trigger caused the cock to fly forward and strike a piece of flint against a steel plate, creating a shower of sparks which fell into a pan of priming powder located at the touchhole. The sparks ignited the priming, which in turn ignited the powder inside the barrel. However, if for some reason the cock was not fully pulled back and locked, so that the trigger could not be pulled, the gun was only "half-cocked" and could not be fired. From this we have the adjective *half-cocked* for inadequately or poorly prepared, and the present term, as in "She went off half-cocked and told everyone about the merger, which in the end never took place." All these terms are actually illogical, since a half-cocked gun couldn't "go off" at all.

goof off, to

To shirk or to laze about. The term originated in the military during World War II and probably comes from the much older noun *goof,* for "a silly or stupid person," from which we also have *goofy,* meaning "stupid or crazy."

gook

Pejorative name for a foreigner, especially one from Southeast Asia or the Near East. The word is believed to come from U.S. military slang for a foreigner, especially a dark-skinned native of Southeast Asia or the Pacific. During World War II the Australians called the Japanese "gooks," while U.S. troops used the word indiscriminately for all South Pacific peoples. During the Korean War the United Nations troops called the Koreans "gooks," which may have come from the Korean word *kuk,* used to signify nationality. During the Vietnam War the word became established once and for all as a disparaging and offensive name for the Vietnamese. Since then it has continued to convey a like insensitivity and hostility toward foreigners ranging from the Arab countries eastward across Asia.

goose step

A marching step in which the legs are held straight and swung high from the hip. This gait, so called for its resemblance to the stiff-legged walk of geese, was used in the military in Germany from the time of Frederick the Great; the German word for it is *Stechstritt.* In Great Britain it was used from 1800 on as a marking-time exercise in military calisthenics and as such was adopted by most European armies until about 1900. The goose step was used by Mussolini's and Hitler's troops during the 1930's and has ever since been associated with fascism, despotism, and blind obedience to authority.

grant quarter, to

> "I ask no quarter."
> —Plato, *The Republic* (c. 375 B.C.)

To be merciful. This term comes from the ancient practice of sparing the life of an enemy who has come into one's power; to give no

Granting no quarter

quarter means to grant no mercy or put the enemy to death. Dr. Ebenezer Brewer cites one possible source as an ancient agreement between the Dutch and Spaniards that a soldier's ransom be equivalent to one-fourth (a quarter) of his pay but then decided that this etymology is spurious. More likely the expression comes from the fact that a victorious army would have to provide its captives with quarters (a place to live), *quarters* having meant barracks or other military housing since the late sixteenth century. To grant no quarter here might mean to provide no housing, or perhaps to kill captives so no housing would be needed. From the same root comes *quartermaster*, the officer in charge of providing housing, food, fuel, and the like for troops.

grapevine

A path for rumors and gossip; an informal communications system. The word is short for *grapevine telegraph*, originating shortly before the American Civil War. The first one was constructed in 1859 between Placerville and Virginia City, California, by Colonel Bernard

Bee, who strung a telegraph line by attaching wire to trees. In time the wire, no longer taut, lay on the ground in loops resembling trailing wild grapevines, whence the name. During the Civil War similar lines were laid by troops, and since the reports heard over such lines often conflicted, the term came to mean unsubstantiated and frequently false rumors.

William Safire cites an even earlier use than Colonel Bee's. Before the war, in the days of the abolitionist underground railroad (for helping slaves escape), the color of the shirts hung on clotheslines signaled danger or safety. Grapevines were sometimes substituted for rope, which was expensive, and so the clothesline telegraph came to be called a grapevine telegraph.

There are several synonyms for the figurative grapevine, also of military provenance. World War I slang called it a *latrine rumor*, presumably for the place where such information was exchanged; World War II troops called it SCUTTLEBUTT; and Gulf War troops called it *goat rope*, presumably for the unreliable results of trying to rope goats.

An older term for an informal communications line, but not originally military in origin, is *bush telegraph*. It was used mainly by British colonists in places such as Africa and Australia, where remote regions are called "the bush."

graveyard shift

A night shift for workers. The name originated during World War I, when for the first time shipbuilders and munitions workers found it necessary to work around the clock in order to produce enough for the war effort. It is still used today for any shift covering the midnight and early morning hours.

great guns

> "Spanking Jack was so comely, so pleasant, so jolly,
> Though winds blew great guns, still he'd whistle and sing."
> —Charles Dibdin (1745–1814), *The Sailor's Consolation*

Intensely, vigorously, greatly. This expression comes from British naval slang of the late eighteenth century, when to *blow great guns* meant a violent gale. However, another meaning, which persisted throughout the nineteenth century, was "important persons" or "big shots." Thus Sir Walter Scott wrote in 1825, "A worthy clergyman, one of the great guns, as they call him." In America in the late nineteenth century the term also was an expletive expressing astonishment, similar to GREAT SCOTT and BY GEORGE.

great Scott

An expression of surprise or amazement. The term, which substitutes Scott for God, refers to General Winfield Scott (1786–1866), who was a military hero of the War of 1812 and became even more popular in America after his victorious Mexican campaign of 1847. He ran for President in 1852, on the Whig Party ticket, but lost decisively to Franklin Pierce. The substitution of Scott for God may originally have been derisive, since the General's detractors called him "Old Fuss and Feathers." Nevertheless, he was an outstanding soldier, serving his country until his retirement in 1861.

Greek fire

General name for an inflammable mixture. The term comes from a primitive but efficient incendiary devised by the ancient Greeks but employed on a large scale only in the Middle Ages by the Byzantines. Bronze tubes mounted on the prows of their galleys spewed forth this inflammable liquid. Allegedly it not only could burn when wet, but water helped it to spread, making it a lethal weapon against wooden ships. No one knows for sure what its constituents were, but it is thought to have been made of quicklime, sulfur, and naphtha. In the nineteenth century the name was used for various mixtures with a similar effect.

Greek treachery

> "I fear the Greeks especially when they bear gifts."
> —Virgil, *Aeneid* (19 B.C.)

A betrayal of trust. The term and idea date from the times of Livy and other Roman historians who regarded the Greeks as full of cunning and trickery. The main instance supporting this claim is the famous wooden horse, which the Greeks offered to the Trojans as a gift and then used to enter and destroy Troy (See TROJAN HORSE).

greenback

A U.S. legal tender note, so called because it is printed in green on one side. Greenbacks were first authorized for use as currency instead of gold or silver during the Civil War. Since then the term has been widely used as a synonym for *dollar.*

gremlin

A mysterious cause of mechanical trouble. This usage comes from World War II, when R.A.F (Royal Air Force) pilots would attribute mysterious faults in their planes to the action of little imaginary elves called gremlins. One fanciful etymology holds that just before the war, members of a bomber squadron serving on the Indian frontier coined the word by combining *Gr*imm's fairy tales, often peopled by mischievous elves, with F*remlin*, a beer from a Kentish brewery that was the only brand available there. The word gremlin appeared in Charles Graves's *Thin Blue Line*, the author having heard it at a Yorkshire airfield. Another writer, however, maintains that the word was current in the R.A.F soon after World War I and that in those days it meant a low-ranking man assigned to the least desirable duties. In any event, the World War II meaning stuck, and gremlin continues to be used as a synonym for mysterious trouble that causes mechanical defects, malfunctions, and similar problems in any kind of machinery.

grenade

A small, hand-thrown missile containing an explosive, a fire-extinguishing substance, tear gas, an insecticide, or some other substance. The word comes from the French *pomegranade*, for the pomegranate fruit, because the military missile, which dates from the sixteenth century, both is shaped like the fruit and explodes much as the seeds burst out from it. In the French army the troops responsible for these small bombs were called *grenadiers*. This name persisted even after grenades fell into disfavor as a weapon, and in both the French and the British military services grenadiers acquired other special duties and often constituted an elite corps. In modern warfare improved grenades were reintroduced and have played a major role since World War I.

ground zero

A new starting point, beginning from scratch. This term comes from nuclear warfare, where it denotes the point at which a nuclear bomb makes impact. Transferred to civilian use, however, it radically changed meaning.

grouse, to

To complain. This mid-nineteenth-century verb originated in the British military and gained currency among American soldiers during World War I. Thereafter it entered the civilian vocabulary.

Guernica

A ruthless attack on defenseless civilians. The term alludes to a small Spanish city that was virtually obliterated by German bombers supporting Franco's forces in April, 1937, during the Spanish Civil War. Later that year Pablo Picasso produced one of his greatest paintings, *Guernica*, in outraged protest over this incident. In the painting, showing a bull goring a horse, the bull represents brutality and darkness, while the gored, frenzied horse stands for the tortured people.

guerrilla

An individual or small group that carries on irregular warfare more or less independently, using such tactics as harassment and sabotage. The word is actually Spanish for "little war," and originally it referred to local resistance against Napoleon's invasion of Spain. The Spanish peasants took matters into their own hands, forming small bands to resist the French, and eventually, with British help, managed to expel them. The word guerrilla remained a permanent part of the English language. Armed opposition to invaders, such as that in Spain, or to an existing regime frequently takes the form of guerrilla warfare.

Gulf War syndrome

A group of unexplained symptoms, often severe, occurring in veterans of the Gulf War, which include skin rash, memory loss, chronic fevers, aches, and fatigue. Although the government and armed forces have denied any particular causes, it is strongly suspected that the syndrome results from exposure to chemicals of some kind.

gun

General name for any portable firearm, such as a pistol, revolver, or rifle. The name, which entered the English language in the fourteenth century, originally meant a stone-throwing, catapultlike weapon. It came either from the Greek *manganon*, a ballista or stone-throwing machine, or, more colorfully, from the Scandinavian woman's name *Gunnhildr*. A ballista named Domina Gunilda was recorded in a 1330 munitions account at Windsor Castle, and further, both *gunnr* and *hildr* meant "war." (This etymology is not as unusual as it seems; see BIG BERTHA.) Modern authorities lean toward the latter theory, holding that soon after *Gunnhildr* entered English it was shortened to gun.

Despite the wild inaccuracy of early firearms, the English used the expression *as sure as a gun* to describe certainty; it was so used by John Dryden (1681), William Congreve (1693), and George Meredith (1859), among others. In the United States one said *sure as shooting* from at least 1853 on.

Less in doubt than managing to hit a target was a gunner's obligation to stay at his post, whence the British term *stand to one's guns* (in America, *stick to one's guns*), meaning to persist and not give way. James Boswell, Samuel Johnson's biographer, wrote in 1769, "Mrs. Thrale stood to her gun with great courage in defense of amorous ditties." A more perplexing use of this phrase occurred in a 1909 newspaper account about members of the staunchly pacifist Society of Friends: "The Quakers stood to their guns, and, without any resort to brute force, finally won." (See also GREAT GUNS.)

gunboat diplomacy

Settling an issue or getting one's way by the threat of force. The term refers to events of the mid-nineteenth century, when the presence of British and American gunboats, along with other naval vessels, coerced the Chinese into making trade concessions. A similar notion was President Theodore Roosevelt's BIG STICK policy. There have been many instances of this strategy throughout history, but the term itself did not come into use until the 1920's.

gung ho

A colloquial term for very enthusiastic. It comes from a Chinese phrase that means "work together" and originated in China in the late 1930's. At that time Japanese troops occupied most of the larger Chinese cities and had a stranglehold on China's industry. An American writer living in China, Helen F. Snow, decided that this problem might be alleviated by forming small producer cooperatives, which would not only help the economy but give employment to some of the thousands of Chinese war refugees. Snow, her husband, journalist Edgar Snow, and a New Zealander, Rewi Alley, formed the China Industrial Cooperatives, a name that was shortened to two Chinese characters pronounced *gung ho*, or "work together." The term was brought back to America by their friend, Marine Lieutenant Colonel Evans F. Carlson, who made it the slogan of his battalion of volunteers, which was formed just after Pearl Harbor. Two companies from this battalion, called Carlson's Raiders, gave the United States one of its first victories of the war when they took Makin Island from the Japanese. In 1943 a war film dramatizing this battle was made, starring Randolph Scott as Carlson and entitled *Gung Ho!* From that time on the expression became widely known. Over the years, however, it became not a rallying cry for cooperation but an adjective describing an overzealous individual.

gunwale

The upper edge or side of a canoe, boat, or other vessel. The word was formed in the fourteenth century from *gun* (the weapon) + *wale* (boat's side) because it was the place for mounting a ship's upper guns.

hack it, to

To cope with, manage, succeed. This term appears to have originated in the U.S. Air Force in the mid-1900's and became widely used during the Vietnam War. William Safire suggests the phrase is another version of *cut it,* as in "cut the mustard."

hair-trigger

Readily activated, easily provoked. An important advance of early-nineteenth-century gunsmiths was the hair trigger, which allowed the firing mechanism of a firearm to be set off with very slight pressure. By the late 1800's this term was being used adjectivally for anything easily set off, as in "Sally has a hair-trigger temper."

half-mast

A sign of mourning. The term comes from the naval practice of flying the ship's flag approximately halfway between the top and base of the main mast as a sign of respect for the dead. The practice began in the seventeenth century or earlier and quickly became widespread. Today flags on flagpoles, buildings, or any other place where they are customarily displayed are placed halfway up the staff when an important person has died. Since about 1950, the term also has been jocular slang for lowering one's trousers partway.

hara-kiri

Suicide or some other self-destructive act. The term is Japanese and originally referred exclusively to the ceremonial suicide practiced by samurai, that is, members of the warrior class in feudal Japan. The Japanese also use the Chinese name for it, *seppuku*. The act originally was performed to avoid falling into enemy hands. About 1500, however, a samurai who was disgraced or sentenced to death would rip open his abdomen with a dagger given him by the emperor (*hara* means "belly," and *kiri* means "cut"). Then his second, a faithful friend he had selected, would finish the job by beheading him and return the dagger to the emperor. Obligatory hara-kiri was abolished in 1868, but voluntary hara-kiri, after some private misfortune or in protest against the conduct of a superior, continued to be practiced. Numerous Japanese soldiers took their lives in this way during World War II as an alternative to surrender. (See also BANZAI; KAMIKAZE). It was mainly after World War II that the term came to be used more loosely in English, not just for suicide but figuratively for self-destruction, as in "The economist regards eliminating all income taxes as a form of economic hara-kiri."

hatchet man

An individual who does a superior's dirty work, such as firing an employee, attacking a political opponent, or the like. The term first was used in mid-eighteenth-century America for an advance soldier, also called the *ax man*, who went ahead of an army moving through the woods, clearing a path for it. George Washington, remembered by schoolchildren for wielding a hatchet against a famous cherry tree, used hatchet men in this way; he also called them *pioneers*.

In the Chinese tong (gang) wars of the 1880's, carried on in America as well as China, so-called "hatchet-armed killers" were paid enforcers who murdered specific tong enemies. The term hatchet man was revived in the mid-1940's in politics and journalism. The political hatchet man (or woman) engages in sharp attacks on opponents or coerces supporters into line. He or she thus clears a path for his (or her) boss, who can then be regarded as "being above" such nasty tactics. Also, a journalist attacking a specific individual or issue is said to be doing a *hatchet job*.

haversack

A shoulder bag used to carry supplies. It originally was a bag in which the cavalry carried feed for their horses, the word being derived from German and Old Norse words for "oats" and "bag." It then became a soldier's bag for carrying any kind of provisions and eventually was extended to similar bags carried by civilians, including hikers, letter carriers, and the like.

havoc

> "And Caesar's spirit, ranging for revenge . . .
> Shall in these confines with a monarch's voice
> Cry 'Havoc!' and let slip the dogs of war."
> —William Shakespeare, *Julius Caesar*

Total destruction or devastation. The word comes from the medieval *havok*, for plunder. To shout "Havoc" was a specific command for the troops to begin looting and massacring a conquered village or town. In England this cry was officially outlawed during the reign of Richard II, on pain of death. Although havoc today still means great damage, *to cry havoc* now simply means to issue a warning, and *to play* (or *wreak*) *havoc with* (or *on*) something or someone means to create confusion or disorder. For example, "The wind played havoc with her new hairdo."

hawks and doves

> "But who does hawk at eagles with a dove?"
> —George Herbert, *The Sacrifice* (1633)

Pro-war and antiwar factions. Doves regard hawks as warmongers; hawks consider doves appeasers and/or cowards. Both terms come from U.S. history. About 1810, referring to the fierce aggressiveness of the bird of prey, Republican Congressman John Randolph called the anti-British extremists in the 12th Congress of the United States *war hawks.* Led by Henry Clay, these southern and western legislators actually constituted a small minority in the House of Representatives but were so vocal in their demands that they achieved a commanding position. In 1811 Clay was elected Speaker of the House. The war hawks cried out that the British were insulting national rights and honor by seizing American ships and impressing seamen. In fact, they were anxious to declare war on England for more selfish reasons: as an excuse to annex Canada, to drive the English from their forts along the Great Lakes (where they were supplying Indian tribes with arms to attack American frontiersmen), and also to take Florida, then weakly held by Britain's ally, Spain.

At first President James Madison was determined to avoid open conflict, but the war hawks gradually won him over, and on June 18, 1812, Congress declared war on England. However, the country was far from united behind this decision. Federalist-dominated New England and other commercial centers along the East Coast violently opposed war, not from any great love for peace but because they felt it would threaten their commercial interests. Two and one-half years later the War of 1812 ended in virtual stalemate. Both sides agreed to stop fighting and restore any conquered territory to prewar boundaries. The Treaty of Ghent made no mention of the grievances that allegedly had started the war.

Some 150 years later the United States found itself similarly divided, at first (1962) over what to do about the Soviet placement of missiles in Cuba (hawks took a firm stand; doves, so called for the age-old symbol of peace and including United Nations Ambassador Adlai E. Stevenson, urged a soft approach). Then came the Vietnam War. The war's supporters again were called hawks and its opponents doves. Each side vilified the other, causing great bitterness on the home front and eventually leading to President Lyndon B. Johnson's decision not to seek reelection. The outcome of this war, too, was inconclusive.

headquarters

The center of operations of any organization. The word, created in the seventeenth century from *head*, meaning "chief," and *quarters*, for "military housing," originally meant the place from which a military commander issued orders and where he and his staff worked. By the late eighteenth century it was being transferred to civilian usage, for the main office of a business, the police, a government agency, or any similar organization.

hector, to

> "Who would have known of Hector if Troy had been happy? The road to valor is builded by adversity."
>
> —Ovid, *Tristia* (c. A.D. 9)

To bully, torment, or browbeat. The original Hector was the oldest son of King Priam and the noblest and most generous of the Trojan heroes described in Homer's *Iliad*. After holding out against the Greeks for ten years, Hector was slain by Achilles, who lashed him to a chariot and dragged his corpse three times around the walls of Troy. For some reason that has never been properly explained, in the seventeenth century the noun hector came to mean a swaggering, blustering bully, from which came the verb form in its modern meaning.

Heil, Hitler

Today, a derisive address to a would-be dictator. The term was the mandatory salute of Nazi Germany, the words meaning "Hail, Hitler." Another expression from the same era is *Sieg heil* (Hail, victory), also used in Nazi Germany.

hep

U.S. slang for aware, well informed, up to date. Although this term's origin is not certain, several etymologists point out that it became popular during World War I and therefore may have come from the drill sergeant's counting cadence for marching, "Hep, hep, hep." A recruit who got out of step was told to *get hep*, that is, wake up and conform; hence hep came to mean knowing one's way around. Exactly the same thing is meant by *hip*, which also came into use in the early twentieth century and in mid-century became the source of *hippie*, the rebel of the 1960's who disavowed the establishment and embraced various forms of personal self-expression.

high-caliber

Exceptional merit in quality or competence. Although the word *caliber* comes from firearms, where it has, since the sixteenth century, described the diameter of a gun's bore, a gun barrel is never described in terms of high or low caliber but of large or small. Since about the same time, caliber also has referred to relative merit or social standing, as it still does. Neither then nor now, however, does high-caliber make sense ballistically.

Hiroshima

Synonym and symbol for nuclear devastation. This Japanese city and military base was the target of the first atomic bomb on August 6, 1945. Ever since, it has represented a portent of the world's fate should nuclear conflict break out.

hold the fort, to

To keep things going until further support arrives. The term is thought to date from the American Civil War. In the autumn of 1864 General J. B. Hood's Confederate force, which had been expelled from Atlanta in September by Union troops under William T. Sherman, swung in a wide arc toward Tennessee, on the very route along which Sherman had advanced. Along their line of march, they called on all the Union positions they saw to surrender. One such position was commanded by General John M. Corse at Allatoona. On October 5, when told to give up in order to "avoid a needless effusion of blood," Corse refused. Supposedly he had received a communiqué from Sherman saying, "Hold the fort at all costs, for I am coming." Today the term is used colloquially and also in a business sense, as in "Hold the fort in the store until the boss gets back from her buying trip."

A similar expression, *hold the line*, likewise comes from earlier military tactics, when a line of troops literally was supposed to prevent an enemy breakthrough. The expression was adopted in football, with a similar literal meaning, and then began to be used figuratively in government and other civilian enterprises, as in "holding the line against inflation."

holocaust

> "Like that self-begotten bird
> In the Arabian woods embost
> That no second knows, nor third,
> And lay erewhile a holocaust."
> —John Milton, *Samson Agonistes* (1671)

Today, a wholesale slaughter, in particular the murder of millions of Jews by Hitler's Nazis before and during World War II. Originally the word, derived from the Greek *holos* (whole) and *kaustos* (burn), referred to a sacrificial burnt offering to pagan gods. By the seventeenth century, however, it was used to mean complete destruction. The Nobel Prize–winning author Elie Wiesel, himself a survivor of Nazi concentration camps, was the first to use the word for the Nazi destruction of Jews, which is the sense in which it is most often employed today.

homage

General reverence and respect. In the Middle Ages, when a lord conferred a FIEF in a ceremony called *investiture*, the knight knelt before the lord and pledged to be his *homme* (French for "man"). It is from this ceremony that we have the word homage, originally meaning a pledge of allegiance and later extended to signify general reverence and respect.

honcho

Colloquial term for "boss." This word, often used somewhat jocularly for the person in charge or the principal leader and organizer of a job, comes from the Japanese *han'chō*, for "squad leader," which was adopted by American occupation troops in Japan after World War II and also was used by them during the Korean War. One often says *big honcho*.

hooch

A shack or hut. This term comes from the Japanese *uchi*, or "house," and began to be used by American troops during the Korean War for both native dwellings and military bunkers. Its use persisted during the Vietnam War and thereafter.

hooker

Slang for "prostitute." Many etymologists trace this word to Civil War General Joseph ("Fighting Joe") Hooker. The Union General allegedly made prostitutes stay in one area of Washington, D.C., near Union Station. Another version attributes the transfer to the general's own questionable proclivities and holds that in tribute to them the women who worked in Washington's brothels were called "Hooker's Division" or "Hooker's Brigade." However, the use of hooker for prostitute is actually somewhat older—the city of Norfolk, Virginia, had hookers in Brick Row as early as 1845—and it has been suggested that the term comes from the idea that a prostitute "hooks" her customer much as an angler hooks a fish.

horde

> "And you're giving a treat (penny ice and cold meat)
> To a party of friends and relations.
> They're a ravenous horde, and they all came on board
> At Sloane Square and South Kensington Stations."
> —W. S. Gilbert, *Iolanthe* (1882)

A very large group of animals or human beings, usually on the move. The original horde was the so-called Golden Horde of Genghis Khan (1167–1227), *Zolotaya orda* in Old Russian, which was probably taken from the Turkish *ordu* or *orda*, for "royal residence." One of the greatest generals of all time, Genghis Khan built an empire stretching from Korea to Palestine, and under his descendants the limits of this realm were pushed west as far as Germany. During the thirteenth century these invaders from the east, called Mongols or Tartars (a name that included many different peoples; see also TARTAR), threatened to bring a new age of darkness to Europe. The name *golden horde* referred specifically to the magnificent tent of Batu, Genghis Khan's grandson, who established an empire in southeast Russia in the thirteenth century, but horde came to be applied to the onslaught of his soldiers.

Although known for their fierceness in battle and in subjugating conquered peoples, the ultimate historic influence of the Mongol horde was immense. They checked the growth of Islam at a time when it threatened European civilization and taught Europe new military strategy and discipline. Nevertheless, it is for their depredation and destruction that they were primarily remembered, and the word horde today is rarely used for a benign force. Rather one speaks of "a horde of mosquitoes" or, disparagingly, of "a horde of tourists" or, with even worse bias, "Asiatic hordes," meaning swarms of people from Asia or of Asian ancestry.

hors de combat

Out of the running. The term is French for "out of the battle" and literally meant being wounded or otherwise incapable of continuing to fight. It began to be used figuratively in English in the 1750's.

hotshot

> "You are a hot shot indeed."
> —James Howell, *English Proverbs* (1659)

Slang for "flamboyantly successful." According to Eric Partridge, the term originally (sixteenth century) meant someone who is excessively eager to shoot—in the same sense that *hotspur* meant an impetuous or reckless person, a hothead. Today hotshot is used mainly figuratively, and often somewhat derisively, as either noun or adjective for a supremely self-confident person who is showily and aggressively successful.

humbug

> "He had merely considered him a humbug in a Pickwickian point of view."
> —Charles Dickens, *Pickwick Papers* (1836–37)

A fake or hoax. This word entered the language about 1740, but no one knows for sure where it came from. Willard Espy gives it a military origin, citing an account in the *Mexican Times* of 1866. Allegedly, during the many wars among the German states prior to the unification of Germany, so many false reports came from the city of Hamburg that people began to say, "That's from Hamburg," meaning "that's not true." And supposedly Hamburg was corrupted into humbug. Eric Partridge, on the other hand, believes it probably came from combining the *hum* of "hum and haw," meaning "to temporize," and the *bug* of "bugbear," an imaginary goblin. As with other words of disputed origin, readers are invited to pick their own favorite source.

hummer, humvee

An all-terrain vehicle widely used during the Gulf War. The name is a kind of acronym for *h*igh-*m*obility *m*ultipurpose *v*ehicle, or HMMV. Diesel-powered, it was faster than the jeep, which it largely replaced in desert warfare. Although its appearance is closer to a tank than an automobile, the hummer later gained some civilian admirers and purchasers.

hundred days

A special period of that length during which important events take place. The term was first used for Napoleon Bonaparte's final campaign, after he escaped from his first exile in Elba and marched across Europe. It actually was 116 days before he was defeated at Waterloo. The term also was used for the absence of Louis XVIII from Paris from March 20, when Napoleon arrived, to June 28, 1815, when he returned to Paris following Napoleon's defeat. In 1933 the term was revived for a period shortly after U.S. President Franklin D. Roosevelt took office— March 9 to June 16, 1933—during which the 73rd Congress passed milestone legislation to combat the devastating effects of the Great Depression, mainly public works and various relief measures.

hunky-dory

Fine, in excellent condition. *Hunky* alone became a popular slang expression during the Civil War, and by the war's end it had been expanded to its present form. Of uncertain origin, it remains in common use.

hush-hush

Secret, highly confidential. Although "hush" for "be quiet" has been used since the fourteenth century, the duplicatory form originated only during World War I, when it was used to describe secret military plans and operations. A planned attack on the German-occupied Belgian coast in 1916 and 1917, which never actually took place, was called the Hush-Hush Operation, and a British force in the Caucasus was called the Hush-Hush Army. After the war the term was transferred to any kind of secret plan or project and is still so used today.

I came, I saw, I conquered

In April, 46 B.C., Julius Caesar celebrated a series of stunning military victories in a short space of time. As was customary, he and his troops triumphantly rode through Rome on chariots and decorated wagons, some of which bore stage sets representing battle scenes. One wagon, however, carried only a simple three-word inscription, *Veni, vidi, vici* (I came, I saw, I conquered), words whereby Caesar referred to the speed with which he had subdued the enemy. Repeated by thousands of Latin students over the centuries, this phrase is still used, often ironically, for other kinds of success.

incommunicado

Unable or unwilling to communicate with others. The word is Spanish and was first used for prisoners of war who were deliberately prevented from communicating with the outside world, lest they reveal their captors' military secrets. It was picked up by Americans during the Mexican War (1846–48) and later was transferred not only to those who were forcibly prevented from outside contact but also to individuals who for one reason or another (politics, business, etc.) preferred not to speak to anyone for a particular period of time.

Indian file

In single file. The term originated during the French and Indian Wars of the eighteenth century, when American colonists observed the Native American practice of having each warrior step in the footprints of the one in front of him, with the last obliterating all the prints. Thus neither the track nor the number of braves who had trodden it could be discerned. Today the term is used simply in the general sense of forming a single line.

infantry

> "That small infantry
>   Warred on by cranes."
> —John Milton, *Paradise Lost* (1667)

Foot soldiers. The term comes from the word *infant*, which has meant a very young child—originally, one too young to talk—since the fourteenth century. In the sixteenth century it began to be used for foot soldiers, who were young and inexperienced compared to knights on horseback.

in harm's way

> "I wish to have no Connection with any Ship that does not sail fast, for I intend to go in harm's way."
> —Capt. John Paul Jones, letter (1778)

In danger. This term originated as the antonym of *out of harm's way*, dating from the mid-1600's, and was used principally as a naval term from the time of the American Revolution. Jones rebuilt the slow merchant ship assigned to him. He named it the *Bon Homme Richard* and soon engaged in a memorable hand-to-hand battle with the British frigate *Serapis*. Although the British were forced to surrender, the battle was too much for Jones's ship, which sank. Today, of course, the term is used in a very general sense, as well as in a military context.

inquisition

Relentless questioning. The word comes from the Roman Catholic Church's prosecution of heresy from the fifteenth to the nineteenth centuries. The Church established a specific authority, a court of investigation, in Spain in 1479; hence it is also called the *Spanish Inquisition.* It was authorized to investigate the opinions, morals, and character of all persons suspected of heresy. Since the principal object was to make an accused person confess to heresy, both to assure his or her ultimate salvation and to uphold the security of society, the Inquisition became associated with all manner of torture and horrible punishment directed to this end. Heretics often were put to death by burning so as to avoid spilling their blood. During the late Middle Ages the Church had instituted another Inquisition, but it was nowhere near as harsh in its treatment of heretics as the Spanish Inquisition, which was conducted more under the control of the Spanish kings than the Vatican. The word inquisition comes from the Latin *inquisitio,* for "inquiry," and today it retains both this meaning and the connotation of harshness bestowed by the historical Inquisition.

in the trenches

Actively working. This term comes from World War I, when it denoted being on active duty. Today it is used in a very general way, as in "He's been in the trenches for a year, trying to negotiate a merger."

iron chancellor

> "It is not by speeches and resolutions that the great questions of the time are decided but by blood and iron."
> —Otto von Bismarck, speech (September 30, 1862)

Nickname for Chancellor Otto von Bismarck, who made Prussia a leading European power and in 1871, for William I, created the German Empire and served as chancellor until 1890. The most powerful statesman in Europe, he earned his nickname through his policy of blood and iron—in German, *Blut und Eisen,* a term he coined in a speech to the Prussian House of Delegates. This policy involved the clever use of war to bring Prussia, and then Germany, to its eminent position. (See also PRUSSIAN.)

ironclad

Firm, unbreakable, strict, or rigorous. The term originally referred to the practice of protecting wooden naval vessels by covering them with thick iron plates and came into common use during the U.S. Civil War. Some such protection had been used earlier (and the U.S. frigate *Constitution*, used in the War of 1812, was nicknamed OLD IRONSIDES), but systematic encasement of ships in metal plate was done only from the mid-nineteenth century on. Later the term began to be transferred to unbreakable agreements, laws that could not be overturned, and the like, and today one still speaks, for example, of an ironclad alibi or an ironclad labor contract.

Iron Cross

A Prussian military decoration instituted by Frederick William II in 1813, during the Napoleonic Wars, which is awarded for outstanding bravery in wartime. It remains a symbol of military heroism.

iron curtain

> "From Stettin on the Baltic to Trieste on the Adriatic an iron
> curtain has descended across Europe."
> —Sir Winston Churchill, speech (March 5, 1946)

A symbolic barrier representing hostile relations between the Communist nations, particularly the Soviet Union and its satellites, and the non-Communist Western nations in the period after World War II. The term was popularized by British Prime Minister Winston Churchill in a speech he made in 1946 in Fulton, Missouri, quoted in part here, but he did not originate it. It had been employed in Germany in May, 1945, by Count Schwerin von Krosigk, Hitler's Minister of Finance, and others, and they probably were echoing still earlier uses, including one by the Queen of Belgium, who in 1914 spoke of a "bloody iron curtain" between her and the Germans.

The term "iron curtain" originally was used in a quite different sense. In the late eighteenth century it denoted a fireproof curtain placed between the stage and audience to prevent the spread of fire in theaters, a practice adopted in France, England, and elsewhere. The name then was used figuratively by a number of writers, including H. G. Wells in *The Food of the Gods* (1904), where he made it a metaphor for a forcible break in communications with society by an individual. In 1920 Ethel Snowden, in her travel book *Through Bolshevik Russia*, may have become the first to use the term in relation to the Soviet Union; arriving in Petrograd, she wrote, "We were behind the 'iron curtain' at last."

I shall return

I won't accept defeat. For the first year or so of Pacific action during World War II, Japanese forces advanced without much resistance, taking the Philippines, Dutch East Indies (now Indonesia), and Malaya (Malaysia). General Douglas MacArthur's forces on Luzon were taken by surprise and, after retreating to the Bataan peninsula, eventually surrendered the entire Philippine archipelago. However, the General vowed, "I shall return," words that were quoted so often that they became symbolic of refusing to accept defeat (especially since he eventually carried out his promise). (See also OLD SOLDIERS NEVER DIE.)

island hopping

Moving from island to island. This term comes from the Pacific campaigns during World War II, which called for amphibious troops to land on enemy-held islands and establish a beachhead. And the American strategy that at last began to turn the tide, attacking Japanese bases here and there but bypassing major enemy strongholds, was called *island hopping*. Although this tactic was not new, the name for it was, and later it was transferred to the tourist practice of moving from island to island during, for example, a Caribbean vacation.

jackstraws

A game similar to "pick up sticks," in which players take turns trying to pick up thin strips of wood (like toothpicks) or straws one by one, without touching any of the others in the pile. The name comes from an obsolete term for "nonentity," *Jack Straw*, which in turn comes from an actual person so named. The original Jack Straw was one of the leaders of the Peasants' Revolt of 1381 and was mentioned by Chaucer. The rebellion was harshly put down, and by the sixteenth century Jack Straw had come to mean a worthless person, a mere straw figure of a man. That usage is now obsolete, but the name survives in the game, which similarly involves small worthless objects.

Jacobin

A political radical. The name originated as the French name for Dominican friars, whose first house in Paris was located on the Rue St. Jacques. During the French Revolution a group of radicals formed a club, at first called the Breton Club at Versailles but renamed the Jacobin Club when it moved to Paris and convened in the former

Dominican (Jacobin) convent. Its members included Robespierre, St. Just, and Marat, who all advocated violent revolution to achieve their aims. At one point the Jacobins virtually controlled France, and their REIGN OF TERROR, whose excesses in eliminating opposition to their cause—real or imagined—became legendary. With the fall of Robespierre in July, 1794, their power came to an end, but the spirit of the group survived in revolutionary doctrine. The party itself resurfaced, but in a much more moderate form, during the Revolution of 1848. Their name continues to be used as a synonym for political radicals anywhere.

jeep

A small, rugged, four-wheel-drive car. It was developed as a quarter-ton, all-purpose vehicle by the Willys-Overland Company for the U.S. Army during World War II and was so popular that it became the one item the Germans most liked to capture for their own use. Its name is believed to come from a character called Eugene the Jeep, appearing in E. C. Segar's *Popeye* comic strips from 1936 on. This character was an imaginary animal that could move at will between the third and fourth dimensions, was invisible while in the fourth dimension, and could answer questions about the future. According to J. E. Lighter, in 1937 the Halliburton Oil Well Cementing Company built a "jeep" truck. Army command cars and heavy gun tractors also were called "jeeps" in 1940 and 1941, as were new army recruits. The current type of jeep, the Willys-Overland's quarter-ton 4 × 4, was selected over Ford's Model G-P and American Bantam's BRC model, but the name Jeep stuck. The design continues to find civilian applications to the present day, mainly because its four-wheel drive and high and low gear boxes make it well suited for cross-country driving.

jerrican, jerry can

A five-gallon can used to hold spare fuel or water for a motor vehicle. Such containers, used during World War II by the German Afrika Korps, first were adopted by the British in Libya and then became the standard unit of fuel replenishment in desert warfare for all the Allied forces. The name comes from the British slang for German, *Jerry*, so used since World War I. (Actually, *Jerry* was English slang for "chamber pot" and was applied to the Germans because their army helmets resembled upside-down chamber pots.) After the war the name continued to be used for any similar container.

jingoism

Excessive patriotism. The term comes from an extremely popular music-hall song by G. W. Hunt that was current during the Russian-Turkish War (1877–78), when anti-Russian feeling was high in Britain and Prime Minister Benjamin Disraeli ordered the Mediterranean fleet to Constantinople. The anti-Russians were called "jingoes," and their warmongering "jingoism." The song went:

> We don't want to fight, but by Jingo if we do
> We've got the ships, we've got the men, and got the money too.
> We've fought the Bear before, and while we're Britons true,
> The Russians shall not have Constantinople. . . .

In earlier times "Hey jingo" or "High jingo" was used by a magician who was making an object reappear (and "Presto" was said when it disappeared).

junta

A small group that rules a country, usually after a more or less violent takeover. The word is actually Spanish for "committee" or "council" and, according to William Safire, was popularized in 1808 when it described the groups formed in Spain during the Peninsular War against Napoleon. Before that, in Spanish it had no connotations of either the military or a coup d'état. In English, however, it acquired military associations because frequently a violent takeover is led, or at least supported, by a military force, whose generals then take over the government. Certainly this pattern was common in Latin America. The word *junta*, sometimes in the form of *junto*, was borrowed into English in the early seventeenth century and at that time was pronounced in English fashion (with a soft *j* as in "jump"). By the time of the Spanish-American War it had acquired its military meaning and had begun to be pronounced in Spanish style ("hoonta").

kamikaze

A suicidal attack. The word *kamikaze* actually can be translated as "divine wind" and originally was used for a providential typhoon that foiled a Mongol invasion of Japan in 1281. During World War II, however, it acquired a different meaning. By 1944 the Japanese were in deep trouble, much of it owing to air attacks launched from American carriers. Since their military code considered death far more honorable than defeat, they hit on the idea of attacking carriers with rocket-propelled manned bombs. For this purpose they organized a Thunder Gods Corps of pilots to launch these kamikaze attacks in which they, of course, were killed.

The kamikaze missions, carried out almost daily from October, 1944, were quite effective, killing an estimated 12,300 Americans and wounding another 36,400. Nearly 4,000 Japanese pilots died in this way. Subsequently kamikaze was adopted into English for any wildly reckless or destructive behavior and later still for a cocktail consisting mainly of straight vodka and designed to induce virtually instant drunken oblivion.

keep your powder dry

> "Put your trust in God, my boys, but mind to keep your powder dry."
> —Oliver Cromwell, speech (October 23, 1642)

Take care of yourself; remain calm so you can act when necessary. The powder Cromwell referred to was gunpowder, thought to have been invented by the Chinese in the ninth century and used in Europe, at first in actual powder form, from the fourteenth century until the nineteenth century, when it was superseded by various kinds of smokeless powder. Igniting wet powder was quite difficult, so it was important to keep one's gunpowder dry, as Cromwell warned his troops just before they entered the Battle of Edgehill. Various kinds of container, called *powder horns*, were devised to store and carry the stuff into the field. In the nineteenth century the term began to be used figuratively and still is.

khaki

A greenish shade of brown. The name comes from the Urdu word for "dust" or "dust-colored," in turn from the Persian *khak*, for "dust." It was first adopted into English in the mid-nineteenth century by British troops serving in India, and indeed by 1857 there was an irregular corps of British Guides called the Khaki Risala (Khaki Squad), which helped put down the Sepoy Rebellion. It then was adopted by several regiments as the proper color for their active-service uniform but was not generally introduced in the British army until the Boer War (1899–1902). During that war khaki also was a slang name for "volunteer."

The color khaki is still used for British and American soldiers' summer uniforms, which themselves are referred to as *khakis*, as well as for many kinds of civilian clothing.

K.P.

> "Poor little me, I'm a 'K.P.'
> I scrub the mess hall on bended knee.
> Against my wishes I wash the dishes. . . ."
> —Irving Berlin, *Yip! Yip! Yaphank* (1918)

Kitchen duties, usually of a menial kind. The term is an abbreviation for *kitchen police* or *kitchen patrol* and originated during World War I, when assignment to menial kitchen tasks became a standard punishment for recruits. The ditty quoted here, related in Elbridge Colby's *Army Talk* (1943), was one of several musical complaints about World War I kitchen scut work.

kraut

Offensive slang name for a German. It began to be used during World War I and is an abbreviation for what was regarded as a quintessential German food, sauerkraut (fermented cabbage). Both it and *heinie*, another slang word for German originating at the same time (this one an abbreviation for the name Heinrich), were resurrected when the Germans again became the enemy during World War II. Some regard heinie as even more offensive because of its other informal meaning, backside or buttocks.

labyrinth

A maze. This term comes from ancient Crete, where at the height of its power, about 1600 B.C., King Minos built at Knossos a huge palace whose many rooms and courtyards formed a maze. According to Greek legend, periodically Minos would demand tribute from the then-much-weaker city of Athens—seven youths and seven maidens, whom he placed in the maze. Unable to find their way, they would blunder into the *minotaur*, a monster with a bull's head and man's body, who killed them with a double-bladed ax, called *labrys* in Greek, and devoured them. Today we still call any person or thing that devours everything in its path a minotaur, and in time the name of the ax was transferred to the maze, or labyrinth. In eighteenth-century England such mazes were a popular landscaping device in formal gardens. Further, physiologists adopted "labyrinth" to describe both the circulatory system and a portion of the inner ear, and it also is used figuratively for any complex entanglement (of relationships, ideas, and the like).

last-ditch

> "There is one certain means by which I can be sure never to see
> my country's ruin: I will die in the last ditch."
> —William of Orange (c. 1677)

Describing a desperate final measure. The last ditch was, in military
terms, the last line of defense. The term had begun to be used figuratively by the eighteenth century, when Thomas Jefferson wrote, "A
government driven to the last ditch by the universal call for lib-
erty." Similarly, to *die in the last ditch* means to resist to the end; it
dates from the early 1700's.

launch, to

> "Was this the face that launch'd a thousand ships?"
> —Christopher Marlowe, *Doctor Faustus* (c. 1588)

To set in action, to initiate. This innocent-sounding word, which
also means to shove a ship or boat into the water for the first time,
actually comes from the Middle English *launchen*, "to throw a
lance." In the fourteenth century it began to be used in the sense of
setting a vessel into water, and before long it was being used figuratively, for beginning other kinds of enterprise. Today one still speaks
of launching an advertising campaign, a new design of automobile,
a business, etc.

The nautical association survives in the noun *launch*, used since
about 1700 for a large open boat employed principally to carry people between a large ship and the shore. This word, however, comes
from the Spanish and Portuguese *lancha*, in turn of uncertain origin
(perhaps Malay, perhaps Latin).

lebensraum

Room to expand. The word is German for "living space" and was
coined by the German historian Heinrich von Treitschke (1834–96),
a staunch nationalist who firmly believed in Prussia's destiny as a
world power that should seize whatever lands it needed. His ideas
were used by the German geographer Karl Haushofer (1869–1946) to
justify German imperialist ambitions: owing to the pressures of
a growing population, Germany "needed" more land. Of course

Germany was not alone in seeking more territory in the form of overseas colonies, and its ambitions were in direct conflict with those of Great Britain and France, which had similar goals. This conflict eventually led to the outbreak of World War I.

Haushofer's ideas were eagerly taken up by the Nazis. One of his students at the University of Munich was Rudolf Hess, who introduced Haushofer to Hitler, and he became one of Hitler's closest advisers. His theories, called *geopolitics* (combining geography and politics) or *Weltpolitik* (world politics), were a cornerstone of Nazi expansion, not so much into overseas colonies as in straightforward annexation of its neighbors, beginning with Austria and the Sudetenland and continuing with the invasion of Poland, Belgium, and so on.

left-wing

Politically liberal, ranging from moderately so to quite radical. Many people think this expression, along with *right-wing*, for politically conservative, comes from the seating pattern adopted by the French National Assembly in the late eighteenth century. The radicals were seated on the left side, the moderates in the center, and the conservative nobles on the right. The term left-wing, however, originated somewhat earlier, about 1700, to describe the *left flank* of an army in the field.

legion

A huge number; a multitude. By the early fourth century B.C., as Rome began to expand throughout Italy, the army was divided into two groups: the legion, made up of Roman citizens, and a second group, made up of Roman allies. The legion, a word coming from the Latin *legere*, "to gather," was enormous for that time—it consisted of 3,000 to 6,000 infantry soldiers and 100 to 200 cavalry troops. It is from its size that we have the current usage of legion, as in "His admirers were legion."

let them eat cake

Lack of concern with the needs of the poor. This term supposedly comes from a statement by Marie Antoinette that helped bring on the French Revolution. However, it actually appeared before she came to France, in Jean-Jacques Rousseau's *Confessions* (c. 1767), referring to an unnamed princess who, when told the country people had no bread, said "Let them eat cake." Nevertheless, the phrase's association with the Revolution and its meaning have survived to the present day.

liberate, to

A colloquial term meaning "to steal" or "to loot." This use of a formerly law-abiding verb began late in World War II, when Allied troops invaded and occupied first Italy and then Germany. Understandably tired of army rations, the invaders, who were regarded as "liberators" of these countries from fascism, began to "liberate" chickens, wine, and other supplies they found to their liking. A similar operation during World War I was called "salvaging," and in the U.S. Civil War, "appropriating," but liberate has remained in American slang in this ironic sense.

lie like a trooper, to

> "A friend of his . . . who lied like a trooper."
> —C. E. Badham, *Prose Halieutics* (1854)

To prevaricate thoroughly and often. This term seems to date from the nineteenth century as a variation on an earlier, seventeenth-century expression, to SWEAR LIKE A TROOPER, a locution still preferred in British usage. Stuart Flexner pointed out that *to lie like a soldier* appeared in 1885, and the Spanish-American War gave us *to lie like a Spaniard*. They all mean the same thing and stem from the legendary lack of veracity found in the military, especially in the lower ranks, who lie to save their skins. The expression *like a trooper* originally meant vigorously and with great enthusiasm.

line of fire

The path of an attack. This term, from the mid-nineteenth century, originally referred to the path of a bullet or other projectile, a meaning that also survives. However, the term is often used figuratively, as in "When Mom starts complaining about Dad's spending, I leave the house to get out of the line of fire."

liquidate, to

"I have not become the King's First Minister to preside over the liquidation of the British Empire."
                    —Sir Winston Churchill, speech (1942)

To get rid of, by cashing in or canceling out or killing. The financial variety of liquidation dates from the sixteenth century, but about 1920 the term acquired a more sinister meaning. It originated in the Soviet Union after the Communist Revolution of 1917, in the Russian word *likvidirovat*, "to wind up," a euphemism for getting rid of anti-Communist elements in the population. This sense later was adopted in English.

lock, stock, and barrel

"Like the highlandman's gun, she wants stock, lock and barrel to put her into repair."
                    —J. G. Lockhart, *Life*, quoting Sir Walter Scott

The whole thing, including every part. Originally this term was used literally to mean all three elements of a firearm. It soon was transferred to the entirety of anything. A nautical counterpart used in British naval slang is *bob, line, and sinker*, the three main parts of a fishing rod; in America it became *hook, line, and sinker*. Although guns have long been made quite differently, lock, stock, and barrel was a cliché by about 1820 and is still used.

logistics

Getting needed materials, equipment, and personnel to the right place at the right time for making a product, providing a service, or pursuing some other enterprise. The term comes from the French *logistique*, originally meaning the military quartermaster's work, of which one of the most important tasks was to house (in French, *loger*) the troops. The term was adopted by business and industry, as well as other enterprises, so that today one may speak, for example, of the logistics of producing a play.

Logistical problem

Long March

"In the wild autumn wind of October
The Central Army began the Long March."
—*Song of the Long March*

The 8,000-mile retreat of 100,000 men and 35 women of the Central Red (Communist) Army and the Chinese Communist Party. The trek began, in September, 1934, at Kiangsi and Fukien, in southeast China, and wound across the plains, rivers, and high mountains to northwest China, ending at Paoan. The Long March was not a peaceful retreat by any means. The Red Army entered into numerous engagements against the Chinese Nationalists (Kuomintang) under Chiang Kai-shek and suffered heavy losses, both through combat and from the harsh conditions they encountered over this great distance. The Long March ended two years, one month, and nineteen days after it had begun, and its end marked a turning point for China. Mao Zedong now was the leader of the Chinese Communists. For a time they fought together with Nationalists against their common enemy, Japan, but by 1940 this temporary alliance was in deep trouble, and in the ensuing civil war the Nationalists were pushed off the mainland to Taiwan and the Communists took over the entire country.

loophole

> "Ere the blabbing eastern scout,
>   The nice Morn on th'Indian steep
> From her cabin'd loop-hole peep."
> —John Milton, *Comus* (1637)

A way out, a means of escape. The word comes from the loophole of the medieval fortress and city walls, through which soldiers could shoot out at the enemy. After gunpowder diminished the military effectiveness of such strongholds, the word was used for any small opening in a wall. By the mid-seventeenth century it was being used figuratively for a small opening through which one might escape, the primary meaning that is still current. "The Internal Revenue Service closes another tax loophole," proclaims a newspaper headline, meaning the tax law has been changed to prevent anyone from getting away with paying less than would seem to be required.

loose cannon

A person or thing that is uncontrollable and therefore apt to cause trouble for its own side. This term alludes to a cannon on shipdeck, which during a storm or combat might come loose from its mounting and roll about, severely damaging the hull and/or injuring the crew. Dating from the first half of the 1800's, the term now is used figuratively, as in "That woman's a loose cannon; you never know what confidential data she'll reveal."

mace

> "Tis not the balm, the sceptre, and the ball,
>   The sword, the mace, the crown imperial,
>   The intertissued robe of gold and . . ."
> —William Shakespeare, *Henry V*

A staff of high office, used on ceremonial occasions. The original mace, whose name comes from the Latin *mattea*, for club, was in the thirteenth century a heavy, iron-headed club used as a weapon. By the fifteenth century firearms had largely replaced this primitive tool, which thereafter became a kind of scepter. It continues to serve as a symbol of dignity (as does the sword), especially in Great Britain, where the Speaker of the House of Commons, the Lord Mayor of London, and other dignitaries use it on special occasions.

mad dog syndrome

The capacity for unpredictable and dangerous actions. This term arose during the Gulf War, when it was applied to Iraqi leader Saddam Hussein.

Mae West

A life jacket. The original Mae West (c. 1892–1980) was an attractive film star who became extremely popular in the 1930's for her comic roles. In the late 1930's fliers in both the Royal Air Force (R.A.F.) and U.S. Air Force began to call their inflatable life jackets Mae Wests, in allusion to the actress's full-bosomed charms. During World War II the name was used for life jackets issued to troops at sea. The name continued to be used after the war but is heard less often now.

magazine

> "The book of books, the storehouse and magazine of life and comfort, the holy Scriptures."
> —George Herbert (1593–1633), *A Priest to the Temple*

A periodical journal containing articles and other contributions from a number of authors. The name comes from the Arabic *makhazin*, originally a storehouse and by 1596 specifically a place for storing gunpowder. The military meaning of magazine persists—a place for storing munitions—but in the eighteenth century the word also began to be used for a periodical. The first publication to use the name was *The Gentleman's Magazine*, whose introduction in 1731 said, "This Consideration has induced several Gentlemen to promote a Monthly Collection to treasure up, as in a Magazine, the most remarkable Pieces on the Subjects above mentioned." Earlier, in the seventeenth century, the word appeared in several book titles, where it denoted a "storehouse of information."

magenta

A bright, purplish red color. In 1859 the Austrians were defeated by the French and Sardinians at the town of Magenta, in northern Italy, just west of Milan. Later that year a brilliant aniline dye was discovered, and the color was named magenta to commemorate the battle, which had been an exceptionally bloody one. That same year another aniline dye, this one a bluish pink, was discovered, and it was named *solferino*, for the other great battle of the same campaign, which took place at the town of Solferino.

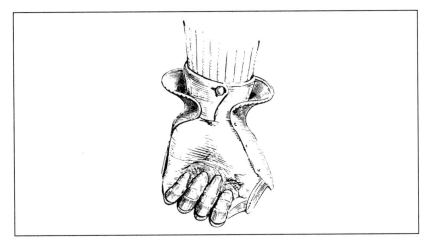

Mailed fist

Maginot line

Any elaborate defensive barrier. The original Maginot line was conceived by and named for André Maginot, France's minister of war from 1922 to 1924 and again from 1929 to 1932. Maginot was determined that the Germans should never again invade his country. To prevent this he had built a line of forts along France's eastern border, from the Swiss to the Belgian frontiers. In 1940 the forts were still in place, but the German army simply went around them, through Belgium, and quickly moved on to Paris. In addition to signifying a defensive barrier, the Maginot line acquired the connotation of a rigid military mentality that insists on following traditional procedure instead of taking a more realistic approach to existing circumstances.

mailed fist

"Ah, who has seen the mailed lobster rise,
Clap her broad wings, and soaring claim the skies?"
—John Hookham Frere, *Progress of Man* (1799)

The threat of brute force. Some believe that this term is a translation of the German *gepanzerte Faust,* used by William II of Germany to his brother, Prince Henry of Prussia, who was beginning a tour of the

Far East on December 16, 1897. If anyone should threaten German "rights" there, said William, then show him your mailed fist. The ultimate origin of the metaphor dates from the late Middle Ages, when armor made of flexible interlinked rings or scales of metal was used to sheathe both knights and their horses against enemy swords, spears, and arrows. The medieval knight was covered from head to foot, and shaking his fist in defiance must have required considerable effort, since the armor, although jointed, was not all that flexible and weighed a good deal. The word *mail*, used for such armor since about 1250, itself comes from the Latin *macula*, for "blemish" or "spot," referring to the holes in the mesh fabric.

managed news

Information given so as to promote a certain interest rather than to be completely candid. The term arose in the cold war during the missile crisis of 1962, when Russian missiles were discovered in Cuba. Here the information given to the public was in the interests of government policy, a practice far older than the current term for it.

maneuver

An adroit or skillful movement or procedure. Although it originally came, via French, from Latin words meaning "to work by hand" or "to do manual labor," in the mid-eighteenth century the word began to be used for the carefully planned movement of military troops or ships, either in tactical exercises or in actual warfare. Almost at the same time, however, the word also began to be used for an agile or skillful movement by an individual or animal that involves craftiness or the intent to deceive. By the nineteenth century maneuver meant a skillfully managed operation or procedure.

The military meaning is still current—troops practicing movements are said to go *on maneuvers*—but we also speak of a clever move in any field as a maneuver and use the verb *to maneuver* in the sense of manipulating or moving skillfully.

manifest destiny

A doctrine of U.S. expansionism. Although the most familiar source of the term is an 1845 editorial by John L. O'Sullivan, diplomat and

Man on horseback

journalist, supporting the American annexation of Texas (then owned by Spain), it was not the first use. William Safire cites biographer John Ward's quotation of Andrew Jackson describing the United States as "a country manifestly called by the Almighty to a destiny which Greece and Rome . . . might have envied."

The term was echoed again and again, usually in the sense of justifying the acquisition of more lands in the continental United States, but in 1898 President McKinley claimed it was the country's manifest destiny to acquire Hawaii, which was duly taken in July of that year. However, by 1900 imperialist ambitions were no longer regarded with universal approval, and today the doctrine is considered somewhat embarrassing.

man on horseback

A dictator, especially a military dictator; also, any strong authority figure. The phrase was used in 1860 by General Caleb Cushing, in a speech warning that an American civil war might end with a man on horseback—like Caesar, Cromwell, or Napoleon—ruling the country. Later the term was used for various military leaders in America who sought elective office—by their supporters for some, such as Ulysses S. Grant, and by opponents for others, such as Dwight D. Eisenhower.

manpower

The number of individuals who at least theoretically are available for work. Although one lexicographer holds that the term originated in World War I, when people were "turned into fodder for statisticians and civil servants," it appears to date from the time of the Civil War. Whatever the origin, the term at first referred to the number of men available for military service. By World War II it had been extended to include those available for war production, and after the war it became a general term for the labor force.

In 1962 the U.S. Congress passed the Manpower Development and Training Act, providing for the training and retraining of workers unable to find jobs at their present trades. The division of the Labor Department dealing with these issues has since been renamed Employment and Training, and indeed the word manpower today is criticized for excluding women, who make up a large percentage of the labor force.

marathon

"The mountains look on Marathon
And Marathon looks on the sea."
—Lord Byron, *Don Juan*, Canto III (1821)

A long-distance race; also, an event of more than normal length, requiring considerable time and/or endurance. The name of the race was first used in modern times in 1896 for an event in the Olympic Games, the first revival of the ancient Greek games. Later (1908) a standard distance for this race was set, 26 miles and 385 yards (42 kilometers, 52 meters), which supposedly was the distance originally run in 490 B.C. by the Greek runner Pheidippides, from the marshy, fennel-covered plain near the village of Marathon (*marathon* is Greek for "fennel") to Athens to bring the Athenians news of their great victory over the Persians. Another version of the story holds that first, when King Darius and his troops were about to invade Greece, Pheidippides ran over rough country for two days and two nights—150 miles in all—to seek help against the Persians from the Spartans. He then ran back in time to help his fellow soldiers defend Athens, and finally, after their victory, ran with the news to Athens. Reportedly he then collapsed and died.

The popularity of the Olympic event named to commemorate this battle, which marked a turning point—had Darius won, our heritage might have been Persian rather than Greek civilization—was such that the name began to be used for other events as well. About 1917 it was used for dance contests in the United States, in which couples danced in a ballroom for as long as they could (fifty hours or longer in some cases). The term has also been applied to concerts (Mozart marathon, Bach marathon) in which many works by a single composer are performed over a time much longer than the normal concert of two or three hours. The *thon* ending appears in such relative neologisms as *walkathon*, originating about 1930 and surviving as a fund-raising activity in which walkers earn contributions of so much money per mile walked.

marching orders

Dismissal from a job; also, instructions to move on. Originally referring to a military command, this term began to be used in more colloquial fashion by the late 1700's, as in "The boss gave Jane her marching orders yesterday."

mark time, to

To wait for something to develop. The term originated from the name of a formal military drill used from the early nineteenth century on, in which soldiers raise their feet alternately as though marching but neither advance nor retreat—in other words, march in place. A British military manual of 1833 instructs that "on the word 'Mark Time' the foot then advancing completes its pace . . . without gaining any ground." Shortly afterward the term began to be used figuratively for any sort of holding action.

marshal, to

To arrange or set out in an orderly way. The verb comes from the noun *marshal*, which originally meant "a keeper of horses"—that is, a groom—derived from the Old High German *marahscah* (mare + servant). From about A.D. 800 the cavalry became increasingly important in warfare, and concomitantly *marshal* became the title for increasingly important individuals, first generals commanding cavalry troops and then, in the French army particularly and some others as well, the most important military rank of all. Napoleon I proclaimed himself Marshal of France and established the BATON as a symbol of this rank. In France a field marshal ranks below a marshal, as was once true in Germany—a field marshal helped select camp-sites and assigned locations to the knights—but in modern Germany and Britain a field marshal is the highest rank.

In the United States there is no military rank of marshal, but the title is used for a variety of officials: a civil court officer who acts as process server and performs other services, the chief of a local police or fire department, or a person in charge of parades and other cere-monies, such as the marshal of a Veterans Day parade. The last, in particular, recalls the derivation of the verb, being charged with the orderly arrangement of the parade's participants.

martinet

A stickler for strict discipline. In the seventeenth century Colonel Jean Martinet of France exhibited such skill in training his regiment that Louis XIV's new minister of war, Louvain, asked him to devise a system of drill to be used throughout the army. Prior to this time, European armies had been made up largely of mercenaries hired to fight when they were needed, and each officer employed his own troops. Consequently military training varied considerably and dis-cipline was haphazard. Louvain decided that his king would be bet-ter served by a regular standing army trained in a systematic way. Martinet's system of drill and discipline was very successful and eventually was adopted in most Western nations. However, the idea of strict discipline for its own sake was at first ridiculed in England, where the Colonel's name became a less-than-flattering epithet, much like drill sergeant. The French never adopted this meaning at all. In French *martinet* means (1) the bird called "martin" in English; (2) a whip similar to a cat-o'-nine-tails; (3) a hammerlike machine tool; (4) a small candlestick. As for Martinet himself, he advanced to the rank of general and was accidentally killed by his

Martinet

own artillery at the siege of Duisburg (1672), an early instance of FRIENDLY FIRE.

MASH

Acronym for *m*obile *A*rmy *s*urgical *h*ospital, whose service at the front lines in the Korean War from 1950 to 1953 inspired a long-standing television series about its wisecracking but dedicated doctors and nurses. The actual unit, consisting of 100 soldiers staffing a 36-bed hospital often packed up to move to the battlefield, was finally deactivated in 1997, and the remaining three MASH units were scheduled to be phased out shortly thereafter, to make way for smaller, more efficient medical units called "forward surgical teams." The TV series, entitled *M*A*S*H* and featuring such characters as nurse "Hot Lips" Houlihan, ran from 1972 to 1983 and is still shown in reruns around the world.

Mata Hari

A femme fatale or siren, a beautiful woman who entices men into danger. The name comes from the stage name taken by a Dutch dancer, Margaretha Geertruida Zelle (1876–1917). She was recruited as a German spy in Paris in 1907, and during World War I she passed on military secrets confided to her by French officers. She was caught in 1917 and was tried and executed by a firing squad. Her trial was widely publicized, presumably to deter other spies, and through it her name became synonymous with femme fatale.

materiel

All the things that are needed to produce a good or service, as opposed to the people needed (See PERSONNEL). The term comes from the French word for "material," and the English version, adopted about 1805, sometimes retains the acute accent over the first "e" (*matériel*). The French used the noun to describe military equipment and supplies, a meaning adopted in English during the Napoleonic wars. (The French noun originally came from the adjective, which simply means "pertaining to matter.")

meat wagon

Slang for an ambulance. This usage dates from World War I. Later the term was also applied to any vehicle in which corpses are transported, such as a hearse, as well as to a police patrol wagon. And more recently still it was used for a hospital gurney.

medevac

An acronym for evacuation by helicopter for rapid medical care. The term originated during the Vietnam War, and the practice of such rescues is perhaps one of that conflict's most (perhaps its only) useful legacies. It has since been applied to civilian use, medevac helicopters being used for medical emergencies by the Coast Guard, state police, and other bodies.

mickey mouse

Trivial, petty. The term was so used in the military in World War II and almost certainly comes from Walt Disney's Mickey Mouse cartoons, which by the mid-1930's had become commercialized and slick in execution, as well as childish and silly in conception. As such it might have no place in a book of terms derived from the military or fighting. However, William and Mary Morris and some other lexicographers believe its use by servicemen is derived from the U.S. Navy's Military Indoctrination Centers, abbreviated MIC, to which undisciplined recruits were sent to shape up, and that MIC then became "mickey mouse" when referring to petty military regulations, such as a white-glove inspection. Whichever origin is true, the expression survives. The cartoon Mickey Mouse was originally (1923) called Mortimer Mouse, but Walt Disney's wife preferred the name Mickey. Disney himself supplied the mouse's voice in the early cartoons.

milk run

Slang for a routine trip. The expression originated in the Royal Air Force (R.A.F.) during World War II, when it was used for regular sorties that were flown day in and day out and therefore were likened to delivering the milk. In the U.S. Air Force a milk run was sometimes called a *milk round*, whereas *milk train* signified an early-morning reconnaissance flight.

million-dollar wound

An excuse for escaping an unpleasant situation. Literally this term means a combat-caused or self-inflicted injury that is not permanently disabling but is serious enough to warrant permanent removal from combat. It probably dates from World War II and was widely used during the Vietnam War and Gulf War. By about 1980 it was also being used figuratively.

Minuteman

Any citizen who is willing to take military action at a moment's notice. The term originated just before the American Revolution, when it referred to a group of armed citizens who were prepared to fight the British at a moment's notice. Their actions at the outbreak of that war, in the battles of Lexington and Concord (Massachusetts), are reenacted annually in those towns on April 19, designated as Patriots Day in Massachusetts. The name *Minuteman* later was transferred to other citizen-fighters and in more recent times to a number of politically right-wing American groups who declare themselves prepared to fight a guerrilla war against Communist invaders. The name also was given to an intercontinental ballistic missile (ICBM).

miss is as good as a mile, a

When you miss the mark, it doesn't matter whether you miss by much or little; it's still a miss. Although this saying was first recorded in 1611, according to Stuart Flexner it became current only during the American Revolution. During the Battle of Lexington (1775), a colonial soldier reportedly shouted these words when a poorly aimed bullet passed harmlessly through his cap. Thereafter it was often repeated and still remains in use.

mock-up

A trial model of a new design. The term originated during World War I, the noun coming from the verb *to mock up*, meaning "to improvise." It was used predominantly in airplane design, where it involved making either a small or a full-size model of the plane, although not necessarily a working model (with engine). In World War II in the U.S. Air Force a mock-up was a panel mounted with a model of aircraft parts, used for instructional purposes. After the war the word was taken up by designers of various products, as well as landscape planners, architects—in short, wherever a model of the design could be used for sales, production, teaching, or other purposes.

Molotov cocktail

A homemade hand grenade. The original Molotov cocktail consisted of a bottle filled with inflammable liquid and was fitted with either a gas-soaked rag or a fuse that protruded from the top. This wick was lighted and thrown at a target, such as a tank, where it ignited and exploded. The heat so generated drove out the tank crew, who could then be shot or captured.

There is some dispute as to exactly by whom and when this weapon was first devised. Some say it was by Loyalists in the Spanish Civil War of the mid-1930's; others hold it was by the Finns, who used it against Russian tanks in the early 1940's and who gave it this name because they regarded Soviet Foreign Minister Molotov as a hated symbol of Russian aggression. (Vyacheslav Milhailovich Molotov, a staunch Stalinist, served as Soviet foreign minister from 1939 to 1949 and again from 1953 to 1956. In 1961, however, he was expelled from the Communist Party because of his long-standing opposition to Nikita Khrushchev, who had just come into power.) The Molotov cocktail was used by guerrillas and resistance fighters throughout World War II, and it continues to be used by various fighting groups who rely on primitive weapons.

mother of, the

The greatest or best of something. This slang term gained wide use during the Gulf War. It is a translation of Iraqi leader Saddam Hussein's expression for a major battle, *umm al-ma'arik* (in Arabic, a metaphor for "important" or "best"). In English the term was quickly transferred and used indiscriminately for any "best" person, occurrence, or the like, as in "That was the mother of all parades."

motor pool

A fleet of motor vehicles available for use by the personnel of some organization. The term dates from World War II, when such pools were used at various military installations. After the war the term continued to be used for similar standby transportation held for government officials, corporation executives, and the like.

mufti

Ordinary clothes worn by someone who usually wears a uniform or robes of office. The term comes from Arabic via French. It appears to have been applied to an army officer acting as a magistrate, a role compared to that of the Arabian *mufti*, a legal adviser expert in Islamic (religious) law. The most important such adviser was called the *Grand Mufti*. However, several lexicographers suggest that the modern usage originated in the nineteenth-century British music hall, where a comedian often would represent an army officer off duty garbed in dressing gown and slippers, an outfit called "mufti." Today we still describe a member of the military in civilian clothes as being "in mufti," but the term is also applied loosely to a judge not wearing judicial robes, a priest or minister in casual clothes, etc.

Munich Pact

A humiliating agreement made to assuage an aggressor in hopes of keeping the peace. It refers to the pact that Great Britain and France made with Italy and Nazi Germany on September 30, 1938, whereby part of Czechoslovakia was ceded to Germany in exchange for a promise that it would take no more land. Ever since, this term, as well as versions such as "another Munich," have been synonymous with appeasement leading to war. (See also APPEASEMENT.)

musketeer

One of a group of close friends engaged in a similar enterprise. Thus the American sportswriter Bud Collins dubbed four early French tennis stars the *Four Musketeers*. The term is a translation of the seventeenth-century French name *mousquetaire*, for a soldier armed with a musket. However, this name later acquired a more specialized meaning, that is, a member of the royal bodyguard who was so armed. Alexandre Dumas immortalized three close friends so serving the king in his novel *The Three Musketeers*.

muster, to pass

"Enough good looks to make her pass muster."
—William Thackeray, *The Newcomes* (1855)

To measure up to a certain standard. The term comes from the assembly of troops who are *mustered*—that is, gathered together—to be inspected. The verb preceded the noun, coming into the English language about 1250, ultimately from the Latin verb *monstrare*, to

Seventeenth-century musketeer

show, and coming to signify "to assemble in order to show." The
military sense survives in *muster in* and *muster out*, to enter and leave
the military service, and still means to gather together troops or a
crew. However, it also is used in a civilian sense, as in "to muster
(up) one's courage before speaking in public." Similarly, to pass
muster has, since the sixteenth century, been applied to a student's
grades, a performer's audition, the quality of a house-painting job,
etc. "And the first verse may pass the musters," wrote George Gas-
coigne in 1575.

myrmidon

A person who blindly carries out orders. In Greek myth the Myrmidons were the loyal Thessalian followers of Achilles in the Trojan War, celebrated for their fierceness. Although at first the word in English simply meant a loyal follower, it came to signify an officer or official who executes the most brutal orders without question, like the officials in Hitler's concentration camps.

napalm

An incendiary substance used in firebombs, flamethrowers, and the like. Although it is associated more with later conflicts, especially the Vietnam War, it was first named and used to bomb enemy territory in World War II; its name is an acronym for *na*phthene and *palm*itate.

Nazi

A person who subscribes to extreme views that include racism and a belief in white supremacy and who takes brutal measures to carry them out. These were the tenets of Adolf Hitler's Nazi (for *Nazional-sozialist*, or National Socialist) Party, which took power in Germany in 1933, fought vigorously throughout World War II, and was finally abolished in 1945. Since then, numerous *neo-Nazi* ("new Nazi") movements have sprung up, not only in Germany but in other countries, including the United States. In 1988 *Time* magazine ran a story about "skinheads" (so called for shaving their heads) who went on anti-Semitic sprees and engaged in other incidents of racial violence. They displayed the Nazi symbol, the swastika, on clothing, banners, and posters, and declared that they considered Hitler's book, *Mein Kampf* (*My Battle*), their bible.

near miss

A narrowly avoided mishap or mistake; also, an attempt that falls just short of success. This term dates from World War II, when it meant a bomb exploding in the water near enough to a ship to damage its hull. After the war its meanings were broadened and came into general use.

no-man's-land

An area belonging to neither of two opposing sides, over which there is no definite authority. The term began to be used in the fourteenth century for the waste ground between two kingdoms; it was so used by the unknown author of *The Chronicles of Edward I* (1320). The name also signified the burial ground of those who died during a plague.

Although no-man's-land often was a disputed territory, the term did not acquire its well-known military meaning until World War I, when it was used for the territory between the thousands of miles of Allied and German trenches. This area was covered with barbed wire and pitted with shell holes made by the artillery of both sides during the three-year-long impasse on the Western front, when the battle line remained virtually stationary.

Since that time no-man's-land also has been used more loosely to describe a situation where one is neither here nor there. In tennis it denotes the area between the base line and the service line, where a player is at a tactical disadvantage, able to hit neither effective volleys nor solid groundstrokes and apt to be passed by the opponent.

nom de guerre

An assumed name or pseudonym, usually taken for a particular purpose, such as writing, acting, etc. The term is French for "war name" and comes from the old custom of every entrant into the French army assuming a new name, especially during the Middle Ages, when knights were known by the device on their shields.

no sweat

Don't concern yourself; there's no difficulty here. This colloquialism originated in the military about 1950 during the Korean War and continues to be used.

nothing to write home about

Quite ordinary, not remarkable. Although it originated somewhat earlier, this expression gained currency during World War I among troops stationed far from home.

nuke, to

To treat or destroy something as though one were using a nuclear weapon. This slangy term originated in the late 1940's as a colloquialism for using an atomic bomb or similar weapon. Later it was transferred to such enterprises as cooking something in a microwave oven, as in "That pizza can be nuked," meaning it can be microwaved. (See also ZAP.)

number is up, one's

One is in serious difficulty or close to death. This phrase was first recorded in the early 1800's, but somewhat later it became widely used in the Royal Navy and U.S. Army, where it signified losing one's mess number because of being killed.

obstacle course

A path or procedure that presents numerous challenges and difficulties. The expression originated in the U.S. military, where traversing a series of obstacles—walls, hurdles, ditches, ladders, etc.—in sequence and within a given time period is part of a recruit's physical training. During World War II the obstacle course at Camp Gruber was notoriously difficult. According to General George C. Marshall, testifying before a Senate committee, a soldier carrying a rifle and a thirty-pound pack had to negotiate a 1,500-foot obstacle course in three and one-half minutes. He had to take off with a shout, mount an eight-foot wall, slide down a ten-foot pole, leap over a flaming trench, weave through a barrier of pickets, crawl through a water main, climb a ten-foot rope, struggle over a five-foot fence, swing by a rope across a seven-foot ditch, mount a twelve-foot ladder and descend to the other side, charge over a four-foot breastwork, walk a twenty-foot-long catwalk about one foot wide and seven feet above the ground, swing hand over hand along a five-foot horizontal ladder, slide under a fence, climb another fence, and sprint over the finish line.

Similar obstacle courses may be part of track-and-field athletic events, and in time the term came to be used figuratively for other than physical challenges—for example, "Going through the university bureaucracy may be described as an academic obstacle course." In Britain the track-and-field obstacle course is called an *obstacle race*, and the term is similarly transferred to nonphysical challenges.

off limits

Not allowed. The term originated in the U.S. military during the late 1940's, when Japan and Germany were still occupied by U.S. troops. In the interests of amicable relations as well as protection, certain parts of a town or particular establishments were declared off limits to military personnel. The term stuck and has since been used to mean both places and practices that are forbidden to students or other selected groups subject to certain rules or discipline.

oil slick

A film left on the water's surface by spilled oil. First recorded in 1889, the term became current during World War I, when it denoted the oil discharged by submarine exhausts, which leaves telltale oil streaks on the water. It continued to be so used in World War II and later was extended to oil spilled by tankers or in some other way.

old fogy

An excessively old-fashioned person; a bore who is behind the times. There is some dispute about this term's origin. One theory holds that it is derived from *foggy*, which originally meant covered with a marsh grass; another says it may come from the French *fougueux*, for "quick-tempered." If either of these is true, the term would have no place in this book. However, there is also a possible military origin. A fogy was an old officer, one who received a *phogey*, that is, seniority pay for having served for at least three years in wartime and five years in peacetime. In America this usage dates from at least 1879, according to the *Dictionary of American English*. Further, for a time fogy also meant an invalid soldier. Both these types could readily be considered old-fashioned bores by younger soldiers, whom they no doubt regaled with oft-repeated stories of former campaigns; hence this seems a more logical etymology than either "boggy" or "irascible."

Old Guard

The stalwarts of any party or movement, conservative and resisting change. The term is a translation of *Vieille Garde*, the name given to Napoleon's Imperial Guard, the elite veteran regiments of the French army. They got better pay, better rations, and better uniforms than all the others, and not unnaturally they were staunch defenders of both the empire and their own prestige and perquisites. Established in 1804, the Imperial Guard consisted of four regiments of Young Guard, four of Middle Guard, and four of Old Guard, as well as four cavalry regiments and ninety-six pieces of artillery. It was they who made the last charge of the French at Waterloo.

In the United States "Old Guard" began to be used for political conservatives as early as 1844. William Safire cites a newspaper article about the conservative Whigs that quotes Napoleon as saying, "The Old Guard will never surrender," and notes that the Whigs did lose to the Democrats that year. The expression later (1880) became identified with the Republican Party and in the 1940's with the most conservative wing of that party. It is most often used as an unflattering description by their political adversaries.

Incidentally, the quotation ascribed to Napoleon is often credited to General Pierre Jacques Étienne de Cambronne, who commanded a division at Waterloo and was called on to surrender. He himself denied ever uttering these words, which probably were invented by a journalist. Nevertheless, a monument to Cambronne at Nantes, France, bears those very words: *"Le Garde meurt et ne se rend pas"* ("The Guard dies and never surrenders").

Old Ironsides

A nickname for any person or object exhibiting particular toughness. It was used in the sixteenth century as a nickname for Oliver Cromwell and then again in the War of 1812 for the U.S. frigate *Constitution*, because British cannons could not penetrate her oaken sides. In 1828 the Navy decided to sell the vessel, and Oliver Wendell Holmes protested in his poem, *Old Ironsides*:

> Ay, tear her tattered ensign down!
> Long has it waved on high,
> And many an eye has danced to see
> That banner in the sky.

Memorized by scores of schoolchildren for generations, the poem had the desired effect, and the old wooden vessel was saved. Today it is the oldest American warship still afloat, and it is visited by additional scores of schoolchildren and other tourists at its mooring in Boston Harbor.

old soldiers never die

A statement made by General Douglas MacArthur at a joint meeting of Congress (April 19, 1951), after being relieved of his command during the Korean War by President Harry S Truman. The full text was "Old soldiers never die, they just fade away," which came from an old barracks ballad. The President believed the General was disobeying orders and trying to dictate policy by pursuing enemy aircraft into China. MacArthur's speech was an attempt to justify his views and actions as he retired from public service.

olive branch, to hold out the

> "No, Warwick, thou art worthy of the sway,
>   To whom the heavens, in thy nativity,
>   Adjudg'd an olive branch and laurel crown,
>   As likely to be blest in peace."
> —William Shakespeare, *Henry VI, Part 3*

To suggest a truce or offer to make peace. The olive branch, along with the dove, has been a symbol of peace since biblical times. "And the dove came . . . and, lo, in her mouth was an olive leaf pluckt off" (Genesis 8:11). The term is used concerning civilian quarrels as well as in military matters.

on the double

Very quickly. This phrase originally meant to march twice as fast as normally, that is, in double time. Originating in the early 1800's, it is used more loosely by civilians.

operations research

The use of quantitative analysis to solve complex problems and devise the most efficient course of action. Both this branch of analysis and its name originated during the two world wars, especially World War II, when military planners tried to apply mathematical and engineering techniques of decision-making to help choose the optimum military strategies and tactics. Since World War II, operations research has been widely used in business and industry (in the areas of transportation, production and inventory control, and scheduling) as well as in many branches of government.

outgun, to

To overwhelm, to outdo. This term originated in the late seventeenth century, when it meant to exceed in firepower. It has been used figuratively since the late 1800's.

overkill

Excessive action, owing to an overreaction or to poor judgment. The term originated immediately after World War II, when it referred to the ability of nations possessing nuclear weapons to destroy far more than was necessary for a military victory. A graphic example in more old-fashioned terms is a firing squad of twenty men aiming their guns at a single person. The term overkill then began to be used by those who believed that an excess of nuclear weapons beyond the amount needed to inflict sufficient damage was wasteful. Within a decade the word was being applied to overzealous excesses of just about any kind.

over the top, to go

To take the final plunge and do something dangerous or notable; also, to surpass a goal. The phrase comes from the trench warfare of World War I, when at a designated time troops climbed over the parapet of front-line trenches to attack the enemy's front line. The "top" referred both to the trench's top and to the open NO-MAN'S-LAND between them and the enemy. After the war the expression survived, assisted by the fact that Guy Empey used *Over the Top* as the title for his World War I novel. After World War II the phrase acquired the additional meaning of going above and beyond what had originally been planned, as in "The fund drive put the building committee over the top," meaning it had raised more money than its original goal.

pacifist

> "I have always been against the Pacifists during the quarrel. . . ."
> —Sir Winston Churchill, *My Early Life* (1930)

An individual opposed to war and in favor of peaceful alternatives to settling disputes. This seemingly obvious term is relatively new. It comes from the French *pacifiste* (and *pacifisme*, giving rise to *pacifism*) and has been around only since the early 1900's. The word began to gain currency during World War I.

palace guard

A leader's inner circle of confidants and advisers. The name comes from the Roman Emperor Augustus's PRAETORIAN GUARD, an imperial bodyguard that under later emperors acquired considerable power. According to William Safire, the term palace guard has been used in American politics since 1791, when James Madison warned that "stock jobbers will become the Praetorian band of the government, at once its tool and its tyrant." Subsequently, it has been used more often for the President's closest advisers and usually in a somewhat critical fashion, by those not included in that inner circle.

palisade

A fence of stakes; also, a line of cliffs. Around the medieval castle, in places where a defensive stone wall was to be built, a preliminary sturdy fence made of wooden stakes, or *pales*, would be built to enclose the site. Later its name, palisade, was applied to other tall vertical phenomena, such as the high cliffs along New York's Hudson River and elsewhere.

panic button, to hit/push the

To overreact to an alleged emergency. The term originated during World War II, when B-17 and B-24 bombers had a bell-warning system so that the crew could bail out when their plane was severely damaged. Occasionally a pilot would push the bell-button by mistake, when the damage sustained was actually minor, causing the crew to bail out unnecessarily. Ever since, the expression has meant to act in needless haste, although about 1950 it took on a more sinister implication with the development of a possible PUSH-BUTTON WAR (activating nuclear weapons by pressing a button). Further, we say "Don't push [hit/press] the panic button" when we mean "Take it easy; don't act in haste or until you know you need to."

The word *panic* itself is believed to be derived from the Greek *panikon deima*, "fear caused by the god Pan," who according to myth caused unwary travelers to flee by making frightful nighttime noises.

panoply

A full array or display. The word comes from the Greek *panoplia*, for a full suit of armor (*pan*, all + *hopla*, armor). That meaning, too, survives in English, but when the wearing of armor declined in importance the word began to be used for a complete suit of ceremonial attire and eventually was transferred to any wide-ranging display. Thus a historian might speak of the panoply of Chinese history or a physician of the panoply of antibiotics.

panzer

A powerful force. During World War II, a vital vehicle of Nazi land warfare was the *Panzer*, alluding to the *Panzerdivision*, a powerful

In full panoply

armored unit. By the early 1940's this term was being transferred to any powerful force or obstacle, as in "Those who believe that the book of Genesis is literally true were forced to defend it against Charles Darwin's panzers."

parade

A large public procession; also, a continual passage of people, events, or objects. From the mid-1600's on, the assembling or mustering of troops for inspection or some other purpose was called a parade.

Within a century this term was extended to other kinds of procession, often in support of some political goal, and eventually to such events as the *Easter Parade*. And because the object of a parade was public display, the verb *to parade* came to be used in the sense of showing off, as in "An arrogant fellow, he loved to parade his expertise on the subject."

parting shot

> "You wound, like Parthians, while you fly,
>   And kill with a retreating eye."
> —Samuel Butler, *Hudibras* (1678)

A final insult hurled as one is leaving, or the last word in an argument. Most writers believe that this expression is a distortion of *Parthian shot*, although there is no firm evidence to support this etymology. It alludes to a practice of the ancient Parthians, who lived southeast of the Caspian Sea and whose empire at one time (first century B.C.) stretched from the Euphrates River eastward to the Indus River and from the Oxus to the Indian Ocean. Mentioned in the Bible (Acts 1:9), they were renowned archers and horsemen and were known for their practice of turning in flight (either real or pretended to lure followers) to discharge their arrows at the pursuing enemy.

passive resistance

> "In this humour of passive resistance . . . Isaac sat in a corner of
>   his dungeon."
> —Sir Walter Scott, *Ivanhoe* (1819)

Nonviolent opposition. Although the practice is no doubt an ancient one, the term came into use only in the nineteenth century, at that time nearly always referring to resistance by colonists and/or natives against the government in power. "Passive resistance was the only weapon to which they trusted," wrote H. H. Wilson in *British India* (1844), although of course in that country rebellion against British rule also erupted in more violent forms, such as the Sepoy Rebellion of 1857.

"Passive resistance is the most potent weapon ever wielded by man against oppression," wrote Benjamin R. Tucker in 1893. But it was not until the organized passive resistance of Mohandas K. Gandhi and his followers, beginning in 1919, that the term and practice made headlines all over the world. Systematic campaigns of civil disobedience continued in India until 1948, when Britain withdrew and India became fully independent.

Today, passive resistance, taking the form of protest marches, sit-ins, economic boycotts, and the like, remains a powerful tool, but it also tends to provoke a violent response, as it often did in India in the first half of the twentieth century.

Pentagon

A symbol for U.S. military authority. A pentagon is simply a five-sided polygon, but in 1943, in Arlington, Virginia, the U.S. government built what was then the largest office building in the world. It was called the Pentagon (for its shape) and housed the U.S. Defense Department. Before long the word had come to symbolize the official U.S. military attitude. According to William and Mary Morris, journalist David Brinkley once defined a Pentagon committee as "a group of the unwilling, chosen from the unfit, to do the unnecessary." The word *Pentagonese* was coined for the bureaucratic jargon that often obscures the obvious and inflates the commonplace and ordinary. (See also GOBBLEDYGOOK.)

personnel

A group of people, considered as a body; also, employees. The word came into English in the early nineteenth century directly from French, where it distinguishes an army's human resources (troops and officers) from its nonhuman assets (weapons, supplies, etc.), called MATERIEL. The term was adopted by business and industry, and indeed its most common use today is to designate all the individuals employed by a business.

Most companies have a personnel department to deal with hiring and other employee concerns. This usage, too, is retained by the military ("All personnel are ordered to return to base," for example), which further developed such euphemistic jargon as *antipersonnel bomb*, a bomb designed to destroy enemy troops rather than bases, vehicles, or other nonhuman targets.

petard, hoisted with one's own

> "Let it work;
> For 'tis the sport to have the enginer
> Hoist with his own petar."
> —William Shakespeare, *Hamlet*

Caught in one's own trap or defeated with one's own weapons. The original petard was a thick iron canister filled with gunpowder, which was fastened to a gate or other barrier in order to breach it by exploding. It was a dangerous weapon, because the engineer who set it off could easily be blown sky-high ("hoisted") when it detonated. Nevertheless, it was so effective that it was widely used. Shakespeare was one of the first to use the term metaphorically; others were John Fletcher (1625), Sir Walter Scott (1826), and mystery writer Dorothy Sayers (1923). Today this somewhat archaic turn of phrase still surfaces now and then—on the tennis court, for example, where the player frustrated by an opponent's short drop shots may finally retaliate successfully by using the same tactic.

phalanx

> "Anon they move
> In perfect phalanx, to the Dorian mood
> Of flutes and soft recorders."
> —John Milton, *Paradise Lost* (1667)

A group of persons closely united by some common purpose or physically massed together. The word comes from the Greek name for the close order of battle in which troops were usually drawn up, originally developed by the Spartans. Scientists also adopted the word for the bones of the fingers and the toes, which are aligned closely, as well as for a bundle of plant stamens.

About 1800 François Charles Fourier, a French critic of capitalism who sought to cure economic and social ills, established some cooperative communities and called them *phalanstères*, French for "phalanxes." Each phalanx consisted of about 300 families and supported itself, chiefly through agriculture and handicrafts, sharing in the profits. About forty such phalanxes were organized in America before 1860, but none survived the Civil War. Among them were the North American Phalanx at Red Bank, New Jersey, which lasted from 1843 to 1856, and the shorter-lived but still remembered Brook Farm (1841–46), near Boston.

philistine

An ignorant, uncultivated person who is hostile to culture, the arts, and the intellect, and content with a base materialistic outlook. The Philistines were a warlike ancient people who fought the Israelites for the possession of Palestine and so were referred to in the Bible as a "heathen foe." In English the term was used in the sense of "the enemy" from the early seventeenth century on. Often used more or less ironically, philistine was applied to drunkards, bailiffs, and literary critics, among others. The present meaning, however, arises from a bloody fight between German university students and the townspeople of Jena in 1693. For the funeral of those students killed in the brawl, the university pastor tactlessly chose the sermon text, "The Philistines be upon thee" (Judges 16:12), whereupon people began to refer to the townspeople of this and other university towns as *Philistern*. The English philosopher Thomas Carlyle (1795–1881), an avid student of German literature, picked up the term and used it in English. It was subsequently popularized by Matthew Arnold in *Culture and Anarchy* and other writings, where he used it as an epithet for a dull, low-brow materialist. By then it had crossed the Atlantic and was used in the same sense by Artemus Ward and numerous later American writers.

phony war

A relatively quiet period during hostilities. The term was invented by U.S. journalists in World War II for the inactive period from the outbreak of the war in September, 1939, until the invasion of Norway and Denmark in March, 1940, and was adopted by British journalists as well. Another name for it was *sitzkrieg* ("sitting war," a play on Hitler's *blitzkrieg*, or "lightning war"). The phony war was interpreted by some observers as reluctance on the part of France and Britain to fight very hard, since they had entered the war mainly because of their commitment to defend Poland (invaded by the Nazis in 1939), as well as reluctance on Hitler's part to engage in active combat against these two strong powers. The phony war ended when Britain tried to land troops in Norway and was turned back and, following the invasion of Holland and Belgium on May 10, 1940, the British government was turned over by Neville Chamberlain to Winston Churchill, who took a far more vigorous approach.

picket

A post or stake used to make a fence; also, a person who stands or marches outside a building or other establishment to express protest. The word comes from the French *piquet*, a pointed stake used in a series for the outer defenses of a castle. The stakes were driven into the ground at an angle, pointing toward any potential attackers. The word also was—and still is—used for soldiers who stand guard. (See the quotation from Beers's Civil War poem *The Picket Guard*, under ALL QUIET ON THE POTOMAC.)

In the labor movement, the term was first used in the 1860's, as both noun and verb, for strikers (themselves called pickets) who were picketing an employer.

piece of cake

Something that is accomplished easily. This expression originated in the Royal Air Force (R.A.F.) in the late 1930's, when it was used for an easy mission. It became widespread by the end of the war. Derek Robinson wrote a book, *Piece of Cake* (1983), about the R.A.F. in World War II, which was made into a popular B.B.C. television series. The expression still serves as a metaphor for something easy to accomplish, much like the simile *easy as pie*, and like it mysterious in its allusion (no one knows why either cake or pie should symbolize simplicity).

pile

A steel and concrete support, tapered at the lower end and hammered into the ground to form part of a foundation or wall. A mass of such supports is called a *piling*. Both words come from the Latin *pilum*, which was a heavy javelin and the Roman foot soldier's most important weapon. *"Pilum inecisti mihi"* ("You hurl a javelin at me") then became a figure of speech for any kind of attack. The word came into modern English, via Old and Middle English, about 1100.

pillbox

A style of hat; a small concrete fort. The original civilian use of the pillbox—a small shallow box, often cylindrical, for holding pills—predates the military by about 200 years, dating from the 1730's. From about 1887 to 1910, however, the name was used for a soldier's cap, and in the 1960's for a fashionable style of a woman's hat. Both were named for their resemblance in shape to a pill container, with straight sides and a flat top. The latter style was made popular by Jacqueline Kennedy, the fashionable young wife of President John F. Kennedy.

During World War I the name also began to be used for a small, low shelter, similarly shaped, usually made of concrete and partially sunk into the ground; it was used principally by machine gunners.

pinup girl

An exceptionally attractive girl or woman whose photograph is displayed on a wall. The term comes from World War II, when servicemen frequently decorated their quarters by putting up pictures of film stars, actresses, and/or their own girlfriends and wives. In the 1950's "pinup" was extended to any attractive person, male or female.

pioneer

> "Come, my tan-faced children,
>   Follow well in order, get your weapons ready,
>   Have you your pistol? have you your sharp-edged axes?
>   Pioneers! O pioneers!"
>   —Walt Whitman, *Pioneers! O Pioneers!*(1891–92)

One of the first to settle a region or enter a field of inquiry. The word comes from the Old French *peonier*, for "foot soldier," one of a special corps of soldiers who walked ahead of the troops with spade and pick in order to make a camp for them. Shakespeare used the word in this sense in *Othello* ("I had been happy if the general camp, pioners and all, had tasted her sweet body"). By the sixteenth century the word meant any kind of advance laborer, and soon it was extended to mean anyone who goes first and prepares the way for others. (See also HATCHET MAN.)

pirate, piracy

"There is nothing so desperately monotonous as the sea, and I no longer wonder at the cruelty of pirates."
—James Russell Lowell, *Fireside Travels* (1864)

A person who uses another's original work without authorization; the practice of such usurping. This usage is a transfer from the nautical sea robber. Nautical piracy dates from ancient Greek times, and the word itself comes from the Latin *piratia*, in turn derived from the Greek. From the early 1500's to the mid-1800's, piracy became a major industry in North Africa, in that one after another European nation paid tribute to the Barbary pirates to win safe conduct for their citizens and shipping. During the same period piracy also was rampant in the Caribbean, sometimes as an extension of hostilities in Europe. Thus, while France and Spain were warring in Italy, the French navy attacked Spanish shipping in the Caribbean. After peace was declared in 1538, lawless pirates continued the raids.

After 1560 the leadership in piracy passed from the French to the English, also at war with Spain. Their first notable pirate was Sir John Hawkins. Another was his cousin, Francis Drake, who became one of Queen Elizabeth's SEA DOGS. Beginning in the late 1600's, the words piracy, pirate, and the verb *to pirate* were being used figuratively for the unlawful appropriation of someone else's invention or work. They are still so used, of course, and we may speak of a pirate publisher who infringes on another's copyright and puts out a pirated edition of a novel or computer software.

point-blank

Direct, blunt, straight at the mark. The term probably comes from sixteenth-century gunnery, although some authorities believe it comes from archery. In either case it meant shooting straight—that is, without the projectile's curving—at an object within a certain distance. Target practice appears to have been used since early times for both archers and gunners, and early on the center of a target was the white "bull's-eye," contrasting with the darker body of the rest of the target. To hit the target, one had to aim for the center, or blank (in French, *de pointe en blanc*, "from a point to the white portion"). Since the center of a target is notoriously elusive, one had to shoot from a fairly short distance to be sure of hitting it. Conse-

Shooting point-blank

quently *point-blank range* came to mean so short a distance that one could not miss.

point man

The person in the lead, the one in a vulnerable position. This term has been used in the military since about 1900 for the lead infantry-man of a squad in combat. Also said to be *on the point*, he obviously is in the greatest danger for drawing enemy fire. Gaining consider-able currency during the Vietnam War, these terms were transferred to politics, where they refer to the vulnerability of the front runner of a group of candidates, as well as other advance figures in a con-troversial situation.

point of no return

A critical point, which if passed allows for no reversal of decision or course of action. The term originated among aviators during World War II, who used it for the point in a flight beyond which there would no longer be enough fuel to return to base. By definition, therefore, the flight would have to continue on to some other destination.

police action

Euphemistic term for a war, specifically the Korean War (1950–53). This conflict was never, strictly speaking, a war, because war was never formally declared. Rather, when North Korea invaded South Korea, the United Nations decided to intervene, and the United States, along with other nations, participated as part of the United Nations force that was sent there. The phrase "police action" was presented to President Harry S Truman by a reporter at a press conference, at which Truman declared that the country was not at war but was trying to suppress a "bandit raid" on the Republic of South Korea. Somewhat earlier, Senator William E. Knowland had compared the U.S. Air Force in Korea to police chasing a burglar, and this simile may have been the source of the term.

poop sheet

A written report or bulletin giving specific information. The term became current during World War II, when it referred to a military drill schedule, and later was extended to any written announcement. The *poop* here is slang for "information."

Portuguese man-of-war

A marine animal that has a large, balloonlike structure with a saillike crest, by means of which it floats on the water surface. Streaming from its underside are large numbers of long tentacles (some as long as forty feet) supplied with batteries of stinging cells, which it uses to paralyze fishes and other animals it feeds on. The animal is so named because its crest called to mind the military sailing ships called *man-of-war* from the 1400's on.

Praetorian Guard

A leader's elite circle of friends and advisers. It is similar to the PALACE GUARD and is derived from the same source. In ancient Rome the *praetor* was a provincial consul with military powers, and his personal bodyguard was called the *cohors praetoria*, or Praetorian Guard. Beginning in the time of Caesar Augustus (63 B.C.–A.D. 14), the Praetorian Guard became the household guard of the Roman emperor, a role it fulfilled until the time of Constantine. During the course of these three centuries the Praetorians acquired numerous special privileges and along with them considerable power, which grew during times of crisis. By the time the empire was in danger of dissolution, the Praetorian Guard had, for a time, unlimited authority. Eventually, however, it was dispersed.

press-gang, to

To coerce. The term comes from a long-established practice of assigning a naval party, called a *press gang*, to impress (forcibly enlist) seamen for military duty. In the Royal Navy, ship captains provided their own gangs for this purpose until the eighteenth century, when the Navy established its own Impress Service. The impressment of American seamen to serve on British ships was one of the grievances that precipitated the War of 1812.

The use of press gangs may go back as far as the thirteenth century and was continued until the 1830's. Incidentally, the *press* in this expression does not mean the same as "force." Rather, it comes from the now obsolete *prest*, an advance on pay that used to be made upon enlistment to make it a legal contract (a contract not being technically valid unless a consideration has been paid).

prize money

A monetary reward offered or won in a contest of some kind. Originally this expression meant the proceeds from the sale of an enemy ship and its goods that had been captured at sea. In the Royal Navy, as recently as 1914, a ship that made such a capture got all of the prize money from it. In 1914, however, the rules were changed, and thereafter all prize money was pooled and shared among the Navy as a whole. The practice of sharing prize money ended with World War II. By then the term was being used for monetary winnings in any competition—a golf tournament, automobile race, etc.

Prussian

Arrogant, overbearing, and militaristic. The bundle of qualities so labeled, and attributed to someone admiringly or, more often, pejoratively, refers to the military machine and attitudes that dominated Prussia, a North European power for two centuries. The largest of the German states, Prussia at its height stretched from the Netherlands, Belgium, and Luxembourg east to Lithuania and Poland, and from the Baltic Sea, Denmark, and the North Sea south to the Main River, Thuringia, and the Sudeten. In 1947 the state of Prussia, still part of the Germany it had been instrumental in uniting, was formally abolished in order to quell the spirit of militarism and aggression so long associated with it.

Beginning with Frederick the Great, Prussia's progress was associated with a number of great leaders, the best remembered of whom was Otto von Bismarck (1815–98). The architect of Prussia's empire, Bismarck, through his system of alliances and alignments, became the virtual arbiter and leading statesman of all Europe (See IRON CHANCELLOR). His domestic economic and social policies were equally influential, creating health insurance and labor laws and rapidly expanding German commerce and industry, as well as acquiring numerous overseas colonies and spheres of influence. Prussia's military might was enhanced by the *Junkers*, the politically reactionary, landowning aristocrats who provided most of the army's officer class; in German *Junker* has approximately the same connotations that Prussian has in English.

pummel, to

To pound with one's fists. This word comes from the *pommel* of a sword, the rounded knob terminating in the weapon's hilt. It in turn was so called because of its resemblance to an apple (*pomme* in French, from the Latin *pomum*, for fruit). Originally *to pommel* meant to beat someone with the pommel of one's sword; in the sixteenth century it was altered to pummel.

pup tent

A small A-shaped tent. It acquired its name during the Civil War, when it was first introduced as a shelter tent. The soldiers, referring to the small size as being more suitable for young dogs than grown men, called it first a *dog tent* and then a pup tent; the latter name has stuck among campers, hikers, and other outdoor lovers.

Purple Heart

A reward for being injured in the line of duty. The practice of rewarding achievements grew out of the medieval custom of conferring knighthood, and indeed this practice is still followed in some places (See under BLUE RIBBON). The Purple Heart, a U.S. Army medal awarded for wounds received from the enemy while on active duty, was created by George Washington in 1782 and was reinstituted by the Army in 1932. It consists of a silver heart bearing a picture of George Washington that is suspended from a white-edged purple ribbon.

push-button war

> "If war were fought with push-button devices one might make a science of command. But because war is as much a conflict of passion as it is of force, no commander can become a strategist until he first knows his men."
> —General Omar N. Bradley, speech

A conflict involving guided missiles and other automated weapons, activated by pressing a button. William Safire points out that since the possibility of starting a conflict so easily has existed, having a finger on the button has become an accusation that one is ready to launch nuclear warfare at a moment's notice. The term dates from about 1945. (See also PANIC BUTTON.)

push up daisies

Be dead and buried. This expression was first recorded about 1918, in one of Wilfred Owen's poems about World War I. It alludes to flowers growing over a grave.

putsch

An unsuccessful attempt at taking over a government, party, or other organization. The word is actually German for "sudden blow" or "coup" and came into wider use in Germany when it was applied to a number of popular Swiss-German uprisings in the 1830's, a chapter of Swiss history that is largely ignored in British and American texts. The word probably never would have entered the English language at all were it not for Adolf Hitler's *Beer Hall Putsch* of November 8, 1923, when he and his National Socialists attempted to force the leaders of Bavaria to form a new government headed by him. Although that putsch was a dismal failure, it made Hitler a popular hero. He was tried for treason and sentenced to five years in prison. He served only nine months, during which he wrote *Mein Kampf* ("My Battle"), which became the Nazi bible. The word putsch also survived and has since been applied, usually by their opponents, to any revolt plotted by insurgents.

Pyrrhic victory

> "Another such victory over the Romans and we are undone."
> —Plutarch, *Lives* (quoting Pyrrhus)

A victory that is as hard (or harder) on the winners as on the losers. The expression refers to the victory of King Pyrrhus of Epirus at Asculum in 279 B.C. over the Romans. In this first really big battle between the Greek and Roman forces, Pyrrhus, who had come to Asculum with 25,000 men, lost his best officers and many of his troops. Ever since, the term Pyrrhic victory has meant a victory so costly that it counts as a defeat.

A similar expression, but somewhat less common today, is CADMEAN VICTORY.

quell, to

> "What passion cannot music raise and quell?"
> —John Dryden, *Ode for St. Cecilia's Day* (1687)

To subdue, to quiet. This relatively innocuous word comes from the Old English *cwellan* and Middle English *quellan*, meaning "to kill with violence" or "slaughter," the object of such death being one's enemies. By the sixteenth century the verb was used mainly in the sense of suppressing disorder, as in quelling a riot, and by 1700 it also could mean simply to subdue, as a mother quells her baby's tears, with no implication of violence or child abuse.

quisling

A traitor, a collaborator with the enemy. The word comes from Major Vidkun Quisling, head of the Norwegian puppet regime that cooperated with the Nazis during World War II. Formerly a military attaché who had served in the Norwegian embassy in Russia and Finland, Quisling became a fascist and formed a National Unity Party in Norway soon after Hitler came to power in Germany in 1933. When the Nazis invaded Norway in April, 1940, Quisling himself came into power and was brutal in suppressing opposition. After the war he was tried for treason and murder (of Jews and other Norwegians), and in October, 1945, he was executed by a firing squad, the Norwegian Supreme Court having reinstated the death penalty for him and other convicted traitors.

Quonset hut

A semicylindrical, prefabricated corrugated-metal building, used for housing, storage, and other purposes. It was developed during World War II at Quonset, Rhode Island, to shelter troops and equipment. The design was modeled after a British structure, the *Nissen hut*, named for its designer, Colonel Peter N. Nissen, in 1930. Although considered a strictly temporary structure, Quonset huts proved to be durable and continued to be used after the war, on campuses as dormitories, to house equipment and supplies on construction sites, and for other similar purposes.

radar

An electronic locating device. The name is an acronym for *ra*dio *d*etection *a*nd *r*anging. The device, which determines the presence and location of an object by measuring the time it takes for the echo of radio waves to return from it, was developed by Sir Robert Watson-Watt in the mid-1930's but became important and well known only during World War II, especially during the Battle of Britain. After the war it found numerous peacetime applications, from stopping speeding cars on highways to locating ships and aircraft when visibility is poor. Further, in colloquial usage the term has been extended to any sensitive pickup of signals, as in "Her radar tells her that he is lying."

raglan

A style of sleeve that extends all the way up to a garment's neckline, instead of being set in at the shoulder. It was first worn and popularized by Fitzroy James Henry Somerset (1788–1855), first Baron of Raglan, who served under the Duke of Wellington and lost an arm at the Battle of Waterloo. He also showed himself a very brave officer in the Crimean War, in which he died from cholera.

Probably because of his handicap, he liked to wear a loose, capelike overcoat with sleeves extending to the neck, which came to be called raglan after him. The coat itself is no longer in fashion, but the style of sleeve (raglan sleeve) is still popular in sweaters, coats, dresses, and other garments.

rally

> "Rally 'round the flag, boys,
>   Rally once again,
>   Shouting the battle-cry of freedom."
> —George F. Root (1820–95), *The Battle Cry of Freedom*

An event designed to stimulate enthusiasm; also, in verb form, to enlist support or to come to the aid of. The phrase "Rally 'round the flag" was ascribed to General Andrew Jackson at the Battle of New Orleans. The word comes from the French *rallier*, originally meaning to reassemble scattered troops. It was used in American politics from the 1830's on, in the sense of rallying around (supporting) a candidate, and also in *rallying cry*, for the watchword of a cause (it was so used in the antislavery movement in the mid-1840's). Today the political rally, seeking support for a candidate or party, plays a role in just about every election campaign. In addition, the transitive verb is still used in the old meaning of gathering together, as in "The captain rallied his team."

Further, in the course of the nineteenth century the word acquired several other meanings: (1) a recovery or increase—in activity in finance (a stock market rally signifies a rise in prices), in strength from an illness, in baseball (scoring one or more runs in an inning); and (2) an exchange between opponents—in boxing (of blows), and in tennis and badminton (of strokes).

R and R

Colloquial abbreviation for *r*est and *r*ecreation, a short respite or vacation. The term originated in World War II and was widely used during the Korean War, when servicemen who had seen considerable action were sent away from the front for a period of time for rest and recuperation, later altered to rest and recreation. After the 1950's the term continued to be used in civilian life for any kind of brief rest or holiday after a period of arduous activity.

rank and file

"There was two-an' thirty Sergeants,
There was Corp'rals forty-one,
There was just nine 'undred rank an' file
To swear to a touch o' sun."
—Rudyard Kipling, *The Shut-Eye Sentry* (1892)

Followers rather than leaders. The term comes from the military, where it is used for soldiers and noncommissioned officers as opposed to officers. Strictly speaking, a *rank* means soldiers standing side by side, in a row, while *file* means soldiers standing behind one another; the commanding officer stands in front of either of these military formations. The expression rank and file dates from the sixteenth century and today is often used for the membership of a large body, such as a labor union or political party, in contrast to its leaders. Similarly, the military expression *to break ranks*, meaning to fall out of formation, was extended to mean to disagree with or refuse to support one's fellows (in a political party or other group).

The word *rank* also refers to each class or grade in the hierarchy of military officers and has been transferred to government and other hierarchies. From this meaning comes the expression *to pull rank on*, meaning to use the advantage of one's superior rank over someone of lower rank; the person able to do so is said to *outrank* the other. For example, "ABC Company's vice-president can pull rank on the personnel director because she outranks him [has more authority than he]." (See also RISEN FROM THE RANKS.)

rappel, to

To descend a steep mountain or cliff by means of a rope. The term comes from the French *rappeler*, a military summons or recall, signaling the troops to return. In the 1930's the word was transferred to the mountaineering technique of descending with the aid of a rope, one end of which is secured at the top while the other is fastened around the climber's body.

rearguard action

Any defensive strategy. In the fifteenth century the *rear guard* simply referred to the back portion of an army, but by the seventeenth century this portion was detached from the main force to protect it against an attack from behind, that is, a rearguard action. In the late nineteenth century the term was transferred to nonmilitary defensive actions, so that today, for example, one might say that a company continuing to sell an old product while marketing a new, improved version is fighting a rearguard action.

rebel yell

A loud, high-pitched shout. During the Civil War the term was used for the blood-curdling yells uttered by Confederate troops as they attacked. Later it was applied to similar utterances, in sports and other peacetime pursuits. Its origin, it has been suggested, may have been a corruption of the British fox-hunting cry, "Tally ho!" Another theory is that it was copied from the war cry of one or another tribe of Native Americans.

The word *rebel* itself, today meaning a person who resists authority, came via Old French from the Latin *rebellare*, "to fight back," in turn from *bellum*, "war." The modern rebel has some degree of fortitude but is not necessarily violent.

reds

Political radicals; Communists. The color red has long been symbolic of anarchy and revolution. The red flag was a symbol of defiance and battle by the early eighteenth century, according to *Chambers' Cyclopaedia* (1728), and had been used as a call to arms in the days of the Roman Empire. It also was used during the French Revolution by the Red Republicans (*républicains rouges*), who wore red caps and were the most violent extremists, not afraid of bloodshed. Again in the revolutions of 1848, in France and in Germany the *républicains rouges* and the *rote Republikaner* represented the most radical elements.

In the twentieth century the Russian Communists adopted a red flag as the symbol of international socialism, and since their Revolution of 1917 the name Reds (it is often capitalized) has nearly always signified Communists or Communist sympathizers.

reign of terror

A period of ruthless oppression. The name comes from a specific time during the French Revolution, from April, 1793, to July, 1794, when supreme power rested with the most violently radical element of the revolutionaries, the Committee of Public Safety and the JACOBINS, led by Maximilien Robespierre. During this period an estimated 17,000 persons—including King Louis XVI and Queen Marie Antoinette— were put to death for supposed opposition to the revolutionary cause, 2,600 of them in Paris alone. However, as often happens in a period of violence, the revolutionary leaders began to fight among themselves. First Jean-Paul Marat was assassinated, and then Robespierre ordered the execution of Georges Jacques Danton. By July, 1794, he had gone too far, and the people themselves rebelled against the Reign of Terror. In this Thermidorian Reaction (*Thermidor* being the new name for July in the revolutionary calendar), Robespierre himself was brought to the guillotine. Since those days the expression reign of terror has been applied to a number of violent dictatorial regimes, including those of François ("Papa Doc") Duvalier in Haiti, Idi Amin in Uganda, the Ayatollah Khomeini in Iran, and others.

rendezvous

A prearranged meeting. The term comes from the French, literally meaning "present yourselves," and in the late sixteenth century was used to order troops or warships to assemble. By the early 1600's the term had been transferred to any kind of meeting, and it is still so used, in English as well as in French.

ricochet

Anything repeated again and again, bouncing back. The word's ultimate origin is not known, but by the eighteenth century it was used to describe the glancing or skipping of a bullet or other projectile with one or more rebounds when it is fired at a low angle. It is the same as the path of skipping stones flung along a water surface. A French military engineer, Sébastien le Prestre, the Marquis of Vauban (1633–1707), who conducted more than forty successful sieges during the wars of Louis XIV, developed a technique for ricochet firing that greatly increased the effectiveness of the siege artillery.

ride roughshod over, to

To act without consideration for another's feelings or interests. The term comes from the seventeenth-century practice of arming cavalry mounts by giving them metal shoes with projecting nails or cutting edges. One wonders whether such armor might not damage the rider's comrades more than any enemy, but to soldiers already down on a battlefield a rearing roughshod charger must have been a terrifying sight. The expression, originating before 1800, is still used today, for domineering behavior, forging on and overriding others, with no respect or regard for them.

rif, to

To dismiss an employee, usually as an economy move. The term is an acronym for reduction in force and was first used in the military but soon was extended to government bureaucracy, business, and industry. Today it is used for any kind of employee layoff, especially in the public sector, such as teachers who are dismissed because the school population is shrinking.

right-hand man

A valuable assistant. The term has been used since the mid-seventeenth century and originated in the cavalry, where the soldier at the far right of the line had a position of special responsibility or command. By about 1800 it had been transferred to an important helper in any line of endeavor.

risen from the ranks

Describing a self-made man or woman. The term originally meant a commissioned officer who had worked his way up from private, at one time a rare achievement. Today it is also used for executives who have been promoted from within an organization. (See also RANK AND FILE.)

risorgimento

A period of renewed activity or rebirth. The word is Italian for "resurrection" and was used for the nineteenth-century revolutionary movement for a united Italy, under King Victor Emmanuel, independent of foreign domination. At the height of this period of strong nationalist feeling, in 1842, came the premiere of Giuseppe

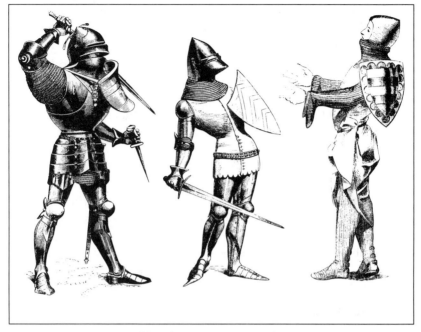

Robber baron exacting tribute

Verdi's opera *Nabucco*, based on the biblical story of Nebuchadnezzar. During the third act the enslaved and exiled Israelites sing a chorus, "*Va, pensiero*" ("Flee, thought"), as a lament for their homeland. At the premiere the Italian audience quickly responded to the music's sentiment as symbolic of their own situation, and despite the law forbidding encores, the chorus was repeated. With this music Verdi became the official composer of the Risorgimento, and the revolutionaries began to use the slogan *Viva Verdi!*—supposedly acclaiming the composer but actually advocating the cause of *V*ictor *E*mmanuel *R*e *d'I*talia (King of Italy).

robber baron

A business leader who becomes wealthy through ruthless exploitation. In feudal times, the powerful lords had complete control over their own lands, enforced by their private armies. Some of the less scrupulous of them exacted tribute from travelers crossing their territory, in effect robbing them of their possessions, and so came to be called robber barons. In the last quarter of the nineteenth century the term came to be used for certain powerful American industrialists—John D. Rockefeller among them—who exploited natural resources, bribed legislators, and used other unethical means to build enormous fortunes. Although in the twentieth century legislation has greatly limited such behavior, a few individuals still have managed to circumvent the law and build large business empires via sometimes questionable means.

rookie

A novice or greenhorn. There is some dispute about the origin of this word, which is a corruption of *recruit*. Some lexicographers believe it originated in baseball in the late 1890's, where it still is used to describe not only raw beginners but the newer team members. Eric Partridge, however, believes it comes from the raw military recruit. It was so used by Rudyard Kipling, who wrote in *The Young British Soldier*:

> When the 'arf-made recruit goes out to the East
> 'E acts like a babe an' 'e drinks like a beast.

Partridge thought rookie was not only a perversion of recruit but a pun on *rooky*, which in British slang meant rascally or scampish. Today rookie simply means a beginner in any field.

rove, to

> "A-roving, a-roving, since roving's been my ruin
> I'll go no more a-roving with you, fair maid."
>
> —Sea chantey

To wander about at random, to ramble. This seemingly peaceable word comes from medieval warfare, where it signified archery practice in which the archer shot at objects positioned at random distances, in order to practice finding the correct range. This usage was extended at first to random utterances—speaking without a particular point in mind—and then to making random movements back and forth.

The noun *rover* also means "a pirate" or "sea robber," a usage dating from the mid-fourteenth century but derived from a different root, from the Middle Dutch or Low German word *roven*, "to rob."

sabotage

The destruction of machinery, disruption of production, and similar calculated interference undertaken to hamper an enemy. The word comes from the French *sabot*, a wooden shoe worn by French peasants, and *saboter*, to make noise with sabots and also to do something badly. Presumably the first *saboteurs* (committers of sabotage) were peasants who rebelled against their oppressive masters, perhaps by trampling their crops. The word came into English in the early 1900's during a French railroad strike in which dissatisfied workers sabotaged the railroad lines. However, it was not used widely until World War I, when resistance fighters in occupied countries (especially France) as well as secret agents hindered the enemy by blowing up bridges, derailing trains, and destroying vehicles and machinery. In peacetime the term is most often used for industrial sabotage.

sack time

Slang for "time to sleep." The term was widely used by American G.I.'s during World War II, but it may have originated earlier, in

Britain, where in nineteenth-century naval slang a hammock was called a sack. (See also SAD SACK.)

sacrament

A solemn Christian rite that is believed to symbolize or to confer grace. This word comes from *sacramentum*, which originally was the military oath taken by Roman soldiers. They were required to swear that they would not desert their standard, turn their back on the enemy, or abandon their general. Traces of this original meaning survive in early Christian usage, the sacrament being considered an oath to God, but the present meaning also incorporates the idea of a holy mystery, which probably was derived from the Latin New Testament. The Protestant sacraments are baptism and the Lord's Supper; the Roman Catholic sacraments are baptism, confirmation, the Eucharist, matrimony, penance, holy orders, and extreme unction.

sad sack

Slang for a pathetically inept person. The name comes from Sergeant George Baker's cartoon character, Sad Sack, who was extremely popular during World War II. He represented a soldier who tried hard to do his best but was not particularly intelligent and was dogged by bad luck, so that he invariably failed at whatever he attempted.

Sam Browne belt

A style of leather belt with a shoulder strap, worn as part of their uniform by police officers, guards, and others. The style was invented by a British officer, Sir Samuel James Browne (1824–1901), a veteran of the Sepoy Rebellion (1857). It consisted of a leather belt supported by a light strap passing over the shoulder, so that the sword it held would not make the belt sag. At first there was a strap over each shoulder, but later it was changed to just one, over the left shoulder, since swords were worn on the left side. The Sam Browne belt was compulsory for British army officers until 1939 (thereafter it became optional) and was adopted in many other armies, as well as being worn by cadets on parade, police officers, and the like.

scalp, to

> ". . . and red men scalped each other by the Great Lakes of North America."
>   —Thomas Macaulay, *Frederick the Great* (1842)

To sell at a price higher than the official one; also, to defeat someone. The term comes from the barbaric practice of cutting or tearing the scalp from an enemy's head, traditional among numerous Native American tribes. By the late 1860's the term was being used for a speculator who turns a quick and unreasonably large profit by means of quasi-legal or wholly illegal practices. For example, a ticket scalper buys tickets to a major athletic event or theatrical performance at regular prices and then, when tickets are scarce, resells his own tickets at whatever the traffic will bear. Similarly, an investment adviser may buy a particular stock and then recommend it to many customers, promptly selling her own shares when the price has risen as a result of her advice. In both cases the seller is figuratively scalping the customers.

The verb is also used loosely to mean defeating someone, as is the related expression, *to have someone's scalp*.

scorched-earth policy

A strategy of burning and destroying crops, buildings, bridges, or anything else that might be of use to an advancing enemy. The term was first used in the late 1930's and probably is a translation of the Chinese *jiāotu zhengcè*; the Chinese did indeed implement this policy before the advancing Japanese armies in 1937, as did the Russians when the Nazis invaded their country in World War II. The practice, however, is centuries old, used since time immemorial by peoples retreating before invaders.

scout

An individual sent to obtain information. The word came into English about 1300, via Middle English from the Old French *escouter*, "to spy" or "eavesdrop" (leading also to the modern French *écouter*, to listen). The primary usefulness of scouts was in warfare, when they not only spied on the enemy but moved in advance of attacking troops to reconnoiter and assess the enemy's strength and defenses. This usage has been transferred in *talent scout*, one who seeks out talented young entertainers, and *football scout*, one who reports on the merits of the opposing team.

The expertise of scouts in the backwoods during the French and Indian Wars and later conflicts fought in jungles, forests, mountains, and swamps probably accounts for using the word for the Boy Scouts and Girl Scouts, organizations that concentrate on developing woodcraft, nature lore, campcraft, and related skills in youngsters with the ultimate goal of character building.

At England's Oxford University a scout is a college servant, a usage that may have derived from the military.

The word has the same meaning as a verb—as in "to scout the other team's lineup." However, the verb *to scout* also can mean to dismiss with scorn or to mock, a usage believed to come from other roots, perhaps from Norse or Germanic words with this meaning.

screaming meemies

Slang for extreme nervousness, bordering on hysterics. According to William and Mary Morris, the expression was first used during World War I for German artillery shells that emitted an exceptionally high-pitched whine before exploding. By the 1920's the term was being applied to a highly disordered mental state. During World War II the name screaming meemies was used for several noisome rockets and mortars.

scrounge, to

To seek out, forage, or borrow with no intention of repaying. This word was London slang in the early 1900's, a variant of *scrunge* or *scringe*, dialect for "pilfer." It came into common use only during World War I, when soldiers used it to describe their foraging. One still speaks of the *scrounger* who "bums" (borrows) cigarettes, as well as of students who scrounge around (aimlessly look) for something to eat after midnight.

scuttlebutt

Rumor or gossip. The original scuttlebutt was a lidded cask used on naval vessels to hold the crew's drinking water. The word itself was a combination of *scuttle*, meaning a hole in a vessel, and *butt*, a large cask—in other words, a cask with a hole in it to allow access to the contents. Presumably the scuttlebutt became, much like the proverbial office water cooler, a place where sailors gathered to drink and chat, and in the early 1900's the word was transferred to the gossip exchanged there.

sea dog

A very experienced sailor. This term dates from the late sixteenth century, when it was used for Queen Elizabeth's sea dogs, pirates who were part secret agents of the crown and part private profiteers. The most notable of them was Sir Francis Drake (See PIRATE). In the early 1800's sea dog began to be applied simply to an experienced sailor, often described as an *old sea dog*. For example, "Jim's been sailing up and down the coast for years—he's a real old sea dog."

secret weapon

Any mysterious or clandestine item or mode of powerful attack. During World War II, prior to D-Day, rumors were widespread that Hitler was about to launch a devastating secret weapon against Great Britain. The term was applied successively during the war to pilotless planes, robot bombs, rockets, and atom bombs. Today it is still in common civilian use, as in "John's second serve is his secret weapon."

shanghai, to

To kidnap; also, to coerce a person into some unwanted situation. The term comes from the nineteenth-century practice of impressing seamen (See PRESS-GANG). Unscrupulous captains would make a man drunk, drug him, or knock him out; when he awoke, he would find himself at sea on an outbound ship that had needed more hands. Since Shanghai was a particularly distant seaport, the practice was described as *shipping him to Shanghai*—that is, sending him on a long voyage—which was later shortened to simply shanghai. Although the practice has long since been abandoned, the expression lives on. It is sometimes used loosely to mean overcoming someone's resistance to perform a task, as in "He was shanghaied into washing the dishes." During World War II servicemen sometimes used the term to mean being transferred against one's wishes.

shell shock

An acute stress syndrome resulting from exposure to active combat. It was so named during World War I, when soldiers living for months in the trenches were exposed to constant shelling by the enemy, and the resulting nervous condition was thought to be caused by both the noise and fear. (See also BATTLE FATIGUE.) The expression is also used loosely to describe the aftereffects of any traumatic experience.

shibboleth

A catchphrase or watchword; also, a password. The expression comes from the Bible. According to the Book of Judges (12:4–6), the Ephraimites, defeated by the Gileadites, wanted to escape across the river Jordan. When asked if they were Ephraimites, they denied it so as to escape, but as a test the Gileadites made them say shibboleth (Hebrew for "stream of flood"), knowing there was no *sh* sound in their language. All those who mispronounced it "sibboleth" then were killed. Allegedly some 42,000 Ephraimites were trapped in this way and slain.

Long after the original significance had been forgotten, shibboleth still meant a test word or a principle to which the members of a group adhere—that is, a criterion for determining the members of a social class or other group. A second meaning still current is that of a catchword or slogan that has been so overused that it has become a meaningless platitude. For example, "My country, right or wrong," is a shibboleth of blind patriotism.

shoot down, to

To defeat an argument or to expose as false. The expression is said to have come from the R.A.F during World War II, from shooting down enemy planes ("to shoot down in flames"), but it may actually have originated in World War I, among aircraft engineers. During that earlier conflict, *shooting gallery* became a synonym for the front line,

Shot his bolt?

and the *whole shoot,* meaning "the entire thing," became the *whole shooting match.*

It was only after World War II, however, that it became necessary to distinguish a *shooting war*—a genuine military conflict—from a COLD WAR. (See also *shot to hell,* under SHOT AT DAWN.)

shoot one's bolt, to

> "Sottes bolt is sone i-schote."
>
> —*Proverbs of Alfred* (c. 1275)

To expend all of one's best effort or use up all of one's resources. The term comes from medieval archery, and by the early thirteenth century it was a familiar proverb: "A fool's bolt is soon shot" (translation of the Middle English quotation above). A bolt was a short, heavy arrow with a blunt head that was fired with a crossbow, and the archer who shot all his bolts at once, leaving none in reserve, was considered a fool.

A related expression with the same meaning, but less common today, is *no shot in one's locker*. In the traditional sailing warship the ammunition was stored in lockers; when the supply was exhausted, the ship could no longer fight. The expression then came to mean that one had used up all of one's cash or other reserves.

shot at dawn, to be

Describing an individual in deep trouble, who faces a severe punishment. The conventional time to die at the hands of a firing squad, following a court-martial or conviction for desertion or treason, was in the early morning hours.

Another term involving *shot* is *like a shot*, which has meant very fast, like the speed of a projectile (bullet, arrow), since about 1800. Charles Dickens used it in *A Christmas Carol*: "The boy was off like a shot."

Still another is *shot to hell*, for "completely ruined," which dates only from about the 1920's, perhaps because before that time the use of "hell" in writing was generally frowned on.

shrapnel

Shell fragments. The word originally meant a type of hollow projectile containing a number of metal balls and a charge of powder, along with a time fuse that made it burst before it reached the target, thus releasing a shower of small projectiles. It was named for the man who invented it, British General Henry Shrapnel (1761–1842), in the early 1800's. The original variety of shrapnel, first used by the British army in Surinam and in the Napoleonic wars, has long since been abandoned in favor of more effective projectiles, but the term continues to be used for shell fragments from any high explosive, whether bomb, mine, or shell, as well as figuratively for small but damaging projectiles.

shuttle diplomacy

Negotiations between two warring nations assisted by a third party hurrying between them by jet plane. This term became current during the efforts of Secretary of State Henry Kissinger to negotiate a peace after the Arab-Israeli War of 1973. The shuttle here is a metaphor for the weaving shuttle that shoots threads of woof between threads of warp.

Sicilian vespers

A massacre. The original source is a massacre by the Sicilians of the French, under Charles of Anjou, who ruled Sicily at the time. On March 30, 1282, which was Easter Monday, the church bells ringing for Vespers in Palermo and other cities were the signal to begin fighting. This extremely bloody occasion became the subject of an opera by Giuseppe Verdi, *Les Vêpres Siciliennes* (1855), with a French libretto by Eugène Scribe. The opera was not particularly successful, compared to Verdi's other triumphs, but served to keep the term Sicilian vespers in the language.

sick man of Europe

> "The Ottoman Empire has the body of a sick old man, who tried
> to appear healthy, although his end was near."
> —Sir Thomas Roe, letter (1621)

Nickname for the Turkish (Ottoman) Empire, which was said to be in decline as early as 1621 by Roe, the English ambassador quoted above, but actually began to fall apart only much later. Addressing the British ambassador, Nicholas I of Russia said, in 1853, shortly before the outbreak of the Crimean War, "We have on our hands a sick man—a very sick man." He all but suggested that it was time the British partitioned the Turkish Empire, but his hint was ignored.

At the peak of its power, in the sixteenth century, the empire extended from Hungary to Mesopotamia and south to Egypt, Tunisia, Algeria, and Libya. The highest tide of success was reached in 1683, when the Turkish army surrounded Vienna, but it was subsequently defeated and, as a result, lost Hungary. By the nineteenth century many more of its valued possessions were gone, among them Greece and Serbia. The fact that most of the Balkan peoples were Christians, although of different sects, gave the European powers an excuse for their "concern" about the empire, which was a Muslim state. Nevertheless, the sick man survived into the 1900's, mainly because the intense rivalries among the major European powers—Russia, Austria, France, Britain, and Germany—prevented them from reaching a unified policy toward Turkey. (See also under BALKANIZATION.) World War I delivered the final blow. Turkey had allied with Germany, and after their defeat Turkey was reduced to its present comparatively small stature.

sideburns

Side whiskers, projecting from the hairline to below the ears, worn with a mustache but without a beard. (In Britain these are called simply *side whiskers*.) Originally called *burnsides*, after General Ambrose Everett Burnside (1824–81), who popularized the style, they became very fashionable. In the late 1880's their name was turned around to sideburns. Burnside fought in the Mexican War and reentered the Army at the beginning of the Civil War on the Union side. He distinguished himself at first and was promoted to major general after his North Carolina campaign, but following a costly defeat at Fredericksburg President Lincoln relieved him of his command in favor of General Hooker. Although Burnside never repeated his early military successes, he remained popular. After the war he served several terms as governor of Rhode Island, and from 1875 until his death he was a U.S. senator.

After the style of side whiskers went out of fashion, the word sideburns was—and still is—used for projections of the hairline forming a border just in front of the ear.

siege

A prolonged battle or period of annoyance and oppression. The word comes via Old French from the Latin *sedere*, "to sit," and denoted a basic tactic of ancient warfare—that is, an army surrounds a fortified place (fort, castle, walled city) and remains there ("sits") until enemy resistance breaks down, at least partly because the defenders are cut off from help and supplies. (See also BESIEGE.) Although this tactic is very old, it is still used in modern warfare. In World War II during the Battle of the Bulge (December, 1944– January, 1945), the Belgian town of Bastogne, held by American forces, was besieged for nearly two months by the Germans, until it was finally relieved by American troops and Allied air support. Such a town is said to be *under siege*, and the attackers are said to *lay siege* to it.

Today all of these terms are used figuratively as well, for illness (a siege of head colds) or other unpleasant occurrences (a siege of locusts, hailstorms, etc.), from which not even machinery is immune (a recent newspaper headline proclaimed that computers were under siege from computer viruses).

Siegfried line

A line of defenses built by the Germans on their western frontier during the 1930's as a response to the French MAGINOT LINE. It is named for the hero of the German epic, the *Nibelungenlied.*

Sieg heil!

A Nazi salute and, by extension, any totalitarian slogan. Literally meaning "Hail, victory," it was shouted out during Adolf Hitler's public speeches.

silent majority

Those who quietly agree with the established policy but do not proclaim their opinions. The expression was first used by President Richard M. Nixon in a television address on November 3, 1969, following a large demonstration against the war in Vietnam. He said, "If a vocal minority prevails over reason and the will of the majority, this nation has no future as a free society. . . . And so tonight—you, the great silent majority of my fellow Americans—I ask for your support."

Since then the term has become associated with the most conservative elements of the population, who support a strong military establishment.

skinflint

A miser, a cheapskate. This term comes from the old flintlock rifle. After repeated firing, the gun's flint would begin to wear down, so that not enough sparks were created to ignite the powder. Most gunners simply replaced the flint, but some tightwads "skinned" the flint, that is, they sharpened it with a knife. Washington Irving made fun of the latter in his *Salmagundi* (1807): "The fool . . . who, in

Skirmish

skinning a flint worth a farthing, spoiled a knife worth fifty times the sum." It was this practice, however, that gave us the word and present meaning of skinflint.

skirmish

> "There's a skirmish of wit between them."
> —William Shakespeare, *Much Ado About Nothing*

A brief, relatively trivial fight. This term, along with football's *scrimmage*, seems to come from various words for a medieval swordfight. (The same roots also gave rise to *Scaramouche*, the boastful poltroon of the Italian *commedia dell'arte*.) Since about 1575 skirmish has meant any kind of brief battle, military or civilian; for example: "Mary engaged in a skirmish with the department store about her bill."

skunk works

A secret manufacturing enterprise whose precise nature and product are a complete mystery. This term dates from the 1950's, when the Lockheed Aircraft Corporation had an experimental division for innovative defense projects, among them the first jet fighter plane, the U-2 spy plane, and the F-117A stealth fighter. Someone at Lockheed named this division "skunk works" after the *Skonk Works* in Al Capp's comic strip, *L'il Abner*, which manufactured Kickapoo Joy Juice (moonshine whiskey). Later the name was extended to any innovative and secret laboratory or project. Ben R. Rich, a former Lockheed director, used the term in the title of his book *Skunk Works: A Personal Memoir of My Years at Lockheed* (1994).

slogan

A catchphrase or word used to identify and/or promote a product, individual, political party, or other group. The word comes from the Gaelic *sluagh*, for "army" or "host," and *ghairm*, for "cry" or "shout," and originally meant "a war cry of the Old Highland clans." Today slogans abound, particularly in politics and in advertising, although they also may still serve as a political-military rallying cry ("Fifty-four/forty or fight!"—"Ban the Bomb!"—"Make peace, not war!" etc.).

smoke screen

A diversion or cover-up intended to hide one's real intentions or simply to deceive. The term comes from naval warfare during the early twentieth century, when smaller vessels, such as destroyers, were assigned to emit quantities of dense black smoke between their own fleet and the enemy in order to conceal the fleet's movements. Later, military aircraft used the same tactic. By 1940 the term had been transferred to diversionary tactics in any undertaking—for example, a welfare provision in a proposed law may be a smoke screen for a tax increase.

snafu

A messed-up situation, as usual. The term originated during World War II in Britain and is an acronym for situation *n*ormal, *a*ll *f*—ed *u*p." The taboo F-word is often euphemized to "fouled" or "foozled." The term was readily adopted by U.S. troops. H. L. Mencken, in *American Slang*, listed numerous offspring, such as *susfu*, for "situation *u*nchanged, *s*till *f*—ed *u*p," *janfu*, for "*j*oint *a*rmy and *n*avy *f*—-*u*p," and *fubar*, "*f*—ed *u*p *b*eyond *a*ll *r*ecognition." None of these caught on permanently in civilian life as snafu did. (See also SOP.)

sniper

One who attacks or criticizes from a hidden position. The word *snipe* came into English in the thirteenth century via Middle English from the Old Norse *snipa,* for the bird, and sniper soon meant a hunter or killer of snipe. The puzzling aspect of this derivation is that fowlers do not usually snipe at snipe but walk directly up to this darting little marsh dweller and shoot it as it flies into the air. There is nothing circumspect or secretive about the procedure. By Shakespeare's time, however, snipe was a term of abuse; in *Othello,* Iago uses it to complain of Rodrigo's stupidity, and Iago was indeed a stabber-in-the-back. It may be from this usage that we get the modern military meaning—one who shoots from a hidden position. This variety of sniping has been a lethal tactic in modern warfare, especially in rough terrain or in towns and cities, which afford many hiding places.

snorkel

An underwater breathing device used by divers. Its name is an anglicization of the German *Schnorchel,* a retractable tube on German submarines in World War II. Such tubes took in fresh air and exhausted fumes and foul air. Soon after the war the name began to be used for diving equipment. It also is occasionally used for fire-fighting equipment that involves using a high pumping platform for fighting a fire in a tall building.

snow job

American slang for a dose of exaggerated flattery used to cover up some real issue. The term was invented by G.I.'s during World War II to describe, for example, persuading one's superior to grant a favor or presenting an elaborate fictional excuse for some misdemeanor, so that the officer was snowed under with words.

soft underbelly

The weakest, most vulnerable part of an organization, nation, or other body. Although undoubtedly originating as a reference to such animals as the porcupine, whose back is well protected, this expression was not used figuratively until World War II, when Sir Winston Churchill discussed the Allied invasion of Italy as an attack on the soft underbelly of the Axis. At least one writer believes Churchill borrowed this phrase from Geoffrey Crowther, editor of *The Economist* from 1938 to 1956. Subsequently it has been used in such references as children representing the soft underbelly of a nation, or Iran being the soft underbelly of Near East politics.

soldier of fortune

> "War which is wont as well to raise soldiers of fortune as to ruine men of fortune."
>
> —Robert Boyle, *Some Considerations . . . on the Style of the Holy Scriptures* (1661)

An adventurer. The term originally was a euphemism for the medieval mercenary who offered his military service to any country or ruler who would pay him. (See also FREE LANCE.) In the nineteenth century it was extended to any adventurer who would engage in undertakings for the sake of monetary gain or simply for fun.

The word *soldier*, incidentally, comes from the Latin *solidus* or *soldus*, an important Roman coin, and hence has a direct relationship to financial considerations. As John Ciardi pointed out, Roman legionnaires, though not all mercenaries, were the most prominent class to work for pay and booty at a time when most Europeans worked the soil and traded by barter, using virtually no money.

sonar

A method for detecting and locating objects that are underwater by means of echoes. The name of this method and the device used are an acronym of *so*und *na*vigation *r*anging. Sonar was first developed and used during World War II to detect enemy submarines and, on submarines, to detect enemy ships. Since then it has been used for various kinds of underwater exploration.

SOP

A mismanaged mess, as expected. The term is an acronym for *st*andard *o*perating *p*rocedure and originated during World War II, among disgruntled service personnel who despaired of the military bureaucracy's ability to accomplish anything promptly, efficiently, or effectively. (See its companion word, SNAFU.)

sortie

An outing or expedition. The word came into English during the seventeenth century from French as the past participle of *sortir*, "to go out," which itself has an uncertain etymology. By the eighteenth century a sortie meant a sally by a besieged garrison—that is, a rapid movement by troops who were under siege to attack the besiegers. By World War I it had replaced *mission* in the sense of an airplane going out on a combat mission. Today it is used quite loosely, as in "After the parade the marching band made a sortie to the refreshment stand."

sound off, to

To speak one's mind very freely. The expression comes from the military roll call, in which each of the assembled soldiers calls out his or her name in turn. By 1918 in the United States the term had come to mean "to speak very openly," usually to complain or to exaggerate.

Spartan

> "The company is Spartan; see how all their wounds are in front."
> —Bassus, *The Greek Anthology*

Austere, frugal, strictly disciplined. The word refers to Sparta, the ancient Greek city-state famous for its well-trained, highly disciplined soldiers. Sparta, with more than 3,000 square miles, and Athens, with somewhat more than 1,000 square miles, were the largest of the city-states. The Spartans had moved into southern Greece as an invading army and fought for generations to win land from the native Mycenaeans. By the time they finally conquered the inhabitants and enslaved them, Spartan military habits were so firmly fixed that they could not be thrown off. Moreover, the Spartans feared the possibility of uprisings by slaves and conquered peoples, so they directed their efforts to becoming a disciplined warrior state.

Although Sparta and Athens were at peace during most of the first two centuries of their existence, by 431 B.C. a disastrous war had broken out between them and their respective allies. The Peloponnesian War, as it was called, dragged on, with some brief interruptions, for twenty-seven years. In 404 B.C. Athens was finally forced to yield, but genuine peace and unity among the city-states was not established for another half-century.

spearhead

The leader or initial thrust of any undertaking. The word came from Middle English in the mid-fourteenth century and meant, as it still does, the sharp, pointed end of a spear—a basic weapon from ancient times and among many peoples. Since the 1920's the word has been transferred to various civilian enterprises, so that one speaks of the spearhead of a fund drive, debate, advertising campaign, and the like. It is also used as a verb, meaning to make the initial thrust.

spoils system

> "To the victor belong the spoils of the enemy."
> —Senator William Learned Marcy, congressional debate, 1831

The practice of awarding political appointments to loyal supporters. The *spoils* come from the ancient Roman practice of a victorious army's helping itself to the possessions of the defeated enemy. The word itself is derived from the Latin *spolium*, "a hide or skin stripped off," which by extension came to mean booty or plunder. "Things conquered in war are said to belong to their conquerors," wrote Aristotle (*Politics*, c. 330 B.C.), a sentiment echoed many times over the centuries, sometimes quite colorfully. In a Senate speech in 1934, Louisiana Senator Huey Long, who raised the spoils system to an art form in modern southern politics, said, "The man who pulls the plow gets the plunder."

Although the concept is undoubtedly much older, it was Senator William Learned Marcy who first popularized the use of "spoils" for political rewards, in a speech defending President Andrew Jackson's appointment of Martin Van Buren as ambassador to England in 1831. Institutionalizing this common practice with the addition of "system" occurred a few years later. William Safire quotes a still earlier political usage of spoils (1812) in the Massachusetts House of Representatives, concerning the "division of the spoils."

In the United States the practice of rewarding supporters began with Thomas Jefferson, who employed it with restraint. By 1829 it was entrenched in the political machines of New York and Pennsylvania, as well as some other states. It was Andrew Jackson who introduced it into national politics on a grand scale, but in fact the "clean sweep" he made during his first year in office removed only about 9 percent of all officeholders (replaced by Jackson supporters), and in his entire two terms fewer than 20 percent of all officeholders were replaced on political grounds (although some historians put it as high as 40 percent).

After the Civil War the spoils system was attacked by various reformers, particularly with a view to setting up a fair civil service system. Although the earliest of these efforts (1871–75) were defeated, several U.S. Presidents challenged the party machine in the matter of apportioning spoils, among them Rutherford B. Hayes and James Garfield. Despite the strength of the Tammany machine, eventually its most blatant outrages were curbed through the efforts of such reformers as Carl Schurz, who called Tammany Hall "one of the greatest criminals in our history, if not the greatest."

In present-day American politics there is no doubt that the spoils system persists, but on a lesser scale, curbed by ethics committees and legal restraints. Nevertheless, the power to make political appointments is a severe temptation; further, individuals in power naturally want to surround themselves with friends and supporters of their policies. Safire suggests that the harsher term "spoils" is now generally reserved for days gone by, and the somewhat milder "patronage" is used for present-day instances of such favoritism.

squad

A small group of persons engaged in a common enterprise, such as a sport or law enforcement. The names for our present-day police squad and football squad come, via French and Spanish, from a Latin word for "square." It was originally—and still is—used for a small number of soldiers who were aligned in a square formation. The modern army squad consists of ten privates, one corporal, and one staff sergeant. Beginning in the late nineteenth century, the word was used for other small groups, in sports, the police, etc., and by 1914 it was used figuratively as well, as in "squads of glasses on the shelf behind the bar."

SS

Enforcers. The term was an abbreviation for Adolf Hitler's *Schutzstaffel*, or protective guard, which was founded in 1923 and became, under Heinrich Himmler, the security guard for the Nazi Party. There were two divisions, the *Waffen* (weapons) *SS*, elite and ruthless combat units, and the *Totenkopf* (deathhead) *SS*, so named for their skull-and-crossbones insignia and black caps, who served as torturers and executioners in the Nazi concentration camps. Ever since, the name SS, along with Gestapo, has become synonymous with cruel enforcement of barbaric policies.

stalag

A prison camp. The word originated in World War II as an acronym from the German **Stammlag**er, a camp for enlisted men who were prisoners of war. There were also the *Oflag*, for **Offizierlag**er, or "officers' camp," and *Stalagluft*, for airmen, which was run by the German *Luftwaffe* (air force). The word might never have come into English were it not for several popular plays and war movies that featured dramatic escapes from such camps, notably *Stalag 17* (1953).

A related word, *gulag*, for the forced labor camps of the Soviet Union, was similarly formed from the Russian *Gulag*, an acronym for the Russian name of the Main Directorate of Corrective Labor Camps. Like stalag, gulag has been extended to mean any prison or detention camp, in particular one for political prisoners.

Stalingrad

Symbol for a heroic stand. The Battle of Stalingrad, which began in the autumn of 1942, marked a major turning point in the European theater of World War II. In August the Germans had begun a major offensive against the Russian city, which lay on river and rail routes whereby oil and military supplies moved north into Russia from the Caspian Sea. By capturing Stalingrad, the Germans hoped both to replenish their own supplies and to cripple the Russian armies. But like the French under Napoleon in 1812, the Germans were weakened by the tremendous transport problems of waging a Russian campaign. They were far from home, while the Russians staged a heroic defense in their own streets and cellars. At last, in autumn, the Russians launched a massive offensive and stopped the Germans cold. Although Hitler ordered his Sixth Army to stand or die, by February the German forces had dwindled to about 80,000 men and further resistance was hopeless. Their general, Friedrich von Paulus, surrendered, and Stalingrad was saved.

After Stalin's death and the repudiation of his policies, the city, which had been named after him in 1925, was rechristened Volgograd. Yet the name Stalingrad survived as a symbol for the heroism of the Russians, and, by extension, for any people making a determined stand against an invader.

standard-bearer

A conspicuous leader of a movement, political party, or other group. The term comes from the officer who carries the military standard, that is, a banner or other emblem on a long pole, thereby creating a rallying point for the troops. This meaning of the word standard comes from the French *étendard*, for "banner;" the derivation of standard in the sense of "criterion" is less clear.

George Washington was among the first to transfer the military use of standard to the political arena. At the Constitutional Convention in Philadelphia in 1787, he called on the delegates "to raise a standard to which the wise and honest can repair." The word standard-bearer has been used in politics to the present day, frequently to mean the candidate who carries the party's nomination.

standby

Ready and available if needed. This term dates from the late 1700's, when it was used for a naval vessel kept in attendance for some wartime emergency. From the 1800's on it has been frequently put as being *on standby*, a usage that continues. Today it often applies to a passenger who hopes to get a ticket or seat on a particular flight if some confirmed passenger fails to appear.

Star Wars

The positioning of military equipment in orbit around the earth to shoot down attacking missiles. This term was used for sophisticated technical equipment employed by allied forces in the Gulf War. The name alludes to the material developed in the film *Star Wars* (1977), which won numerous awards for its technical achievements in depicting an interplanetary hero and his human and robot friends. In 1983 President Ronald Reagan called for a new approach to counter the Soviet missile threat, an idea that quickly won the name "star wars proposal." The term continues to be used to describe highly sophisticated weaponry.

Stateside

In the continental United States. The word was coined during World War II by overseas G.I.'s to mean "back home," and it continues to be used by Americans living or visiting abroad.

steal a march on, to

To gain an advantage unexpectedly or surreptitiously. The term comes from medieval warfare, when a *march* was the distance an army could travel in a given time, usually one day. By quietly marching at night, a force could unexpectedly overtake the enemy by daybreak, or it could come much closer to the enemy than anticipated, in either case gaining the advantage of surprise. In time the term was transferred to any enterprise where anticipating the other's moves achieved an advantage.

Sten gun

A light submachine gun. It was designed by the British in World War II and named for the initials of its inventors' names and the town where it was first manufactured: *S*heppard, *T*urpin, and the town of *En*field. Although not very accurate, the gun is light and effective as a short-range weapon. After the war it was widely adopted by security forces, terrorists, and other armed groups the world over.

stentorian

"Shouting louder than Stentor."

—Lucian, c. A.D. 175

Very loud-voiced. The term comes from Stentor, a Greek herald in the Trojan Wars. According to Homer's account in the *Iliad*, his voice was as loud as that of fifty men combined.

stockpile, to

To collect and reserve a large supply. The term originated during World War I, when stocks of weapons and munitions for the war effort were piled up in warehouses and other storage sites called *stockpiles*. Later the term was extended to similar reserves of virtually any material. After World War II one often heard of a *nuclear stockpile*—a store of atomic bombs and other nuclear weapons and fuels for reactors—but the word is used just as widely for civilian goods.

stonewall, to

"There is Jackson, standing like a stone wall!"
—Brigadier General Bernard E. Bee, July 21, 1861

To obstruct or to stall in order to avoid giving an embarrassing answer. The term allegedly came into being when General Bee so described Confederate Colonel (later General) Thomas Jonathan Jackson after his resolute defense at the First Battle of Bull Run. Jackson always maintained that Bee meant not him but his brigade. Bee himself could not clarify the point, since he was killed in the battle, but the name stuck to Jackson, who from then on was nicknamed Stonewall. Jackson lived less than two years longer, however; he was accidentally shot by his own troops and died of his wounds.

storm trooper

A person specially trained to carry out assault. The word is a translation of the German *Sturmtruppen*, assault troops that functioned during World War I. It has since been extended in such usages as "storm trooper tactics," for violent or especially militant behavior. For example, one might speak of the storm trooper tactics of the Ku Klux Klan or some other militant group or movement.

strafe, to

To damage, or to reprimand strongly. This word comes from the German verb *strafen*, "to punish." In World War I it was used for any sharp, sudden bombardment, especially machine-gunning ground troops from low-flying airplanes. Eric Partridge pointed out that this usage may have come from a German toast of the time, *"Gott strafe England"* ("May God punish England"), but more likely it came from the idea of a particularly punishing attack. World War II newsreels showed some heartrending footage of Nazi planes strafing civilian refugees who were fleeing Paris and other cities about to be occupied by the Germans.

strategy

An overall plan that coordinates all the available means to achieve a particular goal. The word comes from the Greek *strategos*, for "general," and indeed for many centuries the military was the only area in which large-scale planning for effective management was undertaken. (Carrying out such plans is the province of TACTICS.)

Cyrus the Great of Persia (c. 600–529 B.C.) is generally considered the first great military strategist, but an even greater figure was the man who destroyed Cyrus's empire, Alexander the Great. Alexander used, on a grand scale, such basic strategies as keeping some troops in reserve, pursuing a retreating enemy, stockpiling (building up supplies), and using an elaborate intelligence system. In more recent times Frederick II of Prussia and Napoleon Bonaparte of France figure among the outstanding European strategists.

The modern theory of strategy—total warfare, fought with mass armies and engaging all of a nation's resources—was spelled out by the Prussian general and theorist Karl von Clausewitz (1780–1831). For a time in the nineteenth century, *to strategy* meant "to maneuver" (as in "to strategy John into matrimony").

It was only in the 1940's that the wholesale planning and deployment of resources characterizing military strategy were applied to other endeavors, at first in games theory (imaginary conflicts) and then in business, industry, and government policy making. Today every large business engages in *strategic planning* to determine how to make optimum use of its resources in the future. On a smaller scale, individual investors may follow an *investment strategy*, whereby they hope to maximize their returns. The United

States and other nations have a *strategic stockpile* in which they store materials essential for national defense that might not be available during an emergency.

Further, today one is apt to call *strategic* almost anything that serves as a means to an end. During World War II the bombing of cities and the consequent killing of many civilians, hitherto considered immoral, was termed *strategic bombing* and allegedly justified on the ground that it would hasten the end of the war (it did not). Similarly, American and British troops quipped about a *strategic movement (advance) to the rear,* a popular euphemism for retreating. In civilian contexts, one can also *beat a strategic retreat;* for example, "When Fido barks, our letter carrier beats a strategic retreat down the driveway."

stronghold

A place that serves as the center of a group or of a point of view. This term comes from the Middle Ages, when a castle, surrounded by defensive walls and sometimes containing an entire town within them, was termed a *strong hold*. It served as a secure (*strong*) place of refuge to which one could safely retreat (*hold*). Later the term became one word and began to be used figuratively, as in "The Senator's state is no longer a stronghold of liberalism."

subsidy

Financial support of an individual, company, or industry, usually given by a government. The word comes from the Latin *subsidere*. In the Roman armies the *subsidii* (plural of *subsidium*) were troops held in reserve, who would give support and aid when needed. The word became an English one in the fourteenth century, when at first it meant simply "assistance." However, it also signified, in the fourteenth and fifteenth centuries, support granted by Parliament to the crown, and eventually, in the nineteenth century, it came to mean state aid to an individual, organization, etc.

swashbuckler

A swaggering doer of daring deeds. *To swash* originally meant "to dash against," and a *buckle* was the raised boss of a shield. Thus in

Storming the stronghold

the sixteenth century a swashbuckler was a person who made a blustering noise by striking a shield—his own or an opponent's—with his sword, a kind of showing off that even then was regarded with disdain. Shakespeare wrote, "We'll have a swashing and a martial outside, as many other mannish cowards have" (*As You Like It*, 1:2). Although swordplay is hardly a widespread pursuit today, the swashbuckler was perpetuated in a series of popular motion pictures from the 1920's to the 1940's, in which such stars as Douglas Fairbanks, Jr., Tyrone Power, and Errol Flynn represented highly romanticized versions of swordplay and similar derring-do.

swastika

An emblem of Nazism. Until about 1920, when the Nazis adopted it, the swastika, whose name is from the Sanskrit *svasti*, for "good fortune," was widely used as a decorative device in numerous cultures and countries and had no special significance. Since the 1920's, however, in the Western world it has become inextricably linked with Nazism and all it implies—anti-Semitism, fascism, brutal authoritarianism—and, like NAZI itself, stands for those who subscribe to these views.

swear like a trooper, to

To utter vigorous profanity or obscenity. Why the cavalry, whose members are called troopers, should have been singled out for their profanity is not clear. Surely other branches of the service, particularly the maritime ones, could equal or surpass the horsemen. Indeed, in the 1590's Shakespeare picked on the comfitmaker's (confectioner's) wife (*Henry IV, Part 1*, 3: 1), and a few years later (1611) Randle Cotgrave's *Dictionary* listed "swears like a carter" and "swears like an abbot." John Webster chose the falconer (*The White Devil*, 1612) and Peter Motteux, translator of Rabelais, the tinker (1693; it subsequently gave rise to "I don't give a tinker's damn"). The first recorded use of swearing like a trooper was by an unknown author in *The Devil to Pay at St. James's* (1727), and it is this version that has stuck, long after the cavalry lost its military importance. (See also LIE LIKE A TROOPER.)

Swiss army knife

A folding pocket knife with various attachments, such as a corkscrew, scissors, can opener, screwdriver, file, pliers, and numerous blades. It originated in 1884 when the Victorinox Company of Ibach, Switzerland, began manufacturing a pocket knife that became standard equipment for Swiss army officers from 1891 on. Actually, it was an 1897 version, called the "officer's knife" (in German, *Offiziermesser*, still the name for Swiss army knives in German Switzerland; in French Switzerland it is the *couteau Suisse*, or "Swiss knife"), which was the patented ancestor of the modern Swiss army knife. A rival company soon sprang up, Wenger of Delemont, and in 1908 the Swiss government let out contracts to both companies, allowing each to produce half of the knives required by the army. The contracts are still in effect, and both companies call their product, quite legitimately, the official Swiss army knife. However, both also make many different models for other markets all over the world, and numerous other manufacturers produce imitations.

The basic Swiss army knife has a red plastic handle with a white Swiss cross, stainless-steel blades, and a variety of gadgets. One model, measuring 3½ inches by 1¼ inches, resembles a miniature machine shop in that it has twenty-nine different tools from saw to pliers. The knife is prized by hikers, campers, and other outdoor enthusiasts and has been described in this way: "In the wilderness it reminds you of civilization; in civilization it reminds you of the wilderness." In the United States, its largest market (80 percent of total output, or five million knives per year), it sometimes ranks as a status symbol. Nevertheless, Swiss army knives are adored by young and old alike; indeed, we know a seventy-year-old lady, a retired school librarian of decidedly sedentary habits, who literally goes nowhere without her Swiss army knife tucked in her handbag.

tactics

Any deliberate procedure undertaken to reach a desired end. If STRAT-
EGY is the overall scheme, tactics are the actions used to carry it out.
The word comes from the Greek *taktikos*, meaning capable of being
arranged or put in order, and was applied specifically to the art of
arraying one's troops or warships against the enemy. The military
meaning persists, but since the early eighteenth century the word
also has been transferred to civilian matters, in sports (where a team
may use certain tactics to gain an advantage), games (the tactics of
chess, Scrabble, etc.), and any other area where one hopes to
advance (the senator's tactics for winning support for his bill, the
hairdresser's tactics for getting more customers, etc.).

take by storm, to

To become suddenly famous or popular. In the seventeenth century
and even earlier, *to storm* meant to make a violent military assault on
a fortified position. If it succeeded, the position was said to have
been taken by storm. By the late nineteenth century the term was
used to mean suddenly winning great renown, as in "The orator's
eloquence took the crowd by storm."

take evasive action, to

To beat a prudent retreat. The term originated during World War II as a euphemism for a graceful retreat from danger or difficulty. Later, it was extended to mean a disappearing act intended to avoid creditors, being served a subpoena, or other unpleasantness.

take-no-prisoners

Highly uncompromising and determined. This term alludes to the harsh military policy of killing the enemy outright rather than allowing them to surrender and be taken prisoner. In the late 1900's it was transferred to other matters, as in "Our candidate is committed to a take-no-prisoners stand concerning a tax cut."

tank

A large, armored, motorized combat vehicle and, by extension, slang for any cumbersome, unwieldy vehicle or other object. The word appears to have come into English in the sixteenth century from the Gujarati word *tankh*, for "reservoir," and/or the Portuguese *tanque*, for "a pond" or "dammed-up area." Until about 1915 the principal meaning of tank was a large container for a liquid or gas, a usage that persists. During World War I, however, Britain's Major General Sir E. D. Swinton invented a self-propelled combat vehicle armed with cannon and moving on a caterpillar tread. To conceal the nature of this new weapon from enemy agents, it was given the code name tank, to give the impression that it was a storage vehicle of some kind. Tanks were first used in 1916, in the Battle of the Somme, where their real purpose became clear. Today the word is also used loosely to describe a large, clumsy object or person, as in "That tank of a runner will never finish the course."

taps

A signal indicating the end, or death. In the military, taps is the last call at night, signaling lights out. It has been used in this sense since the early 1800's. The modern bugle call known as taps dates from the Civil War. In 1862 Union General Daniel Butterfield, with help from a bugler, adapted the TATTOO call into a new tune. Today taps is played at military funerals and also at many civilian ones, whence its association with death.

tar and feathers

A humiliating punishment. It originally consisted of stripping a person and applying hot tar and feathers. A punishment for theft in the Royal Navy, it was first recorded in the Ordinance of Richard I (the Lionhearted), dated 1189, during the Third Crusade, which stated, "Any robber traveling with crusaders shall be shorn like a hired fighter, and boiling tar shall be poured over his head, and feathers from a pillow shall be shaken out over his head." By the mid-eighteenth century this punishment had become mob practice. It was used by American colonists for those who remained loyal to Britain and refused to support the revolutionary cause. Today it appears to have largely died out, replaced by lynching and other practices of mob justice.

tartar

> "'I'll tell you what I am,' whispered Mr. Creakle, letting it [my ear] go at last, with a screw at parting that brought the water into my eyes, 'I'm a Tartar.'"
> —Charles Dickens, *David Copperfield* (1850)

A savage, cruel individual. This word comes from the Tatars, one of several fierce Asiatic tribes that threatened thirteenth-century Europe. (Although comprising different peoples, they also were often referred to as the *Mongol horde*; see HORDE.) Reputedly primitive in culture and ferocious in battle—they were encouraged to rape, torture, and kill civilians who resisted—the Tatars were considered to represent a new Dark Age. About the fourteenth century the name was corrupted into *Tartar*, perhaps, as Eric Partridge suggested, to imply that these cruel people came from hell, called *Tartarus* in mythology.

In Shakespeare's time and during the seventeenth century, the word Tartar, usually capitalized, also meant a thief and a rogue, but by the nineteenth century it simply signified a savagely irritable or exceedingly severe individual, like Creakle, the hated and feared headmaster of David Copperfield's first boarding school. Similarly,

Tatar archers

the expression *to catch a Tartar* means to seek out something or someone that turns out to be unexpectedly unpleasant or difficult (as in "You're welcome to complain to the boss, but you might find you've caught a Tartar").

task force

A group, often consisting of experts, that is formed to investigate or solve a particular problem. The term originated in the U.S. Navy in the Pacific campaign of World War II and is still used in the military for a temporary group (force) formed to carry out a specific mission (task). After the war the term was adopted by government, business and industry, and other organizations for any special fact-finding and/or problem-solving committee. President John F. Kennedy was particularly fond of the term and set up task forces for foreign aid and numerous other matters. In subsequent administrations the Presidential Task Force (appointed by the chief executive) played an ever more important role.

tattoo

A call signaling soldiers to return to quarters at night. Originally (early 1600's) the call was a drumbeat, but later it became a bugle call. During the Civil War the tune also became the basis of TAPS.

taxi, to

To drive an airplane on the ground to acquire enough speed to rise in the air. This term dates from World War I, when the plane's movement was likened to that of a taxicab, and it soon became a standard part of our language.

tell that to the Marines

> "Tell that to the marines, major, that cock won't fight with me."
> —William Thackeray, *Pendennis* (1850)

You can't fool me; I don't believe it. This expression originated in Britain and was adopted in the United States in the mid-1800's. The alleged basis of it is that sailors considered themselves superior to marines, whom they regarded as gullible greenhorns. However, Paul Dickson claims it was first recorded in Samuel Pepys's *Diary*, with the opposite meaning, that is, the marines could be trusted to tell true from false. From about 1800 on, however, it was used in the present meaning. Byron had it in *The Island* (1823): "That will do for the Marines, but sailors won't believe it."

Thermopylae

Symbol of heroic resistance against strong opposition. The metaphor is based on a battle fought in 480 B.C. between the Greeks, led by Leonidas of Sparta, and the Persians, under Xerxes. The fighting took place at a mountain pass from Thessaly to Locris, only twenty-five feet wide at its narrowest point, where the Greeks held off an overwhelmingly larger force of Persians. Eventually, however, the Greeks were betrayed by someone who allowed the Persians to get behind them, and Leonidas was slain, along with all his troops. It is the brave defense that has been remembered for nearly 2,500 years, rather than the betrayal and its outcome.

Third World

The underdeveloped or developing nations of the world, particularly those of Asia, Africa, and Latin America. The term originated during the COLD WAR and referred to those nations that did not align themselves with either of the two leading world powers—the Soviet Union or the United States—and were wooed by both as potential allies. Because most of these countries heavily depended on foreign aid to support their economies, many of them had, by the late 1980's, aligned themselves with one side or the other, usually according to which was their major benefactor.

throw dust into someone's eyes, to

> "He [Cicero] threw dust in the eyes of the jury."
> —Quintillian, *Institutiones Oratoriae* (A.D. 80)

To mislead. Although they were not the first to do so, it was the Muslims who became known for confounding their enemies by literally throwing dust or sand in the air, an early form of SMOKE SCREEN. Mohammed himself did so in several battles, according to the Koran. "A useful stratagem in war," wrote Erasmus (*Adagia*, 1523), "is to put an army in such a position that in marching up to the enemy the dust may be driven in their faces." And one of Benjamin Franklin's tidbits of wisdom (1767) was "It required a long discourse to throw dust in the eyes of common sense." In any event, the expression has been used figuratively, in the sense of misleading or misrepresenting, for many years.

time bomb

A potentially explosive situation. This name for an actual bomb equipped with a timing device to set it off after a predetermined interval dates from the 1890's and has been used figuratively since the late 1930's. Thus, a newspaper interview with the friend of a stockbroker who shot his boss quotes him, "Len was a nice man who held in his feelings too much; he was a time bomb set to go off."

Tokyo Rose

A propagandist for the enemy. During World War II, U.S. servicemen gave this name to a woman radio broadcaster from Japan who tried to convince them to give up fighting and go home. Beamed from Japan, the broadcasts also played sentimental music that was supposed to make the G.I.'s long for home. The broadcasters were several American-born Japanese women, two of whom were definitely identified, Iva Togori d'Aquino and Ruth Hayakawa. The former was tried and sentenced for treason in 1949 but was paroled after seven years.

The Nazis also broadcast propaganda. A woman broadcaster, dubbed *Axis Sally*, was Mildred E. Gillars, an American who was teaching English in Berlin when the war broke out and who went to work for the Nazis. Her radio program, *Home, Sweet Home*, combining popular music, nostalgia, and anti-Semitism, was beamed to American troops in Europe and North Africa. After the war she was arrested and convicted of treason, and served twelve years in prison. Her British counterpart, William Joyce, was born in America but carried a British passport and was called *Lord Haw-Haw* for the mocking Nazi broadcasts he made from Berlin during the war. After the war he was convicted of treason and hanged.

During the Vietnam War, Trinh Thi Ngo, better known as *Hanoi Hannah*, broadcast from North Vietnam from 1965 to 1975 with messages trying to convince American troops they were an aggressor. She also announced the names of American troops who had died in battle during the previous month and read clippings from American newspapers about antiwar demonstrations. After the war she continued to work in broadcasting.

During the 1991 Gulf War an Iraqi propagandist named *Baghdad Betty* tried to lower the morale of U.S. troops through psychological warfare radio broadcasts.

tomahawk chop

A mock Indian war dance gesture performed at sports events and entertainments. Regarded as offensive to Native Americans, it is supposedly based on an actual war dance.

too little, too late

An inadequate remedy that also arrives too late to be useful. This expression originally referred to military reinforcements that were insufficient or came too tardily. William Safire pointed out that "Too Late" was the caption of a famous 1885 *Punch* cartoon showing a relief column arriving at Khartoum two days after General "Chinese" Gordon had died at the hands of the African Mahdi. The first recorded use of the entire phrase was in an article by Allan Nevins in *Current History* (May 1935), and it was subsequently popularized by David Lloyd George, lamenting the fall of Czechoslovakia, Poland, and Finland into Nazi hands. It has subsequently been applied to a variety of civilian situations.

torpedo, to

To undermine, ruin, destroy. This expression is a transfer from naval warfare, where torpedoes have been used against enemy ships since the American Revolution. The torpedo presumably was named for its resemblance to the flatfish of that name, which emits electric discharges through its tail; it is also called an electric ray. Steamboat inventor Robert Fulton was an early supporter of these enclosed masses of gunpowder and was the first to blow up a sloop in this way, in a British harbor in 1801. He tried to interest Napoleon in the weapon, but the U.S. Navy was far more responsive. During the War of 1812, a line of defensive torpedoes was laid across the Narrows in New York Harbor. Numerous new kinds were invented during the Civil War. A Confederate, Matthew Fontaine Maury, invented the submarine torpedo and ways of planting it that were superior to towing it to its destination, but the war ended before his invention was used. The figurative use of the verb dates from the late 1800's.

Tory

> "Tory. A cant term, derived, I suppose, from an Irish word signifying a savage."
> —Samuel Johnson, *Dictionary* (1755)

A political conservative or a reactionary. The name comes from the Irish *toraighe* or *toraidhe*, for a pursued person or outlaw, and was the mid-seventeenth-century name for Irish Catholic outlaws and bandits who had been forced off their lands and in turn harassed the English in Ireland. In England under King Charles II (1660–85) Tory became a derogatory name for the supporters of the crown, who opposed both the nonconformists (non-Anglican Protestants) and the Roman Catholics. Their opponents came to be called Whigs (see also WHIG). Most of them became reconciled in the Glorious Revolution of 1688, but some Tory extremists remained Jacobites (supporters of James II) well into the eighteenth century, and so Tory became identified with supporters of the Stuarts.

The Whigs were in power under George I and George II, but the Tories returned to power under William Pitt the Younger and remained dominant through the Napoleonic Wars. By then they were no longer associated with the Stuarts but supported the crown and the Anglican Church. From about 1830 on, under their new leader Robert Peel, the Tory Party began to be called the Conservative Party, and the two names (Tory and Conservative) soon became interchangeable, as they are in Britain today.

Although Tory tends to be used mostly for British Conservatives, during the American Revolution the royalists, who supported the British cause against the colonists, also were called Tories.

toxic

Poisonous. The word comes from the Greek *toxikon pharmakon*, for "bow poison," that is, the poison used to smear arrowheads. Although poison arrows have been (and still are) used in many parts of the world since ancient times, the word toxic for "poisonous" did not enter the English language until the 1650's. The same root is responsible for intoxication, or drunkenness.

trench coat

A belted water-repellent coat. The style is so called because it was favored by officers fighting in the trenches of World War I, which often were cold and wet.

trench mouth

An oral infection characterized by painful bleeding gums and bad breath. It is caused by various bacteria and affects mostly the soft tis-sues of the mouth. It was named *Vincent's infection* about 1900, after the French physician J. H. Vincent, but began to be called trench mouth during World War I because it afflicted so many soldiers in the trenches, and that name is still current. Poor oral hygiene and nutrition, stress, and heavy smoking—all conditions endemic in the trenches—predispose one to this infection, which today is treated with antibiotics, dental care, and improved oral hygiene.

Two other conditions were common in World War I. *Trench fever*, also called *Wolhynian fever*, is a rickettsial infection borne by lice. Characterized by fever, weakness, dizziness, headache, severe back and leg pains, and a rash, it is treated with antibiotics; it is rarely seen today. *Trench foot*, or *immersion foot*, is caused by over-exposure to cold, damp conditions, and is treated, like chilblains, by rapid warming.

trigger-happy

Inclined to act violently at the slightest provocation. The early-seventeenth-century gun was set off, like those of today, by means of a *trigger*, which in those early times was also known as a *tricker* and originally (1621) meant the lever that springs a trap. It soon became the name of the small catch that, when pulled, drawn, or pressed, releases a gun's hammer. The present term, literally meaning "eager to shoot," has been used figuratively in politics since the mid-1900's. Various public figures, among them President Richard M. Nixon and candidate Barry Goldwater, were characterized as trigger-happy, meaning they were inclined to declare war precipitously.

Someone who responds rapidly to a suggestion or takes advantage of a situation is said to be *quick on the trigger*. The noun *trigger* itself has come to mean an event that precipitates other events, as in "The rise in interest rates was a trigger for the stock market collapse." The same sense is found in the verb *to trigger*—that is, to spark a chain reaction—as in "Their meeting triggered bitter bureaucratic debates." The forefinger of either hand came to be known as the *trigger finger*, and a *trigger point* is a sensitive area of the body which, when irritated, can cause pain in another part of the body.

In crime jargon a *triggerman* was a hired thug or bodyguard who specialized in gunning down people, but this term has also been used figuratively for someone who initiates an enterprise, as in "The professor was the triggerman for this huge collection of Harvard Business School cases." (See also HAIR-TRIGGER.)

trip wire

Anything that might trip up a person. During World War I, troops that advanced close to the German line often had to cut a wire strung to set off a trap or an alarm. The soldiers called it a *trip wire*, meant literally to trip them up. Later this term was used more figuratively, as in a *New York Times* headline on October 7, 1997: "Looking for Tripwires, Ickes Heads to the Witness Stand." The term today is also used for a small military force used as a first line of defense.

Trojan horse

> "Sing of the building of the horse of wood, which Epeius made with Athene's help, the horse which once Odysseus led up into the citadel as a thing of guile, when he had filled it with the men who sacked Ilios."
>
> —Homer, *Odyssey* (c. 850 B.C.)

A treacherous deception; a guileful stratagem. According to the *Aeneid*, the Roman poet Virgil's account of the Trojan War, following the death of the Trojan warrior Hector, Ulysses (Odysseus in Greek) had a huge wooden horse made. He told the Trojans it was an offering to the gods to secure a prosperous voyage back to Greece. The Trojans dragged the horse inside their walled city (Troy is called *Ilios* in Greek), which until then had stood firm. Under cover of night the Greek soldiers hidden inside the horse, including King Menelaus, crept out and killed the guards, opened the city gates to let in their army, and set fire to Troy. This story not only made the Trojan horse a symbol of treachery but also gave rise to the saying "Beware of Greeks bearing gifts."

In the late 1970's the name Trojan horse also began to be used for an illicit computer program inserted into a legitimate program by criminals, spies, or vandals so as to steal money or information or to destroy memory or scramble data. Also called *trojans*, these programs pretend to provide a useful function, such as a word processor, but actually steal or destroy data. Indeed, some computer experts in the U.S. military warned that saboteurs of this type could extract vital information from a combat zone so as to make missiles explode prematurely or provide intelligence to hostile nations.

troops, the

A body of workers, as opposed to their leaders (See also RANK AND FILE). In American political slang the troops are party workers, mostly volunteers, who ring doorbells, pass out leaflets, and do other menial but necessary tasks on behalf of a party or candidate.

Although a *trooper* is, strictly speaking, a cavalry soldier (See SWEAR LIKE A TROOPER), and a *troop* is a cavalry unit, the word troop comes from the Germanic and French words for "herd," whence it came to denote a company of people—a body of soldiers, police, or, in jocular fashion, any group. Eric Partridge noted that in World War I the British used "troops" to mean "we" or "us" as opposed to the enemy; in the United States today this meaning persists—that is, troops denotes "us" as a group. Further, the verb *to troop* means to flock together or to march, as in "The whole class trooped to the bus stop."

trophy

A prize. The word comes from the Greek *trophe* or *trope*, which meant "turning" or "putting to flight in defeat." Both the Greeks and the Romans put up monuments to commemorate notable victories—a *tropaion* was a Greek monument to victory. Often these monuments were placed on the site of a battle, especially at the point where the enemy had been put to flight. In English this term became trophy, and in the sixteenth century it was transferred to mean an award or honor given for some victory. Today it is common practice to give trophies to the winners of athletic events. A more recent usage, however, is *trophy wife*, usually a second wife, who is married for her extreme attractiveness and accomplishments, which the husband in effect shows off as a winner might display a trophy. The term was coined in 1989 in a *Fortune* article by Julie Connelly, who wrote, "Powerful men are beginning to demand trophy wives. . . . The more money men make . . . the more self-assured they become, and the easier it is for them to think: I *deserve* a queen."

turn a blind eye to

Overlook deliberately. This expression almost certainly originated in 1801, when Lord Nelson, then second in command of the English fleet, was besieging Copenhagen. He decided that his squadron should attack, but his lieutenant pointed out that the flagship had sent up signals to withdraw. Reluctant to obey this order and eager for a victory, Nelson, who had lost the sight of one eye at Calvi, put the telescope to his blind eye and said that he could see no such signal. He did attack, and the French were forced to surrender, a triumph in his career second only to the Battle of Trafalgar.

turncoat

"Turn your coat according to the wind."
—Gottfried of Strassburg, *Apothegm* (c. 1215)

One who changes sides, deserting principle and/or party. The word entered English only in the mid-sixteenth century, although the idea was surely old by then. Fable has it that a Duke of Saxony whose castle lay between French and Saxon possessions had a reversible coat made of blue, the Saxon color, and lined with white, the French color. The side he wore facing out depended on whose army seemed more menacing at the time. This idea appears in several of La Fontaine's fables, and the term was used by Jonathan Swift, Sir Walter Scott, Lord Byron, and numerous other writers.

two strings to his bow

"I wil wel that euery man be amerous and loue, but that he haue ij strenges on his bowe."
—William Caxton, trans., *The Historie of Jason* (c. 1477)

More than one way of accomplishing one's objective. The expression comes from the ancient custom of archers carrying a reserve string, lest one break, and first appeared in English in the mid-fifteenth century. By 1546 it was well known enough to appear in John Heywood's collection of proverbs. In a number of nineteenth-century novels (by Jane Austen, Anthony Trollope, and others) the term refers to suitors and sweethearts—that is, if one love affair doesn't work out, another lover is waiting in the wings. Today the expression still means having more resources in reserve, so that in case of failure one always has an alternative.

tycoon

A wealthy person, a business magnate. This term dates from the Civil War, when it meant "a top leader." Adapted from the Japanese *taikun*, for "great ruler" and the title of the shogun of Japan, it was applied to Abraham Lincoln and Robert E. Lee, among others. After the war it acquired its present meaning.

tyro

A beginner. The word comes from the Latin *tiro*, which was the Romans' name for a raw military recruit. The *i* was changed to *y* in medieval Latin, from which it came into English and then was used for any kind of novice.

U-boat

A German submarine. The word comes from World War I, a short-ening of the German *Unterseeboot* (literally, "undersea boat").

unconditional surrender

A nickname for General Ulysses S. Grant, who is believed to have invented this term. On February 16, 1862, when Fort Donelson was about to fall, he was asked what terms he might accept, and he said, "No terms except unconditional surrender."

underground

Hidden, secret, and usually opposed to the existing establishment. Clearly this description applies to movements carried on since early times by those who regarded a regime as oppressive, but they were not necessarily called "underground." One of the earliest uses of the word in this sense was the *underground railway/railroad*, which, in the United States beginning in the 1820's, was a system for helping runaway slaves escape to the free northern states or Canada. At least 3,200 active abolitionists (those who believed slavery should be abolished) were active in this secret network of hiding places along various routes, whereby fugitives were passed from home to home until they had found safe refuge. Although the network existed as early as 1786, it did not spread throughout the fourteen northern states until about 1830. According to historian Richard B. Morris, its name dates from the time the Kentuckian owner of a slave named Tice Davids pursued him across the Ohio River and, unable to find him, said he "must have gone off on an underground road." During the next thirty years an estimated 50,000 slaves escaped in this way.

During World War II, resistance movements in German-occupied countries, especially France and Belgium, were called *the underground*. Since that time, the term has also been widely used for antiestablishment or nonconformist enterprises of various kinds— not necessarily secret or even particularly subversive. Today one might speak of an underground newspaper that promotes various avant-garde activities in the arts or an underground economy that operates outside the normal banking system.

undermine, to

To weaken, usually secretly and by gradual stages. The term dates from the fourteenth century, when it was common practice for besiegers to tunnel under the foundations of a castle, either to enter it or to weaken the walls. Such tunnels were called "mines," and the foundation then was said to be undermined. By the fifteenth century, to undermine meant "to defeat by underhanded means," a meaning that is still current.

under the counter

Describing an illegal or unauthorized transaction. The term became popular during World War II, when the war effort caused shortages in both essential and nonessential goods. Dishonest sellers then deliberately kept some articles in short supply, hiding their stock under the counter in order to sell it to favored customers and/or at exorbitant prices. (See also BLACK MARKET.)

Unstrung

unstrung

Emotionally unhinged, unnerved. This term most likely comes from the sixteenth-century practice of longbowmen keeping their bows unstrung, or at least with the string loosened at one end, so that the wood of the bow would not lose its resilience. A surprise attack thus could catch them unprepared, and they might feel panicky until they could restring their weapons. By the 1690's the term had been transferred to the emotions, especially in the locution "my nerves are unstrung," in which taut nerves implicitly are likened to a tight bow string.

up in arms

Angry, rebellious. This term originally signified an armed rebellion and was so used from the late 1500's. It began to be used figuratively about 1700, as in "The members were up in arms when the election was postponed."

up to the hilt

To the utmost. This term alludes to a sword being plunged in as far as it can go, up to its *hilt*, or handle. It has been used figuratively since the 1600's, as in "Our house is mortgaged up to the hilt."

U-2

A reconnaissance plane designed for spying. It was developed by Lockheed (See SKUNK WORKS) and made its first flight in August, 1955, during the Korean War. The government originally said it was a weather-reconnaissance aircraft and labeled it *U* for "utility." In May, 1960, the U-2 piloted by Francis Gary Powers was shot down by the Soviet Union, an incident igniting a cold war crisis.

The U-2, in a slightly larger version than the original, is still used. It collects multisensor photo, electro-optic, infrared, and radar imagery, day or night and in all kinds of weather. A popular rock band called itself *U-2* but allegedly chose the name simply because its members liked it.

Valhalla

A final resting place, especially for heroes. The word comes from Scandinavian myth, where Valhalla was a hall in heaven reserved for the souls of heroes slain in battle. They were carried there by twelve nymphs known as the *Valkyrie*, to spend all of eternity feasting. The name comes from *valr*, for "slain," and *hall*, for "hall." Today it is occasionally used for the burial grounds of the great, such as Britain's Westminster Abbey and America's Arlington Cemetery.

vandalism

Doing wanton damage. The word comes from the fifth-century Germanic tribe, the Vandals, who ravaged Gaul and Spain and settled in North Africa. Led by Genseric, in 439 they attacked Carthage, the third-largest Roman city and the last in Africa to fall. From this stronghold they sailed back to Italy, and in 455 they sacked Rome, despoiling it of its art treasures. Loaded with plunder, the Vandals' ships returned to Carthage. Genseric's son, Hunneric, who succeeded him in 477, was even more ferocious but attacked mainly Christians, stealing the treasures and sacred vessels of the Church. The Vandals finally were conquered in 536 and vanished without a trace, but their name was forever identified with the destruction of objects of artistic, sacred, or historical value. By the sixteenth century the word vandal was used in English to describe a wilfully destructive barbarian. The "ism" was added by the French in the eighteenth century (*vandalisme*) and then came into English as well.

Vichy

A symbol of collaboration with the enemy. During World War II the city of Vichy, in central France, long known for its mineral springs, was the seat of the French government under Marshal Pétain that collaborated with the German occupying powers from 1940 to 1944.

VIP

Acronym for *v*ery *i*mportant *p*erson, that is, someone who merits special treatment. According to Ivor H. Evans, the term was coined in 1944 by a British station commander of transport who was responsible for moving planeloads of important individuals, including Lord Mountbatten, to the Middle East. To avoid disclosing their identity in the written orders, lest they fall into enemy hands, he described them as VIP's. The acronym caught on and was used through the remainder of the war. Today it often is used ironically, to describe a person who is actually just self-important.

visor

The front brim of a cap; also, the movable flap on automobile and airplane windshields. The word was first used for the movable portion of a military helmet, which protects the soldier's face, and came into the language, via Middle English, from the Old French *viser*, "to face." Protective face coverings had been included on some helmets from ancient Etruscan times; by the fifteenth century the completely closed helmet (called *close helmet*) was used in many

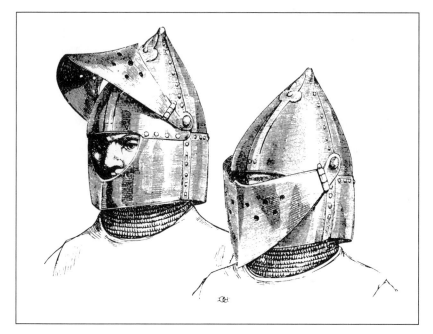

Helmet with visor

European armies. In the 1860's the word visor began to be used for the projecting front rim of a cap, which helps shield the face from sun and rain, and by the mid-1920's shields called visors were supplied for the driver's and pilot's convenience on cars and planes.

walkie-talkie

A portable radio transmitter and receiver. It originally was developed during World War II for use in the fighting services. The rhyming name refers to its obvious advantages of portability and combined transmitting-receiving capability. Even before the war's end, walkie-talkies began to be used by civilian police, and then in many other walks of life, including an inexpensive, simple version used as a children's toy.

walk the plank

Be dismissed or forced to resign. This expression alludes to seventeenth-century piracy. Pirates were not known for kindness to captives. A form of execution they favored was forcing them to walk the plank, that is, walk off a board placed on deck over the water, and consequently drown. Today this term is used only figuratively, as in "With all these layoffs, I wonder when I'll be walking the plank."

wangle, to

To obtain or achieve by whatever means possible; a synonym for beg, borrow, or steal. Although this verb is a few decades older, it came into its own during World War I and is now standard English. During the war it was used mainly as an intransitive verb, as in "Somehow the submarine wangled through." Since then it is more often used as a transitive verb, as in "We hope to wangle some extra vacation days this year."

war baby

A baby born or conceived during wartime. In World War I the term denoted the illegitimate offspring of servicemen, but that meaning is now obsolete. The standard present-day meaning is a child born while the father is on active military duty. War babies usually are not part of a baby boom (a dramatic increase in the birth rate), which tends to occur after a war ends, as it did in the late 1940's (following World War II).

The slang term *son of a gun*, meaning a rogue or scoundrel, is believed by some etymologists to have originally (c. 1700) meant the illegitimate baby of a soldier ("gun"). Others, however, think it may be a rhyming euphemism for son of a bitch, and still others suggest that, gun having been British slang for thief, it therefore came to mean scoundrel.

war bride

A woman who marries a serviceman who is on duty overseas. This term arose during World War II, which was followed by long-term occupation of Germany and Japan and saw numerous marriages between U.S. troops and German and Japanese women.

wardrobe

"Flowers that their gay wardrobe wear."
—John Milton, *Lycidas* (1637)

A stock of clothes or a cabinet for storing them. This word comes from the Old French *warderobe*, originally a compartment used to store and guard ("ward") valuables ("robe") captured from the enemy, including their weapons.

war games

> "Warre is a game wherein very often that side loseth which layeth the oddes."
> —Thomas Fuller, *The Holy State* (1642)

Simulated military operations to help plan strategy and defense and to instruct officers. The name is a translation of the German *Kriegsspiel* (war game), introduced in 1824 by a Prussian officer, Lieutenant von Reiswitz, who actually was improving on his father's design. War games use maps as battlefields in miniature and counters to represent vehicles and troops. Today computers have replaced this chessboard approach.

war horse

An experienced veteran; also, a reliable, oft-performed production. The term originated in the mid-seventeenth century, when it was used simply for a military charger experienced in battle. In time the term was transferred to a highly experienced officer—Confederate General James Longstreet (1821–1904) was nicknamed the War Horse—as well as to veterans of struggles in other areas, such as politics. In the latter sense the term can be used either affectionately or with contempt. In the twentieth century the expression also began to be applied to a play or opera or other production that reliably attracts audiences over the years and therefore is presented so often that it may become hackneyed. Thus, despite their high quality, the operas *La Traviata, La Bohème,* and *Carmen* all have, on occasion, been so described.

war of attrition

A gradual wearing down of opposition or resistance. This term was coined in 1914, when it alluded to the gradual wearing down of the enemy's strength and morale. In a 1915 memorandum to Lloyd George, Lord Kitchener said the war could end either through a decisive victory or by attrition. Since then, the term has occasionally been used loosely to describe a similar action in other spheres, as in "He kept teasing her about smoking, and she finally lost the war of attrition and quit."

war of nerves

A conflict characterized by such psychological measures as threats, rumors, and sabotage, calculated to undermine the enemy's morale. The term entered English in the late 1930's but had been mentioned earlier in Hitler's book *Mein Kampf* (1924), where the strategy was highly praised. Later it was used for the tension between the Soviet Union and the Western nations following World War II, subsequently called the COLD WAR. William Safire quotes U.S. Secretary of States James Byrnes's statement (1946) "that we must not conduct a war of nerves to achieve strategic ends," and the following year Britain's Harold Macmillan used the phrase, too. Soon afterward the expression was transferred to civilian areas, to characterize psychological pressure on an individual, company, government agency, etc. Thus one might speak of waging a war of nerves against a tenured university professor to persuade her to resign.

warpaint, putting on

Colloquial term for applying cosmetics. The term comes from the Native American custom of applying paint to face and body before going into battle. In the 1850's the expression began to be used figuratively, for putting on one's best finery, and within a decade it was used for a woman putting on makeup (perhaps to best her rivals).

warpath, to be on the

> "He has never been on a warpath."
> —James Fenimore Cooper, *The Deerslayer* (1841)

To be extremely angry and prepared to exact retribution. The term originated in mid-eighteenth-century America, when it literally meant a path taken by a Native American war party. In the nineteenth century it began to be used figuratively, as in "She was on the warpath all evening" (Mark Twain, *A Tramp Abroad*).

wars, been to the

Showing signs of injury from a conflict. The term began to be used, according to Eric Partridge, about 1850 and at first simply described the battle scars of military veterans. It soon was extended to include the signs of any harrowing experience, as in "My car's been to the wars; it has 200,000 miles on it."

washout

A failure. In America this term is believed to have come from roads being washed out in a rainstorm and therefore made impassable. In Britain, however, it originated in the military, during the Boer War (1899–1902). It may have referred to a gap or hole caused by violent erosion, Eric Partridge believed, but more likely it came from the rifle range. If a shot landed completely wide of the target, it was called a washout, because on old iron targets such shots were obliterated with some kind of paint or wash. At first washout simply meant a bad shot, but it soon was broadened to mean any kind of failure, including a person or a thing.

waste, to

To kill. This slangy usage may have originated in street gang warfare but became well known only during the Vietnam War. Presumably it alludes to wasting—that is, throwing away—a life.

watchword

> "Our watchword is security."
> —Attributed to William Pitt (1708–78)

A word or short phrase that briefly expresses a principle; a slogan or motto. In the fourteenth century a watchword was a word given to the watch—that is, a password given to military sentries. By 1550 it also was a signal to begin an attack. In the early 1700's the word began to be used in its present meaning of a guiding principle. (See also SHIBBOLETH; SLOGAN.)

Waterloo

> "Every man meets his Waterloo at last."
> —Wendell Phillips, speech (1859)

A final, crushing defeat. The name refers to Napoleon's last battle, on June 18, 1815, near Waterloo, Belgium, which ended in his decisive defeat by combined British and German forces commanded by the Duke of Wellington. The French name for the battle is *La Belle Alliance*, referring to the British-German alliance. The Duke of Wellington also is remembered for a statement he was said to have made a decade later, while watching a cricket match at the famous English public school of Eton. "The Battle of Waterloo was won on the playing fields of Eton," he reportedly said, alluding to the training in sports that prepared young Englishmen for success on the battlefield. The Duke himself and his family denied ever uttering these words, which nevertheless survived as a symbol of certain British values.

The actual Battle of Waterloo was followed by widespread looting of the enemy dead and wounded. Among the items of value were false teeth, made either of ivory or of human teeth; dentists of the time would pay well for these. According to David Howarth, such a haul was made from the field that for years afterward dentures were called *Waterloo teeth*.

Wellingtons

> "The soldier . . . is but a quiet grave man . . . occupied in trivial detail; thinking, as the Duke of Wellington was said to do, most of the shoes of his soldiers."
> —William Bagehot (1826–77), *Checks and Balances*

High rubber boots, extending up to the knee. The original Wellington boot, a style popularized by Arthur Wellesley, First Duke of Wellington (1769–1852), during his campaigns against Napoleon, was a high leather riding boot, with the front part of the top extending above the knee. Later cobblers made a shorter boot, called a *half-Wellington*, which reached only midway up the calf. In the early 1900's the name Wellingtons began to be used for waterproof rain boots, made of specially treated leather or, still later, rubber. They are widely worn in Britain to this day, being very practical footwear in wet weather.

Whig

A member of several British and American political parties of this name. The word first was used for Scottish cattle and horse thieves, who were called *Whiggamer* or *Whiggamore*, or Whig for short. In the seventeenth century it was transferred, first to Scottish insurgents and then to Presbyterians viewed as dissenters and antiroyalists. After the Restoration of 1660, a Whig was an antimonarchist who still sympathized with Oliver Cromwell. By 1689 Whig meant an opponent of TORY, and indeed the Tories used the term abusively. By the mid-nineteenth century the Whigs had become Britain's Liberal Party, and Whig still generally denotes a political liberal in Britain, just as Tory means a conservative.

In America, on the other hand, the first group who were called Whigs were also antimonarchists and later supporters of the American Revolution (whose opponents were called Tories). Then, in 1834, a political coalition of the National Republican party and others who opposed President Andrew Jackson, led by Henry Clay and John C. Calhoun, formed the Whig Party. It survived until 1854, when it was absorbed into the newly formed Republican Party.

whine, to

> "And when they are there, I neglect God and his Angels, for the noise of a fly, for the rattling of a coach, for the whining of a door."
>
> —John Donne, *Sermons* (Dec. 12, 1626)

To make a plaintive, querulous, complaining noise. The word comes from the Anglo-Saxon *hwinan*, which signified the whizzing sound of flying arrows. This meaning persists in, for example, the whine of bullets. By 1500 or so, however, the word had been extended to human and animal utterances, and one still speaks of a whining puppy or a child whining from weariness. By then it had also acquired the meaning of querulous complaint.

white flag

A symbol of truce or surrender. A white flag has symbolized peace since the time of the Roman historian Livy, who wrote of a Carthaginian ship "garnished with . . . white flags of peace." It also meant that the bearer wanted to parley. To this day the bearer of a white flag has, by international custom, safe conduct and may not be fired on or otherwise harmed (a custom not always obeyed in the heat of battle).

Showing the *white feather*, on the other hand, means acting in a cowardly way; the symbolism here is from cockfighting.

writing on the wall

A presentiment of disaster, also called *handwriting on the wall*. The term comes from the Bible (Daniel 5:5–31). While Belshazzar, King of the Chaldeans, was holding a great feast, a mysterious hand appeared and wrote some words on the wall. The King called Daniel to interpret this message, and Daniel warned that it was a sign of the King's downfall. That very night Belshazzar was slain and Darius of Persia took over his kingdom.

Yalta

A seaport on the Black Sea, scene of the last meeting of U.S. President Franklin D. Roosevelt, British Prime Minister Winston Churchill, and Soviet Premier Josef Stalin toward the end of World War II. During this meeting numerous concessions were made to the Soviet Union, and thereafter "another Yalta" became a symbol for naïveté and gullibility in dealing with Communist leaders.

young Turks

Rebels or insurgents, usually of a politically liberal cast. The original young Turks were a reform party established in 1891 to modernize the autocratic Ottoman Empire and give it a constitutional parliamentary government. They raised a revolt at Salonika in 1908 and wrested power from the elderly sultans. Unfortunately the government they formed proved to be almost as repressive as that of the sultans, and their extreme nationalism resulted in as much suppression of Turkish subject peoples as had existed before. Nevertheless, the name is still associated with relatively young activists who rebel against the establishment (party, government, etc.) and seek to liberalize it. A *New York Times* headline of July 21, 1998, described a maverick reform candidate for Prime Minister: "A 72-Year-Old Young Turk in Japan's Premier Race."

zap, to

To bombard with microwaves, radiation, laser beams, electric current, or some other form of energy. This slang word was coined during World War II, when it meant to kill or to shoot, and soon was applied to various peacetime activities. Today one can zap (cook) one's dinner in a microwave oven, zap (tune out) the commercials on a network television show, or zap (kill) Japanese beetles with insecticide.

zealot

> "A single zealot may become persecutor, and better men be his victims."
>
> —Thomas Jefferson, *Notes on Virginia* (1782)

A fanatic. The word comes from the Zealots, a radical, fiercely patriotic Jewish sect founded by Judas of Gamala early in the first century. They were violent opponents of Roman rule and fought fanatically in a rebellion that ended in the total destruction of Jerusalem in A.D. 70. The name Zealot was derived from the Greek *zelos*, which also is the root of jealousy, a feeling that can be characterized by similar excessive ferocity.

zero hour

A deadline or other critical time. Originally, in World War I, this expression, also stated simply as *zero*, was military jargon for the time set for the beginning of an assault. Eventually it was extended to mean any critical time. (See also D-DAY.)

zero in on, to

To focus or concentrate on a goal or target. The term comes from the calibrated adjustments of sight settings on a rifle or other firearm and originated during World War II. Soon afterward it was transferred to any concentration of one's attention on something or someone.

Index